2

1. THE CITY: IN MORTAL AGONY
Sculpture by Zadkine, Rotterdam, memorializing
destruction by German air raids; speaks with
equal poignancy to the world-wide twentieth century
urban crisis.

2. THE CITY: NEW LIFE
Sculpture in the New Town of Hemel Hempstead,
by Yeneesse.

THE URGENT FUTURE

5 70

THE URGENT FUTURE

PEOPLE   HOUSING   CITY   REGION

ALBERT MAYER
Architect and Planner of Environment
Fellow, American Institute of Architects

McGRAW—HILL BOOK COMPANY
New York   San Francisco   Toronto   London   Sydney

THE URGENT FUTURE

40991

1234567890HD72106987

Thankfully to Marion, my wife, whose encouragement and endless patience with night after night of writing and rewriting made this book possible.

W hy *The Urgent Future?* What is meant by this title?

We are in the midst of an endemic and at the present time exacerbated urban-national crisis. It has been accumulating over many decades. But it has only recently begun to be fully recognized. It is likewise now evident that we have had only rather feeble action over the thirty years since we began taking measures, in spite of much purple and indignant language.

We must *now* draw into present programs and action, policies and measures that are, for practical purposes, in the future in the sense that they are not yet even being considered, or are being thought through by only a very few. In some cases we are a little further advanced in action. We must telescope the future, must transform it into meaningful immediacy, must make up for lost time. The most recent national legislation is called the Demonstration Cities and Metropolitan Development Act. But the fact is that the totality of programs legislated in the last thirty years is all on only a demonstration or token basis. High sentiments are expressed in preambles, such as the Housing Act of 1949 whose purpose was stated to be ". . . the realization as soon as feasible of a decent home and a suitable living environment for every American family. . . ."

As an early statement, and for its time, it was adequate. It was even exciting. But in terms of today's crises, such open-ended goals just will not do. Thirty years' work on a totally inadequate scale, continuing tokenism or demonstration, is seen to have accomplished little. Such stated goals are meaningless or even deceptively comforting unless tied to a time goal.

At the rate public housing and urban renewal—our earliest measures, legislated thirty years and almost twenty years ago—and other measures are being implemented through funds made available, it will be one hundred years or more before we reach the pious goals. The 1966 act falls into the same pattern. *The Urgent Future* means that we must urgently debate and we must decide on outside limits of time within which this opulent country will fulfill the various often-stated imperative goals: ten years, fifteen years, twenty years.

Without adding such limits to our intentions, we are in a vacuum. We have no criteria against which to measure anything. The annual budget wrangles in Congress every year are, of course, inevitable. But in considerable measure they occur because X hundreds of millions of dollars sounds like a lot of money in the absolute. But when considered against the quite moderate or even conservative time goal of twenty years for an adequate home for every family, much larger sums and efforts take on a much more reasonable and imperative quality.

In other words, the future is no longer just a vague period to come, but is given limits in time which are seen to be rational, and the very least for which a rational and confident nation can settle. Let us, then, grasp these problems and stride boldly into a future that we have measured and taken the measure of.

The future is urgent in another sense. In our consideration up to now in this country of urban-national crisis and need, we have ignored the realm of underlying dynamics. We have had our eyes on programs that deal with technical-social methods and solutions, which may be an improvement over what has gone before. But we are dealing all the time with changeable details of "super structure," not with the deep underlying actualities which shape them and limit them. If we are determined that existing total government *budgets* are roughly all we are going to go in for, then all we can do is slightly recut the slices which each element can command. If on the other hand, we decide our crisis is such that we must think in terms of growing total national *income* that we can tap, we can throw off the strait jacket that we habitually assume as our maximum expansion in social, physical, architectural-environmental development. Again, if our development picture is circumscribed by assuming the inviolability of our present speculative land-development system and the inevitable accompaniment of spiralling land prices, we build in a factor that negates what we are endeavoring to do in bringing costs in viable relation to incomes. In our discussion of underlying dynamics these fundamentals are brought into focus. We must recognize that the ground rules are obsolete. We must determine to change these archaic ground rules.

Another form of presently submerged urgency is housing, particularly public housing for those in the low-income group. In the surge of awakening to the overall interlinked problems of the city as such, we are tending to downgrade the central importance of housing and excessively homogenizing it into the general picture. In the case of public housing, appropriations are absurdly too low.

For all housing, the current higher rates of interest and unavailability of loan funds have in some areas halved new housing starts. Surely with our well-known ingenuity, we can design anti-inflation measures which do not further deprive those of low and modest incomes as consumers by drastically curtailing the supply of new housing, and as workers by curtailing jobs. These realities make the generalized far-flung programs look funny. Housing in sufficient quantity and at affordable rents, is still and always will be the key and core of any program

There is, of course, much more to it than just time and quantity, more even than the tough realities of underlying dynamics. The quality of life, the visual and emotional content and impact of the environment, the specific ways and the alternatives for optimum accomplishment: These are all essential to a humane world. These are in this study discussed in some depth and extent. But the more these are felt as part of an urgent totality, the more vibrantly appropriate, the more highly satisfying will be the creation. This imperative sense of urgency and of time-goals must permeate our total effort.

This Preface has up to here confined itself to emphasizing those points that are most sharply in my mind as I reflect back over what I've written in the light of realities as they now are, a number of months after the manuscript was completed. I would like for a final moment to shift gears and succinctly convey the total content and intent of this book in its entirety and all its facets by an elaboration of title and subtitles, which can be practicably shown only here:

THE URGENT FUTURE

Addendum: Two important events on the national housing and urban-metropolitan scene took place during the period between the writing of this book, and its publication. One was the reorganization that followed after the Cabinet Department of Housing and Urban Development had been created to replace and greatly broaden the work of the predecessor Housing and Home Finance Agency. The other was the introduction of new and far-reaching legislation in Congress in 1965, which after a year's debate and a number of changes in name became the Demonstration Cities and Metropolitan Development Act toward the end of 1966.

These two major developments have added a sharp timeliness to the total synthesis which this book is intended to present. This book has permitted, even demanded, close comparisons between my proposals and the act's provisions. But one penalty has been that nomenclature has changed. For example, what had been known as the Public Housing Administration became the Housing Assistance Administration under a Deputy Assistant Secretary to the Assistant Secretary for Renewal and Housing Assistance. Likewise the Urban Renewal Administration became the Renewal Projects Administration under a Deputy Assistant Secretary. It was decided to keep the more familiar original nomenclature, and to add an Appendix to make the equivalencies clear. Luckily the Department of Housing and Urban Development had issued just such a document, and this has become the Appendix.

As to the second matter, a section or inter-chapter has been inserted after Chapters 2 and 3 on public housing and urban renewal, to clarify and to highlight our proposals as compared with the provisions of the 1966 act. The 1966 legislation has a number of miscellaneous provisions of positive importance not included in our partial summaries because they are not germane to the specific deep and pervasive issues to which this book devotes itself.

One other element must be noted here. There has been and is a strong tendency, in discussion and action in the urban realm, to speak in quite new terms, in "born-yesterday" terms of new formulas, down-grading or ignoring what has gone before. Thus the previous major vehicles of public housing and urban renewal have in a sense disappeared in language, in favor of demonstration cities, model cities, and housing assistance. But the fact is that unless we directly face the defects of these older programs and creatively build on our experience of them, if we simply jump away with distaste into the euphoria of romantic salesmanship, we lose a great deal or most of the essence of what we should have creatively learned. I have chosen in early chapters to reconsider public housing and urban renewal and to show, creatively re-formed, their new potential. This is not due to any nostalgia but because we can much more effectively project from them as a rebuilt springboard, the imaginative and massive urgent future.

Several developments in the last year have caught up with our proposals. One such is the proposal for sub-cities, which includes the decentralization and sub-centralization of office buildings from the major center, and with particular reference to Harlem in New York as having the added creative factor of deghettoization. The most encouraging, perhaps even exhilarating of the last year's urban developments is New York State's decision to erect a two million square foot building there for many of its operations in New York City.

The embryo of this book was a series of articles in *Architectural Record* in 1964 and 1965, which were done in a most fruitful collaboration with Clarence Stein. My thanks are also due to *Architectural Record* for permission to use the material, which has been greatly expanded, deepened, and diversified, and for the encouragement of its editors, Emerson Goble, Walter Wagner, and Jeanne Davern. I am grateful to Mr. Wyndham Thomas, Director of Town and Country Planning; Miss Hazel Evans, Editor of the publication, *Town and Country Planning;* and Mr. Göran Sidenbladh, Director of City Planning and Building of the City of Stockholm. They helped repeatedly and patiently with information, verification, and photographs. There are many people in this country and abroad who helped in similar ways, and who are so numerous that one can only thank them anonymously.

Albert Mayer

CONTENTS

The new and ever-advancing technology in industry and in agriculture and the mastery of natural forces could be giving us the plenty, the leisure, and, jointly with social science, an unprecedented opportunity for the good life. We should now be able to create for all a life with diminished tensions and more drama; a life of expanded understanding and vision and daily experiences that reinforce them; a life in which drudgery is diminished and transformed into unforced creative activities; a life in which market place and community and the counterpoint of healing nature are easily interaccessible.

But technology and the mastery of nature are causing or permitting a series of galloping maladjustments and uneasinesses. There are massive unprepared in-migrations from rural into urban areas and at the same time out-migrations within our ever-expanding metropolitan complexes. There is massive involuntary and uncreative and even dangerous leisure. The ubiquitous automobile may be considered a symbol of the Jekyll-and-Hyde character of modern man and modern development-deterioration. It enables us to do wonderful things—to visit distant places, to constitute a new family unity, to have, as it were, a mobile hearth. In actuality, it does something of this. But far more does it result in the city's intolerable congestion, in the countryside's despoilment by unbridled road building and anarchic scatter, in excessive distance between living, work, and recreation, in family disorder and disunity. We are not nearer nature, as we could be, but pushing farther away—not only in distance but now in time as well, as the inexorably lengthening journey to work negates the extra leisure of the shorter workday; in the quality of the nature we can reach and the tired condition we reach it in.

The World Health Organization has stated: "The tremendous increase in urban population clearly justifies the warning that, after the question of keeping world peace, metropolitan planning is probably the most serious single problem faced by man in the second half of the 20th Century." In this country, there is beginning to be an awareness of the desperate urgency of the problems. But there is the great danger and even likelihood that effective awakening into action will be excessively, fatally delayed or that actions proposed and taken will not be adequate for the tasks or will lead in wrong directions.

The purpose of this study is to explore the elements in the physical and social planning and development of our urban civilization and how

CHAPTER ONE

CRISIS AND OPPORTUNITY
Part One: Call to Creative Dissatisfaction

these elements can be deployed in order to realize much more fully the promise of the new forces and minimize their wastes and menaces. Its purpose also is to show the inextricability and equal importance of thinking, program, and action, from the near-at-hand local scene through interlinked middle magnitudes to the metropolitan area and the region. Its purpose too is to work out a much closer inter-impregnation of the physical-economic and the social with the visual-spiritual-architectural, and to show that the total human process can be made fully positive and significant and uplifting only when it flowers into nature-based and socially based architectural expression.

Time is against us. We cannot wait on the snail-like gradualism that has characterized progress in urban and metropolitan institutions. Much more determination and decisiveness are called for. They are, peculiarly, now attainable. The administration's 1966 bills which were passed by Congress mark an important, refreshing opening. But as we will see, we must consider them only an opening, and one that in part is leading in wrong directions.

Urgent forces such as population explosion and embryonic forces such as automation insistently demand prompt decisive action. Fortunately the latter could also provide the means. In fact, though current emphasis is rightly on its menace of giant unemployment, the productivity of automation makes almost immediately possible everything we need to do.

To achieve the necessary decisiveness, we must discard the notion that development of any kind, and specifically planning-development, is neutral, so satisfying to the intellect and to common sense that its works will inevitably be accomplished sooner or later. In fact, there must be created a compelling moral conviction and crusading drive, such as in our time nature conservation and civil rights have begun to succeed in crystallizing and refining, to reinforce intellectual conviction, which alone never is or has been enough, and to overcome comfortable-ness, inertia, and vested interest.

Decay, Destruction, Development

As an observer and a hopeful re-former of the urban scene for many years, I have gone through as many years of alarm and elation. I have known continuing and recurring alarm at the intensifying deterioration of our cities and the accelerating expansion of urban decay and disorder; I have known very occasional elation at some fine develop-

ment or prospect of fine development, at the vision of what could be accomplished in this country, at what actually *has been* accomplished in some other countries. Paradoxically, what has kept expectation invincible has been the continuing acceleration of deterioration, combined with the conviction that things are reaching such a critical point that a sensible democracy must finally be awakened to the need for drastic, far-reaching action. Such a time is, pointedly, now. Both the rate and scale of physical and human deterioration have been constantly accelerating in the city centers, on the city fringes, and now far out into the countryside.

Two factors have of late years accentuated and deepened the effects of inherent social, political, and economic weaknesses in our urban-suburban-exurban—in short, urbanoid—system, and thus have hastened our crisis: the population explosion and the internal-combustion-engine explosion. The phenomenal spread of automobile ownership, fast and free promotion of automobile use, and development of road programs for everywhere give full range to anarchic development-destruction.

A hopeful factor is that there is a great deal of discontent, worry, and self-searching—painful recognition of painful symptoms. But unfortunately, many of the deep-seated influences on our situation are not recognized. We have been in large measure fighting the wrong diseases. And our painfully wrought remedies are nearly or quite inadequate to the newer and most damaging illnesses.

We are using up new land at the rate of 1 million acres a year; our population is increasing at the rate of some 30 million, or 15 per cent, per decade, and much faster in the metropolitan areas. Dr. Jerome Pickard states that in 1980 the nation's population will have increased by 36 per cent since 1962, but the population of twenty-one metropolitan regions by 73 per cent: i.e., twice as fast. Population is declining in the farm areas and in the central cities and is increasing at tremendous rates out in the metropolitan countryside.

Syracuse exemplifies this well. From 1950 to 1960 the city's population declined from 220,000 to 216,000. But in the county there was a 70 per cent increase, from 121,000 to 207,000. Yet practically the only available government tools of any creative strength have hitherto been shaped to deal with the central cities' situation, while the outlying regions gallop into the inevitable day when they too must be rescued, at vast expense and heartbreak, by future urban renewal. To what extent 1966 Federal legislative proposals meet these dilemmas and what drastic changes and additions are necessary in them to do the job that needs to be done constitute one of the recurring themes of this book.

Trend Is Not Destiny: Alternatives to Trend

Another troubling factor is that the whole tendency of urban and highway planning and development in this country is to follow *trend,* to study *trend,* to ride with *trend* as smoothly as possible. But trend can be desperately undesirable, however carefully we adjust to it. There is almost no creative recognition that we could be and must be *in creative control,* that *trend* is not *destiny*.

Imagination and statesmanship can take trend into account and in their stride, can distinguish between the inevitable and the alterable and controllable, can bend trend to human and moral purpose. In contrast to irresistible trend, there is a greater than ever wealth of opportunity and choice. But we have to muster the imaginative self-discipline not to get lost among the riches.

The rage for statistics is one index of the enthronement of trend. Yet statistics can often be nothing but a record of reaction and adjustment to unsatisfactory conditions; and they can be accurate but in a high degree misleading. "Megalopolis" and similar coined expressions give some sort of sloganistic comforting sanction to an ultimate compounding of undesirable conditions. "Megalopolis" describes a manifest troubling trend: the oozing together of already amorphous cities into a sort of lava flow hundreds of miles in dimension, from Boston to Washington, from Milwaukee to Chicago, from Pittsburgh to Cleveland. By taking up the expression as the *dernier cri,* the "sophisticated" help themselves accept the condition.

Megalopolis is the apotheosis of trend. It is also stupid and inhumane. Also, it can be resisted, outwitted, re-formed. When their ring of cities known as the Randstad—Amsterdam, Haarlem, The Hague, Rotterdam, and Utrecht—was far along toward Megalopolis, the Dutch decided it was an evil to be countered, that trend could be dethroned. They are diverting much of the urban spread into quite different sections of the country. They have kept green space between cities and green space and farming at the center of the Randstad. In England the overspill of cities is being dealt with by organic New Towns. After the authorization and development of fifteen, there was a lull, and then six more. A new series *and variations* are under way. At this writing, there are a total of twenty-eight New Towns. There are other solutions and other possibilities as well, which I will develop; but also, our existing cities that are already so glutinous and anonymous can be reshaped, after some thinning out, into organic summations of civilization.

Many of the things we do *accentuate* trend. As a quick but telling example:

The sacred cow of highway planners is the cost-benefit ratio. This buys public and business approbation. What does it mean? It means that we plan our throughways and interstate highway system where there is the greatest congestion, where the immediate return is greatest, where the new or expanded facility can make it easier for still more cars and trucks. More revenue, aggravated congestion—and then, another round of such planning. Thus we extrapolate statistics and make trends even sharper. Note that on the radio news we now can ascertain the most advantageous (old) bypasses, to avoid the overcrowded new superhighways. Wits refer to one major superhighway, completed a few years ago, as the longest parking lot in the world.

Originally, in our early history, national policy pushed railroads into *new* areas to create new opportunity and meet new challenge. What has happened to this viewpoint? Now we give trend a big nudge forward, make it more irreversible and harder to manage. Let us, rather, give the cost-benefit ratio a future dimension. Let us take off the statistical man's straitjacket and take a man-from-Mars look at things. Then, let us move, not in circles around the same spots, but in new directions. Let *us* open up new opportunities in new areas, instead of overloading and reoverloading the tired old areas. Again: the planning of the early cross-country railroads had a wonderful adventurous time-and-space dimension which over time has paid off far, far more handsomely in our American adventure than any cost-benefit ratio that would have been narrowly demonstrable.

The Concept of Total Equations

A major concept I want to inject here is that of "total equations." In our current dominant thinking and action, many proposals are justified by apparent return on investment. Many are rejected or not made because of apparent lack of financial return, consequent need of government subsidy, etc. But the fact is that this thinking-action process is based on often narrow partial equations, like any individual commercial operation. The broader public factors of cost and return fail to be considered. For

The City: Symptoms of Disease

1. *Business-monument with confusion behind and around. Seagram Building, New York*

2. *Confusion in what might have been a fine circle, zoning notwithstanding*

3. *Clutter and confusion—any street*

1. *Two-legged jam*

The City: Disease Rampant

2. *Parking desert*

4. *Four-wheeled jam*
(*Remedy intensifies disease*)

3. *Slum, poverty, neglect*

instance, the New York Port Authority is about to build a gigantic World Trade Center in lower Manhattan in New York City. Of office space alone there will be 10 million square feet, plus much exhibition space and incomparable concentration of all kinds of facilities. A fine case is made; and there is a good financial return available. But what of the total equation, and what about alternatives and *their* equations? What will be the money cost of added transportation facilities and operations and the cost, in wear and tear and tensions, of jamming new thousands of people into the already over-crowded tip of Manhattan—already filled with Stock Exchange and Wall Street workers, bank and insurance-company headquarters and brokers, produce exchanges, major law offices? Let us have *total* equations, please; and equally, tell us the characteristics of alternatives.

The cost-benefit-ratio planning of the highway man and the "highest and best use" of the real estate man [1] both thrive on congestion, in the former case increasing it by providing ingenious temporary relief. The new highway is quickly and more massively overfilled, and in turn more local streets and more garage terminals are built. And then, another round—and we happily, lazily assume that the next 100 billion spent will solve what the last 100 billion only made worse. After the beautiful Verrazano toll bridge in New York City was opened, headlines announced that from the very first, the number of users exceeded by 30 per cent the number anticipated. While this is good news for bondholders, it is another case of new facilities spirally encouraging more traffic. The lesson of flood control has not been learned: control the *headwaters* and *minimize* flow, instead of repeating efforts at ever higher costs to handle ever-increasing floods at the mouth of the river.

Consider a prime example of the real estate man's "highest and best use" and the need for total equations to control private decisions in key situations: the 70-story Pan American Building just north of Grand Central Station in New York. The private investors have or will have an excellent return. The city will collect a big chunk of taxes. But what else is there to say, in the spirit of total equations? To one of the most congested spots in the world have been added daily large numbers of

trucks to supply building and tenants and daily thousands of workers to jam the sidewalks, to invade the already jammed stand-up and sit-down lunch facilities, to squeeze into the tight subway space. Suppose, to consider a hypothetical alternative, the site had been turned into a little green park, a low-pressure breathing area in the midst of super-tensions. We don't lose the big chunk of taxes, because there is, for example, a marvelous site for an equal building at the southern end of Madison Avenue at 23rd Street. A skyscraper there would strongly draw the eye; the Pan Am roof sign would be just as prominent. The surrounding area is busy but only mildly congested, and includes a small park. The location is more convenient to both Penn Station and Grand Central than either one is to the other and well placed among other office and shopping concentrations; the Pan Am ticket office could remain at the very heart of things.

On quite a different plane of total equations and of alternatives, several eminent economists have concluded that investment in education produces as high a return as investment in almost any other field and a much higher return than in most. Theodore W. Schultz notes that "the 1958 data appear to support the following rates of return: elementary, 35%; high school, 10%; and to college, 11%." He also quotes some higher estimates. These are hard-boiled figures, taking into account capital investment, earnings foregone during the period of education, and, as return, changes in lifetime earnings.[2] Consideration of such items as additional benefit to family is not included.

This book does not primarily deal with either economics or education. But it is deeply concerned to unfreeze our thinking and broaden our equations to effectively include a larger range of factors and a longer range in time, so that we can permit ourselves to create a new human environment. Consider expenditure on social operations, a very vast increase in which, on the private-equations basis, simply raises budgets, can't be considered because it can't be afforded, etc. In more far-reaching equations—in terms of massively creating rewarding employment and employables, better performance, and savings on remedial institutions—the costs look very different. Altogether, we must radically expand our conception of what is productive work and get out of the habit of thinking that only production of material goods is wealth-creating.

---

[1] "Highest and best use" means the development and use that will, by producing the highest possible private income, result in the highest possible valuation of the land. Only the individual property is considered. No weight is given to problems of increased congestion, effects on traffic and transportation, or social effects or problems.

[2] Theodore W. Schultz, *The Economic Value of Education 1963*, Columbia University Press, New York, 1963, p. 62.

Wholeness and Action

This study is an *action* book, a book to lay the factual base for conclusions and decisions *and* to lead to those overwhelming moral impulses which alone can infuse into conclusions and decisions the necessary conviction for sustained dynamic action.

Economic, technical, and social facts are to be presented here in a more holistic way—more as the interrelated underpinnings of a whole content—than has been done. This is indispensable for producing ideas that are both feasible and revolutionary, as contrasted with only theoretical, utopian, or excessively mechanistic.

The picture of ultimate design to be presented is not only interesting and challenging, but has a pervasive moral and, again, holistic quality which can transform thinking into action and then into crusade. This quality also can transform the innumerable fragmented (though highly sophisticated) and blinkered technical designs, actions, and separate doctrines into effective interpenetrating parts of a rational and exciting whole—a virile, moving vision becoming a program which is achievable and in which man has a dynamic place.

Wherever we as citizens choose or are able to participate in this program—and everyone can do this at some significant level, in some significant locale—we can think and work the more effectively because each of us will be fully aware of fulfilling, not a negligible role, but a mission as important and as indispensable as any other part of the symphony of living in the twentieth century. Burnham's grand and famous dictum still stirs us: "Make no little plans; they have no magic to stir men's blood, and probably themselves will not be realized. Make big plans; aim high in hope and work. . . . Remember that our sons and grandsons are going to do things that would stagger us. Let your watchword be order and your beacon beauty." But let us add: "Do make little plans which the citizen can grasp and energize, plans of excellence and beauty to which he feels intimate allegiance. Make little plans if you want the big ones to have meaning and impact, to be clothed in flesh and blood, and, in fact, to be *truly* executed."

The architect's single beautiful building loses none of its sharpness and poignancy, but enhances them by transformation into an indispensable *contribution* to a total humane system. The architect finally realizes the futility of the single remedy; he retains his skilled and highly evolved touch. The highway engineer is not less but even more fully the highway engineer when he recognizes that his ever more ingenious and many-leveled interchanges alone only temporarily relieve, and ultimately increase, traffic volume and difficulties. He then recognizes that his work is part of a picture in motion, and must be helped by changed and more rationally related uses of land for residence, for employment, for recreation. The public health specialist, the social worker, the educator, the recreation director—all are immensely stimulated when they recognize that there is a *whole man*, not a series of added-up special compartments to be coped with by added-up special departments, and that their specialties are organic parts, fully effective only when they *are* parts, of a joint and mingled program of education, housing, recreation, re-creation. This realization, of course, must be not only an amiable intellectual recognition but an integral part of action.

This is not to say that everyone must be, or act as if he were, a generalist. You always choose your field of special competence and allegiance and struggle tooth and nail for it and with it; but you do this more satisfyingly and effectively when it is a chosen sword arm of a great whole.

We need not fear so complete a consummation of efforts resulting from our holistic view as to remove or dampen personal challenge, drive, incentive. Quite the contrary. By raising our sights, by providing *graded* local challenges, by showing to each citizen the value of his or her previous effort and the opportunity and the need for further contribution—by doing these things we provide exciting new drives and incentives. If, hopefully, we approach our horizon, there are new horizons. Each solution or set of solutions opens up new problems—though, let us always hope and expect, on higher levels than before. Thoreau said: "Only that day dawns to which we are awake. There are other dawns to break. The sun is but a morning star."

Fresh Thinking and Fresh Elements: Some Examples

In order to take a fresh look at our barnacled, deteriorating twentieth century American scene, we must determinedly shake ourselves loose from the web of customary thinking and rash extrapolation. But in then setting out to improve our condition, we don't, in any aspect, have to start from scratch. Radical humane thinking has gone before: Geddes, Howard, Mumford, MacKaye, Stein—a great inspiring body of thinking, exhortation, and example that has been lying almost untouched as far as action in this country is concerned.

1. *More efficiency, more speed in leveling out greater hills*

Disease Beyond the City

2. *Leapfrogging sprawl. The magazine* House and Home *Sept., 1964 says: "Denver, Colorado, from the air, is an almost perfect example of leapfrogging sprawl. Subdivisions have pushed almost to the edge of Cherry Cheek Dam, foreground, eight miles southeast of downtown. Bypassed parcels of farmland are being held off the market in the hope of getting 1980 prices for the land today. The leapfrog has put crippling traffic loads on inadequate roads leading to the new areas, and the growth of ugly strip commercial areas along these arteries makes bottlenecks even worse."*

1. *Supertechnique to meet traffic superfloods*

Trend Enthroned

2. *"Attention motorists this is your new aerial traffic check reporting. Situation hopeless. That is all." (Alan Dunn, The New Yorker June 28, 1958)*

This in itself therefore remains for us to absorb and apply, and to do so is important. Developments since these thinkers wrote have more than borne out the justice of their grim anticipations if not much were done. And in the last twenty years much of Western Europe has successfully applied the substance of their thinking and prescriptions.

This does not mean that these men have said the last word. It will be seen in the course of this study that time and thinking and deterioration have not stood still. A number of examples of fresh ideas and combinations of ideas will be presented. There is new and sensitive thinking on new relationships and potentials. One or two of these may be worth noting here in some detail.

One hopeful sign in this country is that the vastly expanding need for open space is realized and measures are being taken for providing it. These measures take the form of drastic and intelligent extrapolation from existing need to anticipated need, but with practically no change in character. We will, if these programs carry through, have a lot of the county-park, state-park, and national-park type of activity. This consists of outdoor recreation for the day or the weekend or longer, more or less a reliving of pioneering, pitting men or men and their families against nature, challenging them to get along with it. And beyond, there are the wonders and stillnesses of the wilderness.

This is very important, admirable. But much more essential, it seems to me, especially because it is completely lacking now, is a system under which the life of the farm would be fairly close at hand, providing the constant opportunity for the urbanite, and especially the urban child, to have not only feeling for, but actual intimate involvement in, the biological growth processes of nature. He could take part himself in agriculture—the care of the soil, the nurture of dairy herds and poultry, vegetable growing.

The greenbelt surrounding the city, first masterfully conceived as a defense against sprawl and fringe development and as a recreational resource close at hand, offers this opportunity. The farms in it would not only be easily accessible for casual visiting but a fresh and essential educational resource and requirement. Essential? Yes, for city children have completely lost this vital connection. The farmer would be a farmer-teacher, his function becoming more fully satisfying and productive. A new urban generation would develop, at home in organic nature, carrying forward creatively the millennia of human experience and conditioning in nature. As one determinant of the maximum sizes of our cities, this *real* organic countryside should never be more than a half hour away.

A greenbelt land policy and, if required, some farm educational subsidy (small compared to our normal total of farm subsidy) would make this feasible. A further angle to this concept: Many older people of modest means, on pensions or insurance annuities, are moving to small farms in the metropolitan areas. These persons could readily be guided into greenbelts, where they would gladly and profitably participate in the suggested system; and more of our older city people could be encouraged to take up greenbelt life and farming, particularly in view of increasing leisure and earlier retirement. A case of steering and creatively enhancing an incipient trend!

Consider what else could happen in this greenbelt: Forest planting in connection with drainage and flood control. A marvelous humane habitat-zoo, without any internal fences, where there are not just pairs of unhappy animals caged in a kind of denatured circus display, with kids goggling and making faces at them, but actual *self-breeding herds*. Not a pipe dream this, but a brief description of the London metropolitan area's Whipsnade Zoo of some 500 acres, a thrillingly intimate and rich experience in the true quality and scale of animal life.

Thus a number of disparate but connected emerging approaches supply one quite compelling determinant of metropolitan configuration. This is a compact case, not the most important or far-reaching, among a number illustrating new combinations of ideas, needs, multipurpose possibilities. I have set out this greenbelt program somewhat expansively and exuberantly in order by one example to make vivid at the start of this study the humane revolutionary relationships within our grasp.

On a quite different level of relationships and potentials, the massive and poignant race and integration issue is a new situation in the decisive sense that drastic and total things have not been done about it. It has certainly not had any positive and massive attention in planning-development literature or actual urban programs. Planning in this country has been excessively and unrealistically neutral, or "officially unaware." As someone has put it, planners act as though they were in Sweden or Holland, where the populations are racially homogeneous. But one thing is sure: This is not only a matter of civil rights agitation and picketing; this is a central problem of our time. Yet it receives only lip service and pious references; there is marginal and minimal activation. It must have our central and overriding attention, our major radical, creative, and continuing efforts at planning and development, in our present cities and cities of the future. In a later chapter I shall propose a determined, detailed, and feasible program of accomplishment.

Preview

I have said that the purpose of this book is a total theory-and-action examination of our urban destiny and direction. It is not easy to combine a total look with directional drive. To clear the path for our journey, let me here summarize the substance of the major thrusts of this study:

While gradualism is the normal historical mode of this country's progress, we must and do in crises make decisive revolutionary moves. The national urban crisis is *now*. In dealing with it, we must introduce the concept of creative control and creative alternatives, in place of haphazard and unlimited growth. When the operations of a manufacturing firm exceed the capacity of its factory, it doesn't keep adding appendages in all directions. It opens a new branch of predetermined size in a carefully selected location. We will have to absorb this kind of thinking for our cities.

The forms of our decisive action are the massive immediate development of genuine new cities to handle population explosion and the thinning out of central cities; the social, physical, and architectural nontinkering restructuring of central cities which this makes possible; and twentieth-century pioneering in the deliberate channeling of population and enterprise into new regions where we can freely plan and develop our twentieth-century outlook and techniques, joined with active untangling of our megalopolises.

To attain *any* of these urgent objectives involves very large immediate additions to housing supply, especially low-rental, *before* slum clearance—that is, a vast *net* addition of new housing to meet population explosion and beat intolerable slum. Only this will give us the leverage to achieve our great objectives. And only this will provide the massive additional and steadily reliable employment volume that will give building unions the confidence to truly integrate and to allow introduction of the labor-saving cost-reduction techniques they now fear.

We must also:

■ Explore, develop, and vitalize the social base to achieve personal and social participation with a strong sense of identification at all levels, from the intimate and local to the cellular-regional. The expression "cellular" as used in this book is intended to emphasize that the large totalities—the city, the metropolitan area, the region—are not merely large agglomerates, but should be organic structures built up from small living entities, analogous to the human body.

■ Cause this cellular-regional awakening and recognition of the city-in-nature to flower in new architectural-environmental expression, on all scales. This is not to be confused with ordinary beautification conferences and like efforts, which have fervent aims, in general recognize symptoms, run the serious danger of settling for treatment of symptoms and not searching for and dealing with the *organic* cause and process which underly suitability and beauty.

Generalizing from this contrast, the aim in all cases will be to enable the reader to distinguish for himself the very sharp differences that often exist between concepts and courses in urban regional development that in headline or capsule form have very much the same sound. A second major specific example is that of the new towns now building in this country and those proposed in the administration's 1966 legislation, on the one hand, and the quite different New Towns I shall describe, on the other.

Finally, I shall try to inject the recognition that adequate creative program and action are not normal or inevitable, that to shake loose from drift and vested interest and vested thinking and second-rate comfortableness and trend statistics, the opiate of the planner and the people, we have got to join moral fire and personal commitment to intellectual agreement, to bring the issues right to the summit of urgency.

CRISIS AND OPPORTUNITY

Part Two: Response and Program

The challenge that lies before us I have set out by indicating the characteristics of the good, the stimulating life in cities of the modern world, and some thoughts as to how this may be fully attained in physical, social, and architectural terms. Now I shall synopsize the specific points of discussion and proposals which form the chapters of this book. Review, concept, program, action—and their fulfillment in physical, architectural, and human terms.

Existing Tools for Change

Chapters 2 and 3 are given over to description and analysis of government's hitherto most important and powerful tools, both in-city: public housing and urban renewal, for which the Public Housing Administration and the Urban Renewal Administration, respectively, have been responsible. They will be discussed and dissected at length, in terms of their past and present limitations and their prospects, to see to what extent they have met purposes for which they were set up and how they can be structurally modified to do this better, and to see what is required *beyond their stated purposes* so that they may to the maximum serve the new creative and humane environment which are visualized in this book.

In an interlude following these two chapters, I shall underline this discussion by pointing out how these requirements for expanded purpose and these proposals for structural modification compare with, and where they sharply differ from, the provisions of the Demonstration Cities and Metropolitan Development Act of 1966.

Insurance of mortgages for private housing construction is a third powerful government tool. This is carried out by the Federal Housing Administration. It operates in the city, though until lately chiefly beyond the city. The powers and activities of the FHA have been largely noncreative. At worst, they have characteristically manifested themselves in accentuation and limited rationalization of unhealthy development trends: toward outward scatter, toward increased and rigid single-class settlement, toward economic and racial stratification. The FHA has lately started to facilitate some aspects of urban renewal and to reach rather lower into the middle-income market. It has also recently started to emphasize cluster development with community spaces, in place of the ubiquitous single-lot subdivisions. That this is happening some thirty years after Radburn made the first demonstration is an instance of the excessive gradualism and delay in the adoption of creative urban thinking and demonstrations.

Under the new administrative setup that came out of the 1965 act creating the Department of Housing and Urban Development, the (former) FHA now functions directly under an Assistant Secretary for Mortgage Credit and Federal Housing, and there is also an Assistant Secretary for Renewal and Housing Assistance. A notch further down the line under him there are a Deputy Assistant Secretary for Public Housing and a Deputy Assistant Secretary for Renewal. Thus the spearhead quality and function of the PHA and the URA have been seriously modified. That the new chart of organization and operation means a less direct, dynamic, and visibly influential role for public housing and urban renewal is a grave likelihood or certainty.

Last to be noted among the existing tools are our national and state highway policies as carried out and accentuated by the Bureau of Public Roads and the state highway departments. These exemplify the built-in failure of the single remedy and the onward march of trend intensification: more, wider, more multileveled highways and interchanges so as to facilitate increase of traffic, which in turn produces the need for more of the same. The intraurban consequence of this single aim is a fantastic tearing apart of the central city's texture by ingenious land-eating interchange complexes and proliferating parking lots and garages.

The anarchic condition these policies produce is discussed in Chapter 4. In the course of Chapters 6 and 7, I show how we can deal with this anarchic condition structurally and anatomically, by restructuring the city so as to lessen the need of excessive internal movements and by structuring the region by means of New Towns.

Underlying Dynamics of Development

Chapters 4 and 5 deal with underlying dynamics of social and physical development. These are the pivotal chapters. They are pivotal because much of their content flows from the conclusions reached in the earlier chapters as to weaknesses in the development tools, weaknesses stemming from underlying conditions which the present development measures and attitudes toward development do not recognize or cope with. And these chapters are pivotal because I here identify these and other factors which must be recognized and dealt with if the creative policies and measures to be described in the later chapters are to become realities.

Chapter 4 concentrates on existing and entrenched dynamics of development. Typical among the factors to be explored are:

■ Population explosion and automobile explosion. These are well known, of course; but the effects of the one are ignored in active planning and in fashioning development tools; and the effects of the other are actively multiplied by the twin trends of expanded road systems and the ever more uncoordinated use of land that these systems permit and encourage. While our increasing personal wealth and increasing leisure make it altogether likely that the steep upcurve of automobile ownership will carry forward much as predicted, the almost automatic conclusion that this must be paralleled by that much more road system and terminal system may well be dramatically negated by a determined policy of more rational relations between places of living, work, and recreation.

■ The essential nature of the presently dominant shaper and unshaper of environment: the private speculative developer-*cum*-builder operating on minimal or no investment, thriving on differential and accelerated obsolescence and quick turnover. And then, moving on, he leaves gray areas or areas soon to be gray.

■ The results of considering land merely as a private, tradable, highly speculative commodity. Can the land resource be safely left entirely in private hands any more than the water resource?

■ The continuous relentless rise in sales price of houses, in which rising land prices are a serious consideration. This more and more is accentuating suburban segregation and stratification and separation between places of living and places of work for lower-income workers. The price rise forces them to stay in obsolete inferior housing in the city, while industry and their jobs decentralize. And simultaneously, the middle classes continue to move outward, while their office jobs increasingly concentrate in the centers.

Chapter 5 considers underlying dynamics of development in the more creative and projective sense: important existing and entrenched dynamics that need to be reoriented or drastically changed, as well as dynamics still embryonic and not well recognized that we must establish as strong substructure if the necessary structure and superstructure are to be created. Here, as throughout this book, I take a much less deterministic view of trend than now dominates our thinking and action in what goes for planning.

The need for changing our existing dynamics and for building new foundations is presented in the following contexts: Having considered the spiraling rise in cost of land, housing, and community in Chapter 4, we consider in Chapter 5 the successful Swedish experience over the past decades in achieving nonradical but cumulatively drastic decrease in costs of land and construction, and suggest how the lessons learned there could be applied here.

We shall see how we can creatively inject the issue of racial integration into development and *fully* grapple with it, thereby reversing or seriously modifying the current workaday assumptions and truisms and negative trends in this area—an example of confronting and fostering the groundswell of a new era by determined policy and action. We must not only stop destruction and despoilment but take new initiative, not only conserve but change and re-create.

Above all, we must exorcise the lazy optimism that is satisfied with, and even hails, snail-like gradualism. As a nation we are committed to gradualism. Good. But gradualism has to be punctuated by decisiveness if rampant deterioration is not to make the ultimate decisions pointless or after the fact. In the decisiveness of the New Deal that gradualism was overturned, and we hope this will occur in the present antipoverty drive. In metropolitan planning-development we have already fooled around for forty years, and we are still not appreciably advanced. And with each year of inaction or of tiny advance on our side, active anarchy produces further corrosion and erosion.[3]

As the finale of these two pivotal chapters, the reader is presented with some interlinked new concepts and a group of potentials in the social situation that can be much more sharply reflected than before, in the *process* of physical-architectural planning-development as well as in its product. I sketch in the elements of the social base and the place of an activist social science applying its insights to evoke the people's own disciplined initiative and involvement; and how through this evocation we can produce two quite different but subtly related new results:

A new and essential inevitability in planning and architectural expression, based on social content and understanding and firsthand contact among planners, architects, and the people.

A new dimension of creative employment independent of automation, a dimension of humane activity in the infrastructure of community action

which can and will transform present frustration and dismal unawareness into self-expression and civic expression.

As this discussion unfolds, there will be examples of pitfalls, incipient triumphs, triumphs.

Mastering the Trend: New Cities, New Regions, Old Cities Reshaped

Now, coming into the sunlight of our creative specifics, we face the alternatives of unlimited city and metropolitan expansion and mélange, or conscious limitations and nucleations resulting in livability, amenity, accessibility to the green world. Trend, or mastery?

In Chapters 6, 7, 9, and 10, the concepts that can show us the way toward the light are considered:

New Cities and fresh in-city communities.

Restructuring the old city.

Metropolitan planning and federated metropolitan government.

Restructuring old regions, developing new regions, and new ideals of city scale.

We would replace shapeless expansion of cities, anarchic destruction of rural areas, and rural-urban rash with creatively planned New Towns of the most varied types and for the most varying tastes, the nuclei of growth to preplanned size, reasonably self-contained and thus with less need for more and more superroads and for ever-longer journeys to work. We would preserve the countryside as an accessible resource and as a barrier ("the green wall") and would deflate the highway to its reasonable functions. This also gives us the brilliant opportunity and obligation to reduce housing costs by buying cheap land *and keeping it cheap,* to have new communities that would be genuine cross sections of the nation economically and racially. We shall see that these two essential purposes will not be attained by the 1966 legislation, and explain what different measures will need to be taken to accomplish them in fact. Then we shall consider how we can create fresh in-city communities that will reflect, bring into the city, the values of the New Towns.

In Chapter 7 we deal with articulation of the existing amorphous city into organic cells of communities reasonably self-contained and socially confident and capable, by a reconceived urban renewal. The goal is to transform the city, with its remote city-hall power, into a lively structure of varied active and alert local foci of allegiance and participation. The city center is overabsorptive. The large

[3] The administration makes a strong first effort to come to grips with this important problem in its 1966 act, in a section on planned metropolitan development. We will see that we must, from the local level, demand much more, greatly strengthen this initiative from Washington, help its intention by increasingly forcing its hand.

Which Do You Prefer?

1. *Anywhere, U.S.A.—Specifically, near Massapequa, Long Island*

Imagination and Control. Tapiola in the metropolitan area of Helsinki: New city of preplanned size. Living, work, recreation, nature close at hand. Thus, no long daily peak travel to central city

2. *Low- and higher-cost quarters for workmen, professionals, managers*

3. *City center*

4. *And the counterpart: restructuring the old city. Lansbury district in London*

15

1. Recently, on the 245-acre farm that is Sacramento, California's Gibson Ranch County Park, ranch manager John Day demonstrated hand-milking of a cow to a group of interested children. When Day directed a stream of milk into the mouth of one of the boys, the youngster jumped back in surprise. "It tastes just like real milk," he cried. The farm is twenty minutes from the center of Sacramento.

Needed: Nature Close-in. The Greenbelt: Twentieth-Century Thinking and Attainable Reality

2. *Developing a new trail. Nature Center on the outskirts of the small city of Stamford, Connecticut. Part of the school education program of a "tributary" population of 200,000, within half-hour radius. Such centers, catalyzed by the National Science for Youth Foundation, require 50–100 acres of land and generally include a working museum.*

3. "Where do the lamb chops grow?" Nature can be confusing for the city child. (*New York Times Magazine Section, Jan. 31, 1965. Article by Fred and Grace Hechinger*)

surrounding city matrix is deprived of glitter, deprived of prideful elements of identification. City hall may be even more remote than Washington. Socially, politically, recreationally, architecturally, in terms of employment, we want to create lively organic districts—subcities—in our great cities and in our medium-sized cities. Within these districts, we reconsider the cell of neighborhood in the light of the new tests of integration and of educational modernization. This is Chapter 7.

A regional constellation satisfying the requirements and potentials of our epoch involves the rational development of our metropolitan regions as a whole, and the civic and/or institutional arrangements to effectuate unified regional policy, a form of federated metropolitan government. This is Chapter 9.

Then, true twentieth-century pioneering! We consider the promotion and development of alternatives to cumulatively increasing the population of our very large metropolitan areas. In our twentieth century, with its marvelous new developments in communication by planes and cars, by television and telephone, by electronic techniques, a great sector of industry and employment is no longer tied to big centers or regions with their increasing diseconomies. We should make every effort to channel population and work opportunity to other areas of the country, where we can more fully apply our twentieth-century vision and social and technical advances. And, in this, there are national and state policy implications, as well as intimate and painful local decisions and facings up. A drastic and searching policy debate is required, and tough policy decisions need to be made, to create an adequate and far-sighted program and to convert it into action. This is Chapter 10.

Chapters 6, 7, 9, and 10 build our major theme. But in this book there is a parenthetical chapter, as it were, dealing with a vital element in the physical and functional configuration of neighborhood, district, city, New Town, and region: Chapter 8 on the central city center. The future function and scale and indeed vital existence of the central city center are in a state of doubt. Physically and financially huge works to solve its problems are under way, which may or may not carry with them permanence or optimum answers. We consider the two cases:

■ The great city (numerically). Here the present phenomenon is giantism, with the city center sucking up into itself all that prestige and vanity, those twins of insecurity, can manage to do—depriving many centers of less huge cities of the stimulating

elements that they simply cannot compete for in this weird market; and depriving their own city sub-areas of desperately needed excellence, of self-identification. I have read that the Metropolitan Museum of Art in New York has 360,000 separate items, and am quite willing to accept the figure, give or take 50,000. (I wonder whether anyone really knows.) This is megalomaniac hoarding—warehousing, rather than fostering culture. Within the city, there is another absurdity, the absurdity and diseconomy of superconcentration of governmental functions in a center, when much of the city's actual work is spread through the total city.

■ The middle-sized city, on the other hand, must conceive and work up a good deal more cultural variety and freshness and quality for its center, if it is not to give up its waning magnetism and functions to the great cities, on the one hand, and to the youthfully resourceful outlying centers, on the other. Here, with our twentieth-century resources, we can compose dramatic answers that will probably more than outshine, with a very special quality, the massive cultural-entertainment installations of the great cities. We will see.

Synthesis and Sublimation: Environment Shaping and Architecture

A paramount thesis of this book is that planning-development reaches its full potential only when it finds physical-visual-spiritual expression in architecture, and that architecture flowers only when the architects, the creative environment shapers, have a constantly renewing contact with natural and social scientists, and very directly with people. Underlying that contact, and a precondition of it, is the fact that the architect's works should be cradled in, and grow out of, the topographic and biological and physical facts and manifestations of nature.

The historians seem to agree that the intensive degradation of the city and its schism with nature began in the middle of the eighteenth century, with the in-migrations and slum crowding of low-paid workers (the "urban villagers" of their times). A century later, the great Olmsted, looking backward in anger and forward in dismay, created a beautiful actuality and vision in his great naturalistic parks, from New York's Central Park to San Francisco's Presidio; and later, Charles Eliot formulated and activated Boston's girdling metropolitan park system. But such works unfortunately turned out to be interludes, by and large. The continuing lava flow of the city and the great metropolitan eruption of the last decades, combined with bulldozer technology, have massively ignored or degraded physical and biological connections and have submerged respect for the integrity of natural terrain. One recalls the accurately descriptive jingle:

> Cut the trees and no lament,
> Fill the valleys with cement.

The climactic eleventh chapter of this book deals with the crucial preconditions of architectural expression and the ambient conditions of today, and relates both to the great need for an ultimately satisfying architecture of environment.

This chapter deals also with the role of design in infusing beauty and fitness at each scale from the very small to the very large, and includes examples to show how this role flows from a harmonious, thoroughgoing, and humane understanding of human and ecological needs in living, working, receation, and re-creation.

In the end, architecture, created physical environment, cannot lie. Whatever our verbal proclamations or self-assurances, the highest creative skills are still devoted to those elements which really represent the power and intent of the time. To make democracy visceral and not just verbal, we must be sure that those skills actively embrace daily life and the institutions of the people, are not just monuments to the powerful, whether they are kings or businessmen or art patrons.

Toward Decentralization of Excellence

In our cities we are used to centralization of architecture—on our Fifth Avenues, in our civic and cultural centers, in monumental skyscrapers. But we must produce uplifting architecture in people's daily lives. We must have a decentralization of excellence—in daily installments, with neighborhood foci. Cities, and civilization, cannot afford squalor or dullness, whether by neglect, by intent, or in support of moral Puritanism and the economic "minimum standard."

Our architecture now is typically more concerned with façades and masses than with quality defined in ambient space; less concerned with community architecture and community creation than with the single glamorous building or building group; less concerned with daily life and reaction than with the "public image" or the monument of the huge concern. What we must create runs all the way from the daily environment close at hand to the noblest regional complex.

This does not mean that we want a great-scaled

Washington Monument in the backyard, or even in the community center, for the architectural expression must be hierarchical, in scale and proportion. What it does mean is that each small community must not only meet the functional requirements of open green and developed space, but find its expression in living design, and so be deemed as worthy of care and attention and talent as the largest complex at the regional scale. Thus the "interstitial areas" between projects must no longer be leftovers or just areas where clean-up, paint-up drives flourish and wane. More inspiring elements are needed. We require, let me repeat, the decentralization of excellence. The local community must be the theater of serenity and stimulation, of work and repose, of social life and of private life, and each citizen must identify with it and be involved in its creation and support. In short, *texture* of the city-region has to rise to the quality of the excellent plan, from the small playground to the great dam. In contrast to this we have scenes of boredom and seas of parking in housing developments and around shopping centers.

We also have to trace and gain the potential grand simplicity of the regional scale. For here, too, there is degeneration, for instance, the degeneration of regional architecture in the highway system. The original elegant cloverleaf has become a tangle of spaghetti. The original brilliant simplification and systematization of traffic flow has given way to serpentine absurdity of volume complication.

We can actually transcend what has gone before. But we cannot do it on either the small scale or the large scale if we are trying to give architectural shape to what is essentially anarchy and indiscipline.

Toward New Peaks of Excellence

I have emphasized the small scale and the decentralization of excellence. There are two reasons for this:

The hinterland of daily living, in the interstices of the great city and beyond, has been neglected, and needs radical, talented, and devoted revisualization.

The central summits themselves will gain in purity and total distinction, when they become the culmination of decentralized excellences, rather than just forceful, if stirring, intruders in the city scene. There must be no attempt at displacement of the great peaks or at any leveling out, but a total articulated enhancement.

Epilogue and Prologue: The Urgent Future

These problems of great depth and immensity face us in attempting to create conditions for the good life in the twentieth century:

First, can we, in the welter of international and national problems and urgencies, convince enough people with enough fire to place the character of our life environment high in their thinking and action priorities?

Second, if this is accomplished, can there be injected as moral vision the knowledge that personal and civic excellence can overcome inertia, and the habitual comfort of the second-rate?

Finally, having, we hope, attained these intellectual and moral transformations, can we put our creative forces effectively into the field *in time*, before accelerating current disruptions have irrevocably changed the dimensions and nature of the multiple problems?

Our final chapter, then, will be summation, exhortation; then, may one hope or anticipate?—jubilation.

CHAPTER TWO

PUBLIC HOUSING AS KEY TO COMMUNITY

Public housing, including particularly the principles and actuating forces underlying it, is the key to any satisfactory urban and regional development program. It is *not* just an unpleasant hangover, a residual necessity incidental to relocation of those displaced by new highways, urban renewal, and other public works.

My unorthodox thesis, furthermore, is that the country's and the Congress's solemn commitment to achieve proper housing *and communities* for all Americans cannot be carried out without the ingredient of a greatly expanded subsidized housing program, not only to provide better housing for citizens of very low income and low-middle income but also to open the way to proper community development through the entire spectrum of our neighborhoods and urban areas.

The tortured history of public housing, its straitjacketed, nonevolving character, its imposed and accepted penury of spiritual outlook, its involuntary isolation—these might at first thought make the proposal of such an enhanced role seem absurd. But let us consider the factors in great part accounting for the past and present state of public housing. And let us then consider what immense progress, progress that might even be called a flowering, has recently become quite visible, both physically and socially. And finally, with this background, let us see the true potential of public housing.

Symbols of a Shabby Past

Public housing has been the prisoner of its original opponents and detractors, its character to an almost unbelievable extent determined by them. They managed to attach a stigma to the program and to propagandize public housing into a position apart from the main stream of things. Housing officials, Federal and local, have always been excessively on the defensive. They sought to escape attack by being undeniably "virtuous": starkly penurious, inoffensive, squeezing down space, minimizing community facilities. There was great competition to achieve this kind of "virtue." The generally depressing results alienated support. The specific legislative handicaps, such as the prohibition against commercial facilities in housing developments and the requirement that families had to move out when their incomes had increased beyond rather narrow limits, had sharply deteriorating social effects.

Public housing has been the butt of criticisms whose targets are really the assorted ills and shortcomings of our urban society and polity. The circumscribed public housing effort alone couldn't begin to overcome these, but as a major visual landmark, public housing became the easy symbol.

It has been too glibly associated with the economic and color ghettos which are the result of unwillingness of the white-middle class to permit diffusion and integration, i.e., insistence on retaining its own exclusive white preserves. Public housing has been identified with juvenile delinquency and vandalism. We now know that this is not valid,[1] that delinquency and vandalism are a society-wide social-economic-educational problem particularly characteristic of our time. This is epitomized by the following headline in the *Christian Science Monitor* of September 28, 1963: "Affluent Hoodlums Test Rye, N.Y."—Rye being a wealthy and highly exclusive suburb in Westchester County. The first sentence reads, "Privileged children of upper-income homes, who amuse themselves with petty thefts, vandalism and party-crashing, are the object of a city-wide clean-up drive." The details of the case of Darien, Connecticut, are by now almost legendary. Similar experiences in upper-middle-class suburbia are noted in newspapers all over the country.[2]

Combined with these elements, we have a strong reaction from the excessive original hopes and expectations. We all naïvely thought that if we could eliminate the very bad physical dwellings and surroundings of the slums, the new sanitized physical conditions would almost per se cure the social ills. We know better now.

---

[1] I have recently seen figures on the notoriously publicized Pruitt-Igoe-Vaughn public housing complex in St. Louis. Police-department figures on index crimes (a technical classification which means the more serious crimes, excluding minor crimes such as pilferage) for the period 1959 to mid-1963 show considerably lower incidence per 100,000 persons there than for the city as a whole, and far less than half the incidence for the Fourth District in which it is located. And, significantly, the rate in Pruitt-Igoe-Vaughn went down in this period by over 50 per cent, while the other two rates remained practically stationary. In 1964, the figures were Pruitt-Igoe, 1,553; city at large, 3,559; Fourth District, 7,626. As another example, a study by the Family Court in Chicago in May, 1963 (the latest one made), showed a significantly lower actual crime rate in public housing than in adjacent areas.

[2] In San Jose, California, the high school has recently been suffering broken windows and other damages of vandalism. The malefactors are the children of well-paid industrial workers (in the $7,000-to-$8,000 bracket) who own their own homes in local subdivisions. This superficially less spectacular example actually emphasizes the presence of delinquency throughout the range of social classes.

Present Evidences of a Humane Future

But this is not the end. Public housing, lately stung and roused by the criticism it has had, has in the last few years begun to do things about its situation creatively. Out of the hard and harsh ground of criticism (in some measure justified, it is true), in the last few years we have new growths, new attitudes, visible new progress, not yet adequately noticed. Finally, PHA Commissioner Marie McGuire's buoyant determination has been giving to these beginnings sustained lift and drive.

For example, public housing is coming to be seen having a role in *renewal,* as community and civic asset, not just shelter; as beacon and focus, as neighborhood enhancement. One kind of illustration is presented by Miami, where on sites within an over-all city area of over a square mile, the Miami Housing Authority has programmed 900 units of low-rental housing. There are to be three 200-unit developments whose community spaces working with adjacent schools add significantly to the usability of these facilities. The remaining 300 units, to be placed in scattered vacant areas in groups as small sometimes as only a couple of houses, will remove the litter-spotted character of the general area and encourage adjacent improvement. The result will have a visual and social impact and upgrade a susbtantial part of town.

Another case is that of a much smaller city, Mt. Clemens, Michigan. There the housing commission developed a total of 160 units over twenty sites, with the effect of refreshing the city by injection of fresh design into a number of locations. The houses constituting this scattered stimulation have won several competitive architectural awards.

Another new approach in a number of cities, notably Cleveland, where it started about six years ago, is the community recreational facility planned and built by the housing authority for the elderly low-income citizens of one development, but sized for, and actively used by, the elderly generally from areas quite beyond that development. In small cities, it is often the only such available resource, and it is the skill and experience available to the housing authority that have initiated and carried it through.[3]

---

[3] I was fascinated by the Public Housing Administration's *Senior Citizens Centers: Coordinating Community Interest,* published in April, 1963, a guide winding step by step through the problem of arousing interest, conducting surveys, forming citizens' committees, augmenting funds by finding private contributions and other city funds, and later,

Still another type of example of outreach into the community beyond: in New York's Jefferson Houses there is the East Harlem Plaza, a multi-purpose outdoor asset, with fiesta design and atmosphere, much used by those in the development itself for family and group recreation but also reaching out into the whole East Harlem subcity with its concerts, festivals, and art shows by local part-time artists. The members of its managing committee of twenty-five come from all over the area. Audiences vary from just parents and teachers for a local school show to hundreds and even sometimes thousands for abbreviated opera.

Cultivation of Social Action: Leadership and Competitions

Pushed and self-pushed into it in the last years, some public housing bodies have become engaged in genuine social analysis, in pathfinding, in imaginative programs, all leading to social action and achievement for the participants.

The Chicago Housing Authority, for one, has sought out and has systematically encouraged leadership—in its larger projects, please note, as well as its smaller ones. In its Rockwell development, there are nine building presidents, an operating newspaper office, teen lounges, meeting rooms, etc. Under the presidents, tenant committees control laundry-room use, playground supervision, and gallery and elevator use, in some cases with rotating monitorships. The organization functions independently, and has survived several changes of authority manager and changes in staff of other agencies. An urban grass-roots burgeoning of active democracy and responsibility has been achieved.

In Knoxville, the local authority's low-rent Western Heights was a cop's headache until about two years ago. Captain Huskisson, head of the city's crime prevention bureau, is quoted: "Almost nightly we'd get a call on broken windows, smashed street lights, garbage cans set afire. But we haven't had a call there in over 18 months, maybe two years." Analysis and parents' mass meetings produced a Boy Scout troop and a junior police department. The selected junior policemen were issued identification cards and honored by being encouraged to "check in" with the Knoxville Police.[4]

Another fairly recent mode of social exploration and social effort by local housing authorities has been to emphasize competitive achievement in the creation and maintenance of more satisfying surroundings. One set of such efforts in particular has brought about a dramatic reversal of cliché. It had been almost an axiom that flowers, flowering shrubs, and blossoming trees were "out" in public housing landscape design because they are inevitably plucked or destroyed. This assumption has been turned upside down. For a considerable time now, there have been a large number of developments all over the country (and the number is growing) where flowers are almost as prevalent and conspicuous as in the middle-class suburbs and the source of as much pride to the families and groups who plant them—and who gain various forms of public recognition.

The formally competitive effort flourishes, of all places, in the public housing developments of the big cities, including Chicago and, most recently, New York. Prizes are offered and widely competed for in two classes: public areas, where the effort is organized, sometimes on a project-wide basis, and small front and back yards, where the effort is made by innumerable individual tenants. And very often, there are no protective fences: public opinion and determination are the *social* fences! In Chicago, the day of judging and awards has become an annual festive day of celebration and parade.

Two things are becoming widely recognized. The creation of better visual appearance and space use has an important positive psychological and social effect, in fostering pride and identification, which the worthiest clean-up, paint-up campaigns can't attain to. At the same time the plus results are not automatic, may be quite ephemeral or negligible, and may fortify cynicism—unless the physical effort is preceded by, and synchronized

---

organizing the operating committees of the elderly themselves. This publication is a real contribution, simple and direct, to the ideal of effective citizen action and physical-social result. It is partly based on the successful consummation of a program for senior citizens in Temple, Texas.

[4] This kind of undertaking and experience is widespread.

Thomas E. Harris, executive director of the Hunter's Point Boys' Club in San Francisco, has noted that 150 boys' clubs have been set up within or near public housing projects, in many cases in physical quarters made available by housing authorities. He mentions specifically that housing authorities in Seattle, Portland, and Los Angeles have helped to set them up. Ray W. Sweazy, director of the Urban Relationships Service of the National Council of Boy Scouts, delivered a paper in October, 1963, before the National Social Welfare Assembly, in which he noted the initiative of Miss Marion Neprud of the Public Housing Administration, starting in early 1962, which has flowered into close cooperation between housing authorities and Boy Scouts. This has since produced 200 scouting units in Chicago housing projects, over fifty in Dallas, etc., etc.

with, social interest and participation. There is a movement to achieve this, a movement being called "juvenation" which is just now beginning to take place. The East Harlem Plaza and several others, in New York, Washington, and St. Louis, illustrate this fresh dynamic combination of architectural quality and social eagerness.

Self-criticism as a Spur: Visible Results

These preceding descriptions, if they were taken to imply complacency or paint any overoptimistic picture, would be misunderstood, for public housing still has very far to go to accomplish what it must accomplish in urban society. One must call sharp attention to the disturbing fact that the bad image of public housing is prevalent not only among the real estate people and the middle-class public but also among those for whom it is meant. In the course of his study on relocation from the West End of Boston, Chester Hartman notes that over a long period only 17 per cent of the slum inhabitants in the nation who had to be relocated moved into public housing. In the specific area studied, 74 per cent of the persons questioned said they would not want to move into public housing.[5]

But the big point is that public housing *is* self-critical, that it is no longer static but has in recent years taken important new strides and is evolving. We are well beyond the beginning of sensitive creative policy and operation. Even in architectural appearance, I have been surprised, in visits around the country within the last few years, by how many pleasant developments there are, and surprised to find indeed that there are some brilliant ones—though certainly the bulk are still grim, dull, drab, as is generally true of our middle-class housing and of our luxury housing too.

In Easton, Pennsylvania, Hugh Moore has done a little-known jewel of a public housing development on very difficult terrain; Aaron Green's magnificent one in Marin City, California, is better known. Emanuel Turano has done a delightful one for the aged in Greenwich. Meathe and Kessler's single homes and row houses in Mt. Clemens, Michigan, are by far the best work in the city. (The preceding examples are also by far the best work in their respective cities.) Toombs, Amisano, and Wells have done a development on challenging topography that is the best complex of domestic architecture in Atlanta. All these are fairly recent.

[5] "The Limitations of Public Housing: Relocation Choices in a Working-class Community," *Journal of the American Institute of Planners,* November, 1963.

Looking at any of these works, I think that no one, casual visitor or discerning critic, would react with "Oh! Public housing!" or would fail to recognize the special synthesis among architect team, authority, indweller, and site that they embody.

All of this social and architectural progress encourages me. It is part of a new ferment, a new outlook, and a new grasp. What I have seen and learned in the last two years has definitely reconverted me to the view that there is new accomplishment and realistic promise.

There is also visible now architectural-social accomplishment not so striking as the examples just noted but perhaps even more significant. I have seen, for example, Krohn Homes in Phoenix by the architects Leschner and Mahoney and Villa Espagna in San Juan, Puerto Rico, by Rafael Carmoega. What characterizes these is an unpretentious humanity which is the product of a genuine grasp of local idiom and feeling. Without achieving really distinguished architecture, the design of these developments expresses this grasp and even rises some grades above it. This might be called the beginnings of local vernacular.

Bases of a New Approach

Consider now the tremendous factor, beginning to be felt and put to use, of the modification and lightening of negative pressures and rules on low-rent housing:

■ Easing of the income-rent ratios, permitting families to stay who have raised their incomes, with the resulting possibility of retention of local leadership timber. One of the blackest marks against public housing is that it is becoming more and more confined to lowest incomes and "the other America" of miserable poverty. This does not seem to be inherently necessary. Abroad, it is not and never has been so. But an enormous and persistent effort must be undertaken and supported to reverse the trend here.

■ Permission to include commercial facilities, even small shopping centers: not only a release from the absurd inconveniences and even hardships of having to go a distance for every little item, but a livening effect on the tempo of living and congregating. In Europe such facilities have always been allowed and quite normally included.

Adding all the above observations together, we see building up a whole change of outlook and body of sympathy, skill, research, and performance which will soon be seen to be a priceless community asset. Jettisoning public housing five years ago in its then form and outlook might conceivably have made sense; as of now, this would be social folly and waste. Situated at the heart of things— near the home and the family—local housing authorities are in a very special position to bring together agencies and departments to act, not departmentally, but as catalyst for the whole man, the whole family. And they have started to do so. Here are a few of the agencies which find a common focus and habitation in public housing and which have felt and responded to this new current: National Homemakers Services, National Committee of State Garden Clubs, American Red Cross, child welfare groups, Boy Scouts and Girl Scouts, Boys' Clubs, the U.S. Department of Agriculture Extension Service. In view of prevalent urban and suburban delinquency and other problems, at all levels and locations, this vital across-the-board mobilization has been an important new force in the urban scene. It is in fact a precursor of some of the new elements in the 1966 demonstration-cities legislation.

What is needed also is sustained public observation and strong public criticism of public housing— creative, encouraging, expectant criticism, not a dismissing shrug.

Alternatives: What Role for Private Enterprise?

All sorts of alternatives to public housing are proposed: private enterprise, new private development with subsidy, neighborhood rehabilitation, rent supplementation. Of course, rehabilitation has a real place as an instrument for countering neighborhood deterioration. But it does not meet the major, indeed desperate need for more low-rental housing to relieve the shortage at the low-income level. As to private enterprise, in its normal developer sector, what housing solutions has it to show that anyone can think seriously of it as an alternative? What desire or capacity for the social aspects and civic aspects which are so essential? [6] The troubling question of well-located land for low-rent housing is no easier of solution under private auspices, because the moment normal private enterprise got earnestly into integration at low

---

[6] I omit for the moment the consideration of genuine institution-based cooperatives and public interest groups and of direct investment of important magnitude by large institutions such as insurance companies and pension funds. These lie in a very different sector of private, or rather nongovernment, enterprise which is discussed later in this chapter and in Chap. 5.

and low-middle income levels, as distinguished from middle and high-middle levels, where the minorities can be only a sprinkling because of economic conditions, precisely the same opposition and harassments would arise. These must be met in either case by much greater public decisiveness and determination. And local housing authorities must themselves show more vision and decisiveness, backed by the Department of Housing and Urban Development, source of their funds and subsidies. That there is building up incipient and more than incipient local experience and opinion to back such a policy, we will see later.

The cost differential between public and private work is more of a question, and certainly must be threshed through. But figures I have seen from New York comparing costs of straight public housing, regulated private (Mitchell-Lama) enterprises, and cooperatives are anything but conclusive.[7] The problems of material and construction standards, durability, and maintenance are probably crucial in explanation of cost differences. How to reduce the inflexible costs of housing has *at all levels* not had the scale of research it requires. The prevalent practice of partially meeting the cost problem by paring down living space is not only inconvenient but socially shortsighted. Almost nothing has been or is being done to drastically reduce the costs of conventional construction. The remarkable progress of the mobile home, no longer just an index of American mobility, in drastically low costs and in volume (currently 20 per cent of all housing starts) injects a threatening and yet hopeful immediacy.

Two New Kinds of Effort

There is a special ingenious effort to involve private enterprise in low-rental housing and at the same time to destratify socially and economically. This is taking two forms:

One is to take families of the low income levels that would need the level of subsidy of public housing but, instead of placing them in a total public housing project, to place them in a private middle-class development or middle-class neighborhood, in small numbers compared to the middle-class bulk. The Federal government pays the difference between what a family could afford and the commercial rental, without its being known who is

---

[7] Mitchell-Lama is a New York State law offering builders special inducements in exchange for limited return on investment.

1. *The dismal stereotype:
"Decent, safe, and sanitary"*

**Public Housing:
Newly, Transfiguration.
The New Impulses.
In Architecture: Freshness,
Community, Insight,
Distinction**

2. *Mt. Clemens, Michigan*

3. *Easton, Pennsylvania*

4. *Marin City, California*

1. *Community deliberations: Tenant Council Meeting. Cabrini Homes, Chicago*

Vitality in the Housing Community

2. *Tenant music-makers: Philadelphia. Passyunk Homes*

3. *Outdoor dramatics: Philadelphia. Richard Allen Houses*

4. *Fooling around in the play area: Redlands, California*

the publicly aided tenant and who are the unaided tenants. The major purposes are to produce a democratic kind of mix in the areas the low-income families enter and to avoid excessive concentration of low-rent enclaves. This rent-supplementation method was provided for in the 1965 Federal Housing Act, and is now in operation.

The other method is to build a fairly large development which is part public housing and part private housing for middle-income people. The design is such that there is no obvious or invidious labeling. As individual family incomes rise or fall, the government-subsidized or unsubsidized status would change accordingly.

An example of the first method is an experiment in New Haven. A large family is located in an essentially middle-class neighborhood of single houses. In addition to the mix and the anonymity, there is in a number of cases still another advantage: the houses occupied, frequently substandard or run-down to begin with, are rehabilitated with the aid of the housing board. Thus there is a brake on neighborhood deterioration, or upward push. This has a healthy civic effect. A variation of this method is being tried out in San Francisco. Under a demonstration grant from the Federal government, the San Francisco Development Fund, a nonprofit corporation, is acting as agent to arrange for a number of low-income families to buy into an essentially middle-income cooperative.

There is a serious hidden disadvantage to these approaches, which may be termed "residual stratification." The most promising of low-income families are selected because this minimizes danger of failure and because in the scattered situations, special social services are more difficult to provide. These approaches, one of them now embodied in the nation's housing law, are very likely, then, to skim off the best of the low-income families and leave the regular subsidized public projects with a still more prevalently low-stratified group. Thus there is a chance that the remedy may be worse than the disease.

This is not a curmudgeonly remark. In a *Journal of Housing* article, two participating staff members of the New Haven Redevelopment Agency, having noted various problems of the New Haven experiment, then say, "For these reasons, careful selection of families to live in scattered housing, be it publicly owned or rental assisted, is a necessity." [8] In an account of the San Francisco enterprise, it is stated, "Sixty low-income families who give promise of

increasing their income will be chosen for this project." [9]

The second kind of effort seems relatively free of this danger, however. In a pending proposal with important possibilities, the Lavanburg Foundation is the private partner of the New York City Housing Authority. There will be over 1,000 of the low-income families and a similar number of those of middle income. This is development of a neighborhood, with lively community facilities, in which both groups will participate—as well as outsiders.

These situations have been given space here because they are interesting in themselves and, especially, because they seem a good specific illustrative case of equipping the lay reader himself to distinguish, to make the kind of alert personal exploration and valid comparisons of proposals he may hear about which he should get into the habit of making, whether in the realm of public housing or elsewhere.

I would not be understood as totally condemning such efforts as New Haven. Special circumstances—e.g., in New Haven, the need to find quarters for extra-large families and the opportunity for neighborhood rescue—would justify them. But such efforts should always be a minor number or proportion, so as not to run into the danger of residual stratification. We will know more about the limitations and potentials when we begin to see what develops from the 1965 Housing Act's rent-supplementation section.

The major and vastly predominant solutions for democratizing our living conditions should be three:

■ The joint foundation-authority type described above.

■ Further liberalizing the allowable rent-income ratios to permit retention of upward-mobile families as a leavening influence in normal public housing developments.

■ Design of large housing projects to produce natural varied subgroupings or subcommunities within the total, so as to gain the advantage of intimate and varied social-physical scale and large-scale low-overhead services, and so as to achieve architectural-social refreshment of a whole area in the city: i.e., injection of new and varied qualities peculiarly possible in the large scale.

Public Housing as Key to Development

It is one thing to take the position that low-rent

---

[8] Joel Cogen and Kathryn Feidelson, "Rental Assistance for Large Families," *Journal of Housing,* no. 10, 1964.

[9] *Rent Subsidies,* Department of Public Affairs, Community Service Society of New York, November, 1964, p. 7.

public housing should be a continuing enterprise, quite another to assert that it is, as I maintain here, key to urban development. Why is this so, and how can public housing fulfill this function?

The *why* has been fairly touched on in preceding discussion of the social and architectural searching and techniques that are beginning to flower and of the discovery that we have in public housing a policy and administrative tool much more responsive and creative than we had suspected. Its contribution is needed at higher income levels also —for example, its uncovering of tenants' responsibility and purpose, its effectiveness in replacing *anomie* and resignation with local democratic action. In the incubator of the public housing body we may be developing a more needed and more potent set of citizen impulses and practice than in the hallowed and fairly healthy but limited home-ownership situation. This is the creative side of public housing, a strong contrast to the stereotype of the anonymous rabbit warren. To put a point on this, I quote a public housing tenant: "The people who live around me are no longer preoccupied with rats, roaches, and mountains of garbage. I found that more than half the people have an active interest in their building and neighborhood. They are concerned with safety, cleanliness, beauty, and recreational facilities."

In short, then, public housing is the key to urban development because it, more than any other tool of change, has the power to move us toward true urban development. As for how public housing can fulfill this function, I have examined varied cases of its role as *renewal*. But many more things need to be done:

We need to go seriously further in legislative improvements than the two important modifications already noted: the new higher incomes allowable for families remaining in public housing and the possibility of shopping liveliness.

There is the need, for social health, of appreciably greater economic spread of tenant income, *within* developments or in closely related developments. Cooperative sales should be allowed—an objective to be kept constantly in mind—to tenants who begin to have the means to buy, in previously regular public housing developments as well as in such special cases as the San Francisco cooperative discussed above.

Also in the direction of social health, there is no question of the need and value of social scientists and social workers, for creative operation and management and for the injection of their insights into planning and design. While in one way or another various housing bodies have managed to employ a sprinkling of such professionals, new specific authorization is needed to make such counsel available to housing authorities on a fruitful scale. There is, in fact, a vast and pressing need for the insights of social science and the skills of social work in relating people effectively to their fast-changing—and often suddenly changing—urban environment.

We must deal with the population explosion and with industrial decentralization. As of now, low-income workers are still by and large confined to the inner city because of the availability there only, or chiefly, of slum rents or public housing which they can afford. Private enterprise is building so-called "New Towns," or fringe developments, those one-class communities which have at best only a thin layer of economic variation. The needed ingredient here is public subsidized housing, as in the English New Towns. It must no longer be chained to the inner city.

And within the city, one critical point needs fresh reexamination and fresh emphasis. Thirty years ago, in the early beginnings, Lewis Mumford, Henry Wright, and I wrote a series of articles in *The New Republic* devoted mainly to urging the thesis that public housing should *not* be equated with central slum clearance but should also, and possibly mainly, be done on vacant land, inlying and outlying. We were not able to influence the course of events. This issue is desperately worth rearguing as even more applicable now. The crucial point is *added supply* and not replacement; and unless there is much greater locational choice available within the cities and in the metropolitan areas, the ghettos and the excessive journeys to decentralized industry will worsen.

As a seeming paradox, it is a fact that the past and current formula of new subsidized low-rent housing only to the extent of an equivalent amount of slum demolition actually delays and frustrates genuine social-physical slum elimination. Unless we *first* increase supply, the remaining slums remain equally crowded; and indeed they and other areas become more crowded (and profitable) with increasing population. Thus the visual and middle-class–emotional satisfaction of some fairly immediate slum clearance must be rationalized and revolutionized into a big program of new construction promoting genuine cumulative slum *elimination*.

Needed: State and Local Initiatives

One standard complaint against public housing

1. *Public effort: Chicago.*
   Park View Apartments

Flowers in Public Housing Developments

Tenants' private and public flower gardening is a characteristic feature both North and South. Individual, social, and corporate eagerness has discouraged vandalism and diminished indifference.

2. *Festival atmosphere: Chicago. Bridgeport Housing*

3. *The home garden: Norfolk, Virginia*

4. *Invitation to compete*

is that there is too much centralization and rigidity and restrictiveness in Washington, which controls the allocation of capital funds and annual subsidy, and a resultant lack of adventurousness and experimentation. Whatever may have been the truth in previous years, I am satisfied, after recent periods of close contact at the various levels, that the contrary is more nearly true: that such boldness and initiative and new directions as are apparent have come mainly from Washington.

There is indeed a quite exciting and adventurous new development sparked by the Housing Act of 1961: deliberate experiments by varying combinations of Washington, local housing authorities, local citizen groups, and universities. These are taking place not only in the places, such as Boston, Philadelphia, New Haven, and New York, but in a number of possibly unexpected places around the country, such as Michigan City, Indiana; Rapid City, South Dakota; Glassboro, New Jersey; and Anchorage, Alaska. The demonstrations run from a number in unstratified housing in unstratified neighborhoods for low-income and middle-income people, including cooperative ownership in some cases, to self-help in order to lower costs in new housing and in rehabilitation, to inexpensive cooling in hot climates; i.e., they run a wide gamut of social and technical and sociotechnical operations.

However, pursuing the thinking further and in a more essentially positive direction, it is just too bad that practically the only source of financial initiative and subsidy funds is the Federal government. There has been practically no other financial initiative.[10] But it is highly desirable for states and cities to get a move on, to pass legislation and authorize funds which would both produce some desperately needed increase in the volume of public housing and produce fresh and varied local approaches. It has always been a major glory of the American system that states did take initiatives, that localism leavened the whole system by trying things out and often pointing new ways.

As citizens, we have the insistent obligation and the high opportunity to give up easy whining and inject positive direction of housing into state and local affairs. While satisfactory housing and stimulating community life are a national interest, they are more traditionally, warmly, and satisfactorily a local concern. For example, the substantial number of local citizen housing associations should awaken and turn to a much-belated new role as determined proponents of fully creative state and local action. And what about the local unions aggressively pushing along these lines and for cost reduction, any ill effects of which should be more than counterbalanced by higher building volume?

Altogether, the saying is, "Don't just stand there!"

Size of the Needed Program and the Social-Architectural Challenge

We face today, a series of many-faceted choices in urban and regional development, and public housing has an indispensable role to play in making them. Its impulses and resources and experience and, above all, its recently emerging integrating outlook have a great deal to offer as a versatile ingredient in vitalizing the communities of the city and region. This being so, let us get some idea of needed quantity and urgency of program.

For all the controversy that has accompanied public housing from the beginning, one might think that large amounts had been built. The fact is that there has been absurdly little in the more than twenty-years that congressional legislation has provided for it. William Grigsby says that at a rough approximation, over 5 million families live in substandard quarters.[11] In the almost thirty years since public housing first started, a total of *under 600,000* units have been built, started, or reached active planning. While some people who live in slums could afford to command somewhat better housing, the vast majority could not. Over two-thirds earn less than $4,000 a year, and one-third earn less than $2,000. The 1965 housing legislation set higher yearly public housing totals than this thirty-year average of 20,000 units a year, i.e., 60,000 a year for four years. A significant touchstone is that in the year 1965–1966, the rate of local housing authority applications for help to Washington is over six times the average, or twice the new yearly rate. But the real gap is this: there is still no stated period by the end of which every family or indi-

---

[10] Except in the significant cases of New York State, Massachusetts, and Connecticut. There are a number of other state commissions with regulatory functions. But only a handful—those of California, Hawaii, Illinois, Pennsylvania, and Rhode Island—have real significance. New Jersey in late 1966, started a Department of Community Affairs, which may well be a trailblazer.

[11] William G. Grigsby, "Housing and Slum Clearance: Elusive Goals," *The Annals of the American Academy of Political & Social Science*, March, 1964, p. 112. This is a conservative *low* among responsible estimates. For example, Boris Shishkin, representing the AFL-CIO, noted that "close to 15 million dwelling units are still substandard" in testimony on March 3, 1966, before the House Banking and Currency Committee.

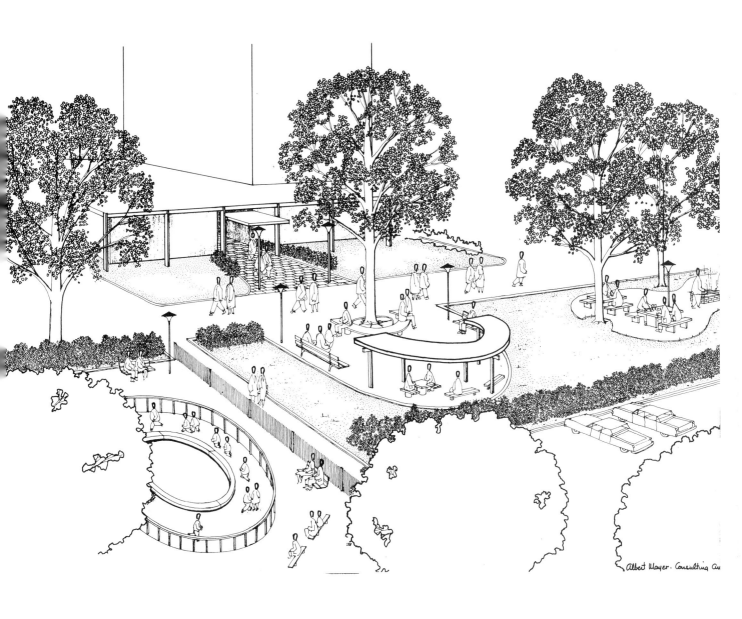

Public Housing. New Impulses:
Community Out-reach into the Surroundings:
A Neighborhood Community Center and Social-Recreational Area

Sketch is for St. Louis public housing. Other examples: Mall in public housing,
Washington Southeast, in Chapter 3: East Harlem Plaza of Jefferson Houses,
described in this Chapter, shown in Chapter 7 as illustrating another issue also.

vidual should be enabled to live in a livable home in a vital community. We must set a goal of, say, twenty years and come up with a program of between 250,000 and 300,000 public housing units a year. This is certainly conservative but begins to make sense.[12] And to reemphasize points made before, a large number of these should be built on vacant land immediately, and a sizable proportion should be compulsory for New Towns, if we are going to attain the stated and essential purpose of democratic mix. This will require new legislative expansion, and *that* requires real, animated debate, now.

It is customary, in this kind of advocacy, to compare the specific expenditure with the astro-

[12] From the total of 5 million substandard housing units we can deduct, say, 1 million to 1.5 million which can be satisfactorily and economically rehabilitated. However, we must add a minimum of 2 million for demolitions and relocation (for urban renewal, roads, etc.), population increase, and accumulating deterioration in twenty years. We thus arrive at a minimum for public housing, taking account also of those who can be accommodated by the rent-supplementation method, of between 250,000 and 300,000 units a year for twenty years.

Please note that such a rate is for *public housing only* and does not include *anything* for middle income and above—i.e., a *net* annual addition of public housing of *not less than* 200,000 units a year, above presently provided yearly totals.

The figures for a total annual volume of housing across the board should be of the order of 2.5 million. Thus our public housing figure, though a great increase over what is presently provided, will come to only 10 per cent of a total program.

nomically greater expenditure for defense, for Vietnam, and for outer-space exploration; and then to go on to say how little we are seeking in comparison, etc. These are completely valid evocations, but let us use a more workaday measure of comparison: The annual cost of our agricultural subsidies is something over $3 billion. We would require, based on experience to date, $90 million subsidy per year for every 250,000 units of public housing, about 3 per cent of the agricultural subsidy. And *our* subsidy produces construction jobs; it's not just bookkeeping.

On another plane, it should be noted that the design of public housing communities is increasingly being considered an important challenge by architects. While to most major firms the prestigious office buliding, the new university library, and the airport terminus are still the glittering assignments, and housing is a filler-in, younger talented architects are being attracted to the creation of community. The examples cited previously for outstanding excellence have largely been done by younger architects. This whole question of the relationship of architects and architecture to public housing and its social texture is the urgent social-architectural challenge.

In determination of the scale and location and community design quality of public housing: we are at this specific crossroads. We must pass through it and, hopefully, move on at a much faster pace. This is the political challenge to the citizen.

We now deal with the work of urban renewal, the development of its range and vision and the actual performance of its seventeen years, and its possible future course. The Urban Renewal Administration has been the Federal mechanism set up to make grants to local municipal bodies to carry out the work of urban renewal. May I say initially that the thinking and vigor and action of the last few years, under William Slayton, URA Commissioner until 1966, greatly surpassed the previous pedestrian plodding and irresolute intent. Slayton had an important part in galvanizing the municipal renewal agencies, which as in public housing are the determinants of the character of the actual programs.

The Housing Act of 1949 and subsequent acts marked an exciting stride forward in the philosophy and policy and legislative framework for the social-physical development of our cities and metropolitan areas. It provided for "the realization as soon as feasible of a decent home and a *suitable living environment* for *every* American family, thus contributing to the development and redevelopment of communities and to the advancement of growth, wealth, and security of the nation [italics mine]." In Title I of this Magna Charta of urban renewal, it was provided that the Administrator "shall encourage the operations of such local public agencies as are established on a state or regional or unified metropolitan basis or as are established on such other basis as permits such agencies to contribute effectively toward the solution of community development or redevelopment problems on a state or regional or unified metropolitan basis."

The first-quoted provision extended the original public housing legislation of 1937 to include, as part of the obligation of supplying a decent home, provision of better environment and community. In the second quotation, we see the dual intention to further the solution of community development problems on a much broader basis than merely housing and to promote metropolitan action.

Objectives and Practice

It was only in 1964—fifteen years after this act! —that Congress made it possible for the Urban Renewal Administration to make disposition of cleared land it was acquiring for low-rent public housing units on the same basis of write-down as that given to programs sponsored by private enterprise. An extraordinary lag, an extraordinary dichotomy, and an important milestone reached fifteen years later than it should have been! As of

CHAPTER THREE

URBAN RENEWAL AS CREATIVE CATALYST?

the end of 1964, around 20 per cent of renewal projects had public housing units scheduled or in place, a total of about 27,000 units, still a very small number in proportion to the total relocations of something over 160,000 families for urban renewal alone. For a number of reasons, we must not make too much of this low ratio. But it is a crude index of a total increase in stratification of residential areas by urban renewal. Also, it sheds some light on the severity of the relocation problem, particularly in view of the fact that by far the largest part of the nation's approximately 200 square miles of cleared urban renewal area has been residential slum. The 1966 act, at long last, requires most urban renewals to provide a substantial number of units of standard housing at low and medium charges.

In its Title I, as quoted above, the 1949 act encourages local agencies on a metropolitan basis. Urban renewal as it operates is strictly on a political-city basis. Of course this is a terribly tough nut to crack, and we must not excessively blame the URA for failing to crack it. At the city level, urban renewal is in some places making a serious contribution in an overdue coordination and synchronization of the planning and activities of municipal departments. This includes the enforcement side of the building and fire departments, health and sanitation, and in some cases, housing and planning policy and open space and park activity. In short, in the best cases, as in Boston and New Haven, there is a sort of vice-mayor for development.[1]

Title I provisions call for elimination of slums and blighted areas and for maximum redevelopment by private enterprise. Congress, in calling for slum clearance so emphatically, had not learned from accumulated experience in public housing that slum clearance, while satisfying to the civic emotions and the eyes, produces grave negative effects socially, because it entails maximum social-community disruption, and, because in this era of scarcity of low-rental housing of *any* kind, it has maximized the total of families that had to be relocated and minimized the available supply of housing.

[1] However, a great big caveat here. As so often happens in our country, the pendulum may be swinging too far in the other direction. An excessive homogenization of the administrative setup is visibly emerging. This may have two basic ill effects. On the one hand, it blurs the sense of mission and singleness of purpose of the public servant or commission whose intense interest is, for example, in low-rent housing or code enforcement. On the other hand, the citizen finds it harder to identify and deal directly with someone who counts and who can help him in his particular need.

Congressional Purpose and Local Objectives

In a basic way, urban renewal has strayed far from the purpose expressed in the act of 1949: "a decent home and a suitable living environment for every American family." This seriously stated purpose has been very much minimized by most of the cities undertaking urban renewal. In general, the main interest of the roughly eight hundred cities that are engaged in urban renewal is twofold: to tear out several visually prominent disreputable and economically underdeveloped areas, especially near the center of the city, and replace them with a glittering galaxy of buildings and spaces; and second, to reattract presently centrifugal commercial and shopping volume, to "fight back against the suburb."

About one-quarter of urban renewal projects are not residential at all. Another quarter will have over 50 per cent of their acreage in nonresidential uses. And where there is residential use, it is predominantly for higher-income families, who are always accommodated anyway, and some middle-income families. No one can claim that the glittering office buildings, apartment houses, and department stores being built are providing a decent home and suitable living environment for Americans. In fact, this component of home and environment, really the minimum component, is frequently altogether absent, the people simply being displaced to other areas.

This change-over is defended on various grounds, principally the important one of restoring city pride and self-confidence and a festive reflection of this in major projects to attract visitors.[2] We need the glitter. But we imperatively *now* need a great deal

[2] One of the most usually cited advantages of the kind of urban renewal we have is increased property taxes of the after as compared with the before (i.e., slum), often a spectacular figure. But if the new facilities created meet a demand and fill up, it means that there was need, and the new facilities would have been built on the chosen site or on another; hence the total tax-collection increase would be more or less the same. (Witness the "urban renewal" or "urban redevelopment" that takes place regardless of official action or encouragement: for example, the huge Century City in Los Angeles, which cost about $200 million; the two huge new centers in Dallas, a city which has no urban renewal authority; the complete redevelopment of Park Avenue below 59th Street in New York, with massive office buildings by many builders; Stuyvesant Town in Manhattan by the Metropolitan Life Insurance Company; Sutton Place in New York; Georgetown in Washington; Old Town in Chicago.)

Official urban renewal does promote a general atmosphere of buoyancy. But the advantage of the spectacular specific before and after instances of increases in tax collections is very much open to question.

Urban Renewal: Before and After. Where Are the People?

Photographs from brochures dealing with two cities. Each shows the old slum of the city, ugly and troubling, and then shows the glittering and quickly satisfying contrast—the new project. In the dozens of such brochures I have looked through, none show pictures of where and how the displaced people live. This absence speaks eloquently in general, and with not enough exceptions, for the interest and outlook of urban renewal. Where are the PEOPLE?

1 and 2. New York City: Kips Bay. Slum into high rental

3. Detroit "Corktown" slum into 4. Headquarters of Florists Telegraph Association

more of the pervasive substance of better housing and living communities for all Americans. And to reinstate this element, we surely need active public debate.

There is, hopefully, some concrete local ferment on this issue. Consider, for example, this report from the Cleveland *Plain Dealer* of May 28, 1965 (some five years after urban renewal had got under way):

> Councilman Leo A. Jackson said it was emphasized (in a closed-door session of the city council) that business leaders must support the residential urban renewal programs if the businessmen want full cooperation of council in (nonresidential) programs such as Erieview II.
>
> Jackson, Chairman of council's urban renewal committee, has been holding up legislation on Erieview II and six new projects because he has been dissatisfied with lack of progress in residential urban renewal programs such as Glenville and University-Euclid.[3]

Positive Efforts by the Urban Renewal Administration

While the URA in Washington went along with this basic *de facto* change in primary purpose, it made some effort to broaden and deepen the prevailing crude thinking and action, to bring back the higher purpose and action—though these are still to be realized by deeds. More immediately, a partial restoration of focus has been in terms of neighborhood conservation and rehabilitation made possible by the Housing Act of 1954. This is in some cases having an important effect on local neighborhoods, in physical-visual-restorative terms and in local self-confidence.

To begin with, the URA insisted on the *workable program* as a prerequisite. This is in effect a demand for some kind of over-all city plan to effectuate the purposes of the act; for a plan dealing with segregation; and for some proof of citizen involvement on a "civic leaders" basis and/or on a locality basis, the latter particularly in areas where conservation or rehabilitation is to take place. The URA also introduced the concept and practice of the general neighborhood renewal plan and the community renewal plan. In capsule, these involve breakdown and particularization, area by area, of what is proposed to be done to the whole city on a

[3] In the 1965 mayoralty election, the incumbent Democrat came within two thousand votes of being defeated by a Negro Independent, this being one of the main issues on which the mayor had been challenged.

long-term basis, as well as rough time scheduling. But these plans and corresponding developments are well in the future, at varying points in the future. In fact, with the creative partial exceptions of Philadelphia, New Haven, Baltimore, Newark, San Francisco, and St. Louis, urban renewal consists of one or more fairly unrelated large projects mostly in areas that were slums and now, because of the city's development since these slums originated, have become areas where private enterprise sees or thinks it sees profit for minimum or zero investment, and for an economic group quite different from that which really needs the benefits of urban renewal.

Restructuring and Slimming Down the City

As for *restructuring* the city in a positive sense through urban renewal, this is just not happening. The confused, traffic-bedeviled structure of our cities, even the more forward cities, is not being unscrambled and restructured by urban renewal into entities approaching closer local self-containment of living, work, and recreation. Further, the heavy concentration of *new* construction and functions closely in one large area of the central business district means increase of traffic between it and the other portions of the city. I know of only one exception. Eastwick, the huge vacant-land renewal in Philadelphia, appears to be aiming at attaining both an economic-social mix and considerable industrial and other local employment, so that in this one case, if it fully eventuates, travel and crosshaul are likely to be substantially reduced.[4]

While the loss of population by the city should not go too far, to a certain point it has essential merits, in permitting more humane space conditions and in creating green areas, the lack of which was a major cause of our original out-migration from the central city. But instead of making the most of opportunities for slimming down, urban renewal, as it is practiced, proceeds on the underlying and spoken premise that there was some optimum congestion at the point in time when population and

[4] I feel in duty and in truth bound to note exceptional cases even though they are exceptional. The reader must be fully aware that these *are* exceptions—to feel discouraged, not encouraged. He should also be on the lookout for exceptional situations in his own city and do all he can to make sure that they are utilized to their maximum potential as community-building and city-restructuring element. As an example, a current opportunity in Washington which should be seized is that of taking over for such purposes the 313-acre site which the National Training Center is giving up.

visitors were at their peak: a sort of golden age of congestion. For example, Victor Gruen notes with regret that the population of Boston declined by 7 per cent from 1920 to 1960; that in Cincinnati 209,000 people visited the core in 1945, and only 171,000 in 1960.[5] If it can be accepted and used as a new starting point that our major cities should slim down somewhat further still, we will be in a position to create superior central cities.

De-development by Dislocation and Relocation

As for social restructuring, the essentially discrete-project nature of urban renewal and its essentially private-profit character mean essentially economic stratification, by way of middle-high-rental housing and office buildings. And this means massive dislocation of the previous inhabitants, who by and large can afford only very low rents and are, in vast predominance, the color minority. Improved measures for humane relocation since the early devil-take-the-hindmost days are a tribute to massive local democratic protest and to URA responsiveness and pressure on local authorities. Everybody finds some kind of reasonably good roof, a sizable number even improve their shelter. But they generally *pay higher rents,* and from the point of view of city development and social tensions, the results are, by and large, definitely deleterious. The city power structure is happy and can point with pride to the glistening new project areas which have replaced the old junk. But the vastly greater nonspotlighted nonproject areas of the city, the many, many "invisible parts," are being de-developed because there are haphazard influxes of displaced families into them, with negative social effects on those displaced and on the recipient areas. This haphazard de-development, resulting from continuing displacement by renewal and other public operations (highways, public buildings, etc.), makes much more difficult the ultimate real renewal or revitalization of the city when urban renewal finally gets around to such areas. What to do?

A Proposal for Housing in Place and for Reciprocal Renewal

First, I wish to propose the concept of "reciprocal renewal" development undertakings. At present we have large renewal projects on land redeveloped mainly by private enterprise, public institutions, and sponsors of cultural-civic-governmental centers.

[5] Victor Gruen, *The Heart of Our Cities,* Simon and Schuster, Inc., New York, 1964, p. 90.

However, by and large, the miscellaneous previous occupants—the families displaced and the displaced commercial and industrial users—are reaccommodated in the same area only to a minor extent or not at all. They are scattered haphazardly, or go out of business. Reciprocal renewal would mean that for each redevelopment of the glittering kind, there would be several corresponding developments so conceived and so located as to offer the displaced, not just nonleaky shelter *anywhere,* but new quarters more advantageously located with respect to places of work, to social resources, to recreation, to integration.

An analysis would initially be made of the types and places of work of those who are to be displaced. Some would be found to be working in service jobs near their existing homes near the center (where the initial redevelopments that are the key developments in this plan are usually found); they should be rehoused there or nearby. Many would be discovered to be working in recently decentralized industry near or beyond the outskirts; they should be rehoused nearer their jobs. On the basis of this analysis, the reciprocal developments would be plotted out and scheduled for carrying out simultaneously with, or before, the initial key development or developments. The large, glittering development would have a number of counterpart developments so located that they would in, say, four or five locations begin to effectuate a rational city and transportation plan. Thus, instead of the sort of undated or postdated check which the URA community renewal plan represents, there would be vital, progressive *development* of the interrelated nuclei, a plan *by means of* the renewal process.

Problems of Private Development

This concept is more complex and less spectacular than the single spectacular projects whose *sine qua non* is profit or the prospect of profit. This means that a large part of urban renewal will not appeal to the professional private developers as it generally does now. That problem has to be faced, and should be faced at the earliest moment.

In the first place, the essential dynamics of urban renewal as of now are in the hands of the private developer. He depends in residential building largely on the upper and middle reaches of the market. Where he has tried to work at a substantially lower income level, as in Longwood in Cleveland, it has not worked out.

And even if it should work out, it is not these razor-close situations, in terms of investment at low

1. *Before*

2. *Participation*

Urban Renewal in Place: Before and After

Baltimore, Harlem Park area. To achieve in-place transformation involved the Community Organization Dept., Neighborhood Council of the forty-two blocks, Block Council of each block: success following early trial and error. Importance of social factor, dedication, participation.

3. *After*

4. *Social activity*

profit, that appeal to the professional developer, in any sizable quantity. His kind of building operation is in situations of zero or close-to-zero equity investment and for a narrow market.[6]

There can still be room for the professional developer, and he can go further down into the residential market by way of special low-interest FHA 221(d)(3) and (in New York State) Mitchell-Lama enterprises and by way of the new rent supplementation. But the tacit or spoken premise that he is the prevalent mainstay of urban renewal and that, mainly, projects should be selected on which he can be expected to submit a bid stands in the way of the program's becoming a true sword arm of positive urban planning and development.

Long-view Private Investment and Public Interest Groups. Integration

A very determined drive needs to be made to involve public interest groups and "long-view private enterprise" groups such as pension funds in the field on a much larger scale than presently: directly, as equity entrepreneurs and policy formulators, not supinely, by way of making a mortgage loan to the speculative builder. There are some fine examples. In San Francisco, the International Longshoremen's and Warehousemen's Union–Pacific Maritime Association pension fund has built St. Francis Square, a delightful middle-income cooperative development whose fairly low charges are made possible by FHA 221(d)(3) low-interest financing. When I visited there, I was given the equally gratifying racial composition: 56 per cent white, 24 per cent Negro, 10 per cent Chinese, 10 per cent Japanese. The importance of this new sector of private enterprise cannot be overestimated. A significant example of a public interest group doing this kind of thing is the Wheat Street Baptist Church in Atlanta. By the same combination of urban renewal land and the FHA's low-interest financing, it is producing a 520-unit low-middle-income development through a nonprofit corpora-

tion. Rentals there begin at $69.50 a month. Church organizations such as the Community Renewal Foundation in Chicago are beginning to do fine work. Note that such developments have an active policy of racial integration, not merely a compliance with legal requirements. In Chapter 5, I discuss the especially fine examples in New Haven of the operations of public interest groups and their active integration policy.

The point must be underlined: such instances will have real impact only when there is great expansion from their present specimen status to a much more frequent and characteristic form of creative entrepreneurship, taking on a much larger portion of the urban renewal spectrum. This is the new hopeful dynamic which must be pushed.[7]

Development of New Housing before Slum Clearance

A second major proposal I wish to make is that carefully located and planned residential reservoirs, particularly low-rental, should precede slum clearance. Thus we would be liberated from the squeezing-in and squeezing-around process that goes with the constant endemic shortage of low- and low-middle-rent accommodations. In extreme cases now, people are relocated in one area and a few years later are again relocated by clearance. Perhaps a complete change of legislative intent is necessary here to permit the agencies to undertake a realistic reapproach. The vacant land may be available within the city. Or, more probably, it is not, in adequate quantity; and this becomes one more reason for pounding out a metropolitan housing and urban renewal setup.

A consequence of the policy of groups of reciprocal projects and of freer use of vacant land would be that slumminess or degree of slumminess would no longer be the principal factor in choosing locations for urban renewal and for new housing. This is a distorting factor, because there is absolutely no logical connection between what makes for suitable and advantageous future locations and the fact of past slumminess. I know a case where the selection for the first urban renewal of 100 acres of slum adjacent to the central business district but not in it will seriously delay or make impossible the redemption of the shaky, blighted, and gray "100

---

[6] It should be noted that the private developer's customary residential market is now well on the way to being overbuilt in spite of the generally optimistic market analyses that are always forthcoming. This is not yet fully evident, because in most cities there is some unsatisfied demand to start with, and the first operations skim this cream. But even now there are some serious cases of underoccupancy, such as Plaza Court and Grand Forest in St. Louis, and Society Hill in Philadelphia. The boom-and-bust element in the induced easy-money financing of high-rental apartments must not be overlooked.

[7] The New York *Times* on June 21, 1966, carried the encouraging news that several large Protestant denominations, including the Episcopal Church and the United Church of Christ, have committed themselves to a large revolving fund for such operations.

per cent" blocks in the central business district proper, because the demand for property on which to build in the center of the city simply is not large enough to require or absorb the total area available in both sections, for a good many years at least.

Relocation Again: Demonstration Programs and Serious Gaps

The process and results of relocation are viewed very differently, depending on where you sit and what lens you are using. The Urban Renewal Administration noted with satisfaction that 80 per cent of those relocated move into standard housing, better housing. What it didn't note is the severe reality that monthly rents for displaced families go up sharply. For example, the median rental of those displaced from the Western Addition renewal in San Francisco rose from $39 to $58. The ratio of rent to income rose from 17 per cent to 23 per cent. In Boston's West End, median rentals rose from $41 to $71. At such income levels as those of most slum dwellers, this may be catastrophic. And in the case of Negroes the rises are even more drastic than such figures indicate, because of the drastically restricted supply open to them.

Optimistic figures by the URA are just not enough. It is anticipated that in the next eight years there will be 825,000 families displaced by urban renewal and by highway programs (four times as many as have been displaced so far). This figure comes from the report, early in 1965, of the Advisory Committee on Governmental Relations, which also noted that relocation in some cities had been hampered because of critical shortage of alternate housing. Citizens of good will must see to it that urban renewal speedily meets the real human issues. If the virulent right-wing opposition, for bad reasons, and the liberal and minority groups, for good and humane reasons, both oppose urban renewal, the program needs urgently to look to itself. The URA acknowledged in early 1965 that over seventy cities and counties had rejected urban renewal in the previous four years. If it is not to increasingly encounter and deserve such repudiation, we must insist that it quickly and drastically solve this problem, or *we* will need to join the opposition.

But no matter how much more delicately and maturely and reciprocally urban renewal proceeds, there will be some displacement, with social tensions of many kinds. We must take much more positive account of them—deal with them creatively through social analysis and social work. This must have three aspects: working among those being displaced, preparing them for relocation; observing and preparing the localities into which they are moving and will move; and continuing to keep buoying up the situation of both the in-migrants and the old residents in the de-developed localities after the moves have taken place.

Both local housing authorities, in the case of public housing, and urban renewal authorities have in one way or another tentatively begun but quite inadequately managed to get into this area of social thinking and action. Much more is needed in both to produce effects on people and environments.

The social facets of relocation are the subject of several demonstration projects. A notable one is presented and discussed in a publication by the District of Columbia Redevelopment Land Agency, *Community Services and Family Relocation.*[8] But there are two things to say, sharply. It is extremely late in the day for this indispensable work to be done in only a handful of cities. It should long since have been an across-the-board requirement. We have now been doing urban renewal for seventeen years. We must shift gears; the volume of clearance and urban renewal must be limited, not by the availability of sponsors for new medium- and high-rental buildings, but only by our willingness, capacity, and dedication in maximizing supply of low- and low-medium-rental housing and in handling displacement creatively.

Demonstrations should much more quickly become requirements and norms. We cannot afford the creation of any more social debris. Also, and this applies to almost all demonstrations: their duration is too short (six months to two years generally). Their prolongment and incorporation into the permanent system should be provided for.

Finally, there have been no adequate studies of the psychological and social effects of displacement and relocation,[9] nor of the state of mind of the vastly greater numbers of city people who are not directly involved at all—particularly those near to an urban renewal enterprise which lavishly upgrades its own internal area with handsome or pretentious buildings, swimming pools, terraces, and so on. Very many of those not directly affected will be at the very bottom of the community renewal program time totem pole. The minor

[8] District of Columbia Redevelopment Land Agency, 919–18th Street, N.W., Washington, April, 1964.

[9] However, "Grieving for a Lost Home" is a start in this connection. By Marc Fried, it appears in *The Urban Condition,* Basic Books, Inc., Publishers, New York, 1963.

sprinkling of minority occupancy they see in these new high-priced quarters will not seriously make the psychological and physical situation of these many thousands any happier.

The Resurgence of Civic Allegiance

Urban renewal has made one very positive contribution, or at least the time spirit in which urban renewal has been born has done so. And certainly this contribution has been fostered by the URA's operational requirements of a workable program, etc. This is the spiritual and social contribution of a new or renewed feeling of allegiance to the city as a concept and as a place to work and live, a feeling for one's own part of it and for it, the kind of feeling that makes one try with determination to make it better to live in. This appears on both the city level and on the locality, or neighborhood, level. The *Daily News* in Philadelphia has articulated it fervidly: "We are showing the nation, again, leadership in meeting problems in the 20th Century, as we did in the 18th Century." Again from Philadelphia, which deserves a prominent place in this context, Gustave Amsterdam, chairman of the redevelopment authority, is quoted by *Time*: "It's fashionable in Philadelphia to be interested in the city. I'm only one of dozens of men who are getting great exposure to city problems. It's a delight to see them inspire one another." [10]

On the smaller scale, there is the Upper Roxbury section of Boston, now known as Washington Park, a deteriorating and deteriorated neighborhood. Here citizens of all levels and colors have participated "to promote a program of community betterment and brotherhood," as it is put by Otto and Muriel Snowden, directors of Freedom House, the local settlement house spark plug. A team of social workers began with an idea and wound up with a strongly supported and officially accepted urban renewal plan covering some 500 acres. The final public hearing on the plan by the Boston Redevelopment Authority was attended by 1,200 local people. A vote was taken, and all but three voted in favor of undertaking it. The ingredients of the plan had been developed block by block, initially by the citizens in each block, ultimately by the redevelopment authority's planners working with citizens. The intimate *community process itself* produced tremendous human values and growth long before the renewal project got physically

[10] *Time,* Nov. 6, 1964, p. 70.

under way—a bright contrast to the usual uncertainties and tensions and resentments.

While citizen support can have its darker side—often having a class character, tending to be more developed among upper-income groups than among the poorer groups and more developed in the centers of civic power than in the neighborhoods—the resurgence of civic allegiance is a notable mid-twentieth-century fact. It is our job to further change its too usual power orientation. The assignment is to take hold of it and to make its permeating effects more people-oriented, less property- and investment-oriented.

The Need for Representative Support

The fact is that the Urban Renewal Administration never stipulated just what "representative" means, and in most of the cities that mean business (I am here using the phrase in two senses) a "power structure" has emerged, or rather has formalized itself into compact, continuous structure from a probably long-standing ad hoc, sporadic existence. For the most part, this power structure consists of members of business and industry, banking and real estate. This group can and does lay cash on the line for research and market analyses and campaigns for bond issues and cultural centers, etc. Its view of development (as of many other things) may be thought of as a sublimation of the chamber-of-commerce type of interest and outlook. It has, however, a much smaller, more potent, and more tightly knit membership, representing great economic scale and concentration; i.e., it forms a sort of oligarchy. The new insights and requirements of urban renewal and redevelopment have produced the new systematized form of power structure, have made clear who has the say.

This is a potentially dangerous crystallization. While quite civic-minded within its lights, such a group tends to see the problem of displacement and relocation of low-income and minority tenants and of small businesses as the inevitable price for what it considers the vastly greater benefits. But as Lowdon Wingo has said:

> The critical policy question is not only how much the community is prepared to give up to realize the goals implicit in the master plan but *who* gives up *how much* so that the fruits of the plan can be realized—quite frequently by others. This perspective has led the uncritical liberal to the implicit conclusion that the importance of the social goals realized by the planned transformations of urban environments always outweigh the

Urban Renewal:
The Knife Edge

For discussion and proposals for interpenetration, see pages 43, 44.

Urban Renewal:
Long View Investment
by Labor Union Joint Pension Fund

St. Francis Square, San Francisco. Handsome, racially integrated, middle income. See also illustrations Chapter 5.

current individual and group values which must be forgotten. It is by no means obvious that this is the case.[11]

A requirement needs to be set up, and methods evolved, by which the mechanism and experience of this power group are opened up to include intimately and effectively the representatives of labor, of minority and locality groups, and of consumers of shelter. This may avoid the explosions that take place when such elements are ignored, and suddenly wake up. There are enough illustrations to warrant expectation that we can get positive direction from such an opened-up group if we discriminatingly recognize the actual differences among its members. Such a group can give real meaning to the label of "representative support."

On the locality base again, the famous Hyde Park–Kenwood resurgence of civic allegiance and of creative leadership-participation in Chicago is an example of an essentially middle-class success story. And ultimately successful, after much travail, has been the experience of The Woodlawn Organization, also called TWO, in Chicago. Starting with a frustrated, bitter local group that felt it was ignored in original urban renewal planning, this has become a grass-roots enterprise of 40,000 members, mostly Negro, led by local clergymen and other local people with their own technical planning advisers and proposals. Initially catalyzed by Saul Alinsky's National Industrial Areas Foundation and financed by several philanthropic foundations, TWO is now much more locally self-sustaining. Sparked by determined picketing, after four years the city council approved development plans satisfactory to the TWO group and its allies and to the University of Chicago. The first construction move of the recently accepted plan is now taking place. The Kate Maremont Foundation of Chicago is starting a series of restorations, including alteration of small flats to larger ones for larger families, itself an unusual development. This Woodlawn case is endlessly fascinating, and endlessly documented by its own local newspaper, the Woodlawn *Booster,* and numerous others.

There are other Washington Parks, Hyde Park–Kenwoods, Woodlawns; and the animation, skill, devotion, sense of worthwhile action in place of frustration; the self-discipline, leadership, and even sacrifice that these have evoked are exhilarating.

[11] "Urban Space in a Policy Perspective," in Lowdon Wingo, Jr. (ed.), *Cities and Space: The Future Use of Urban Land,* The Johns Hopkins Press, Baltimore, 1963, p. 5.

But there are not many; and they are nothing like as totally numerous as the unsung, unheard, uncrystallized numbers of people listlessly relocating, shifting around, re-relocating. The resurgent groups are the glory of urban renewal. The challenge to us to multiply, *genuinely* multiply them (and not just on paper, with hand-picked leaders) should be seized as one of the great opportunities to restore the spirit of the city and of the "least of these."

Creative Dispersion of Renewal

Now for some other measures—on a different scale, of quite different character, but pervasive—by which the city's population can much more generally share *currently* in the now highly concentrated improvements, by installments, as it were.

In the first place, all our cities are terribly lacking in park and recreation areas, particularly in fairly small ones near at hand. I propose that every urban renewal enterprise that gets government aid must set aside a given area for public park (i.e., not just the project's private open spaces). This should be the case in business and industrial areas as well as, of course, in residential areas. For the former there are in our cities far too few examples; such as Bryant Park in the heart of New York and Lytle Square in Cincinnati. Even though postage-stamp size (3 to 5 acres, actually), they are delightful oases; with their counterpoint of green and shade and momentary leisure they so do much with so little to provide relaxation from the city's workaday tensions.

Another proposal applies particularly to renewal areas, including university expansion, which are sharp gouged-out chunks of steadily increasing concentrated enclave area, sharply demarcated psychologically and physically from their surroundings. (See a striking case in the illustration from the Washington *Star.*) The universities should consider the creative advantages of a practicable degree of decentralization and of subcentralization with growth, rather than follow the rage for accretion in one area (e.g., Columbia University in New York). And in place of the sharp straight-line edges with their visible exclusionary implications, our urban renewals should have fuzzy edges—on *both* sides and both physical and social. That is, on the "residual community" side, occasional small squares and park spaces, a spill-over of the new project atmosphere, as it were. And reciprocally, I want to develop minor casual public-oriented elements just within the renewed enclave side, so that there are definite planned and casual contacts between the two areas. The goal: a sharing, psychologically and physically.

And now I go a great deal further, though I am still in the realm of relatively minor expenditure. We know that it will be ten, fifteen, twenty years before urban renewal really permeates the square miles of the great nonrenewal matrix, what I have called the bottom of the community renewal program time totem pole. In these great wastes of undated-check community renewal programs, we must immediately undertake and effectuate a master plan of development of small architectural and functional foci which will be visible evidence of ultimate intention, local allegiance-arousing magnets which will provide emotional lift to drab areas. I have done or helped catalyze and create a number. They work. One case is noted here and illustrated by before and after shots. Replacing the dingy open areas between the sections of the bazaar-like East Harlem Market in New York, several festive small sitting plazas have been installed, partly paid for by the stall holders themselves. They are important and welcomed oases.

But we need not just occasional specimens in less than a handful of energetic and imaginative exceptional places; rather, we need a universal movement of individually small-scale actions. And teams of architect social workers to plan with the people. Physical-economic renewal, of course. But renewal above all of the spirit and spirits of people, and thus democratization of urban renewal. Note that as conceived and executed, these small individual efforts involve a spirited financial partnership between city government and private local people and involve maximum participation by local people in conception and actual working. This small-scale multicentered renewal has the seeds of *continuing* renewal; the habit of local self-appraisal and self-help takes root. Particularly important are the architectural and functional foci. With virtuous code compliance and paint-up activities alone, many areas trying to achieve rehabilitation do not have the necessary staying power. The verve does not last.

The City Center and the Future

The city is an interwoven complex of phenomena and actions, such that, in a book devoted to it, almost any topic could be appropriately considered in any of a number of places. Thus we shall now briefly touch on one aspect of the city center that comes in much more fully as part of the main discussion of this subject in Chapter 8. One serious

weakness of urban renewal, a weakness characteristic especially of middle-sized and smaller cities, has not yet become compellingly and alarmingly evident. Early examples may be successful due to an accumulated backlog of need, but the seeds of delayed nemesis lie within. The central business district has generally deteriorated, for various well-known reasons, and lost ground to the peripheral centers, in terms of shopping, residence, and to a smaller but probably growing extent, office buildings and entertainment. The characteristic answer of the middle-sized city is to improve highway access to the central business district by a loop limited-access highway off the interstate system, to provide increased parking within this loop, sometimes to develop a main shopping street with a pedestrian mall. The endeavor here is to offer convenience equivalent to what is available in the outlying centers. On the side of positive content, land is redeveloped for these standard uses: new office buildings, revamped or rebuilt stores, tall apartment houses, and a cultural-civic center.

The big question is simply this: Why should you want to go there? These new or reborn standard attractions are simply not sufficiently potent, not decisively superior to the peripheral centers in total variety or in, say, shopping chic. And when really outstanding style or entertainment differentials are sought, there are in most localities major cities not excessively far by automobile or plane, where the real glamour lies, as of now.

Beyond this, at presently allowed high densities and with the total amount of land available in the central business district and in excellent locations adjacent to it or farther out on main local arteries, we really have a surplus of land and will experience a blight of surplus in the core. This will happen unless we restudy allowable building densities and devise and adopt new and vital land uses, both to creatively utilize the potentially excess areas and to build a potency of attraction which the standard uses by themselves do not have.[12]

One of the pragmatic handicaps facing the adoption of such magnetic developmental conceptions is the shibboleth that in urban renewal, private enterprise must do all but a very minimum. Some of the necessary new creative elements to be dis-

[12] In later chapters we will come to grips with what the metropolitan key center of the future can really hope to be, and should be, in the light of the forces operating in the second half of the twentieth century; what new or special developments should contribute to its new status and new quality dimensions vis-a-vis the out-lying centers, and vis-a-vis the great metropolis.

cussed later are somewhat experimental, inherently not profitable, or not profitable enough. But they are humanly expansive. And to be this, is what the city owes to itself and to the region.

Summation: The Vital Issues Facing Urban Renewal

The quality of urban renewal varies vastly from city to city in two respects: from the spottiness of one or several large single projects to a high degree of comprehensiveness of a physical city pattern and connection between its parts; and from the mainly visual content of the large-scale central real estate transformation to a content that includes a degree of social concern, making for social growth during the renewal process itself and afterward. The fact that some cities have gone so much farther than others in these respects, under identical Federal requirements, is both encouraging and discouraging. This should get a great deal of searching attention from Washington and from the cities themselves. The fact that we *can* do as well as we do in a very few places is a challenge to do very much better in the others.

But even in the most sensitive New Havens and Baltimores and Philadelphias, we have need of systems of deliberately reciprocal projects and need of vastly more vacant-land, low-rental housing operations, in-city or beyond. We need much more of skilled social diagnosis and practice. And even in cities with the most searching community renewal programs with their timetabling in terms of decades, there must be *now* a series of permeating focal undertakings in communities all over the city, as an immediate earnest of the city's concern for *all its* areas and people, not just the lucky (or unlucky) few touched by the concentrations of renewal; and all the people must be creatively involved in this process.

We must also use urban renewal to restructure our cities for minimal crisscross of travel and traffic. Urban renewal can do this by building up better distribution of subcenters of residence, work, and recreational activity, and by reversing the push to increasing economic segregation in new developments and ethnic segregation in new developments and relocation areas.

We must restructure in two other senses. Note again that the most forward-looking cities have placed the urban renewal director in a position where as a sort of vice-mayor, he with authority pulls together all "development departments." This is indispensable; and in particular it is absolutely

crucial in respect to education. An essential ingredient of success in urban renewal is the excellence and the location of schools—excellence to retain and attract back people with children who can afford to move out of the city, wise location to serve as an instrument for integration. New Haven is a fine example of both the new administrative setup and the result in schools; Boston is a fairly strong example. If the city each of us lives in isn't "with it," we the citizens must go strongly into action.

Urban renewal must face the issues of the future function and quality of the center of the central city in the metropolitan region, whether that city is large or middle-sized. As noted above, in middle-sized cities we must evolve a more fertile array of stimulating land uses and activities, diminishing current reliance on "more of the same only better" standard uses. In the great (population wise) centers, a drastic reanalysis and discipline will need to replace the voracious sucking up of all conceivable facilities and congestion generators into one area. Finally, it is indispensable that there be urban renewal on metropolitan basis if our high expectations are to be attained in these and other regards.

Public housing and urban renewal, with the new social substance, the democratic social character we insist on infusing into them, are indispensable to any development. But we must not lose sight of the fact that even thus elevated, they can take us only part of the way to the goals of our century, the fully creative vision and capture of a new urbanism and urbane life. It is with these instruments *and* with New Towns, greenbelts, the metropolitan galaxy, new regions, and other freeing physical and ecological concepts and implementations that we will be able to achieve, in both large totality and intimate scale, an ambience of landscape and of architecture that will wholly express and maybe electrify our twentieth century.

Postscript to Chapters 2 and 3: Comparison and Contrast with the 1966 Demonstration Cities and Metropolitan Development Act.

Among the major objectives of this book are the following:

■ To present a cumulative picture of the community-city-region in its dilemmas and in its potentials for re-creation and new creation.

1. *Before*

Needed: Creative Dispersion of Renewal

One of several plazas serving Park Avenue market and its neighborhood in East Harlem, New York City: in a crowded teeming area, a festive social, functional, community enhancement; and at night, gossip, television, domino tournaments. Such creative dispersion is a rarity.

2, 3. *Now*

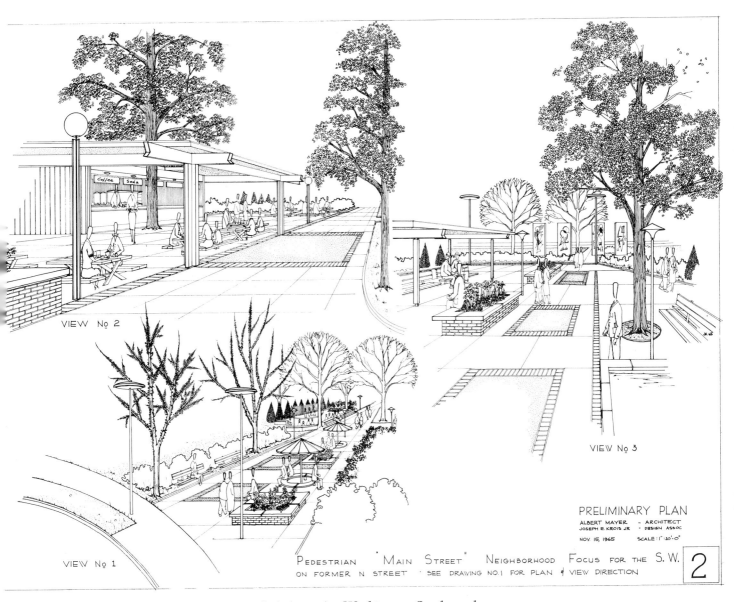

VIEW No 2

VIEW No 1

VIEW No 3

PRELIMINARY PLAN

ALBERT MAYER – ARCHITECT
JOSEPH E. KROIS JR – DESIGN ASSOC

NOV. 15, 1965   SCALE:1":20'-0"

PEDESTRIAN "MAIN STREET" NEIGHBORHOOD FOCUS FOR THE S.W.
ON FORMER N STREET · SEE DRAWING NO.1 FOR PLAN & VIEW DIRECTION

2

4. *Sketch for a Pedestrian "Main Street." A focus for Washington Southeast low-income area*

■ To communicate a strong sense of the high importance and the urgency of the problems that picture presents and to the individual a sense of the immediate direction he himself can best take as a participant in solving them.

■ To enable each participant, lay citizen or design-involved professional, to acquire a valid understanding and active opinion on, and make a choice between, proposals which at first sound either very much alike or equally desirable.

With these thoughts in mind, let us pause to compare the 1966 act on demonstration cities and the views on public housing and urban renewal just expressed in Chapters 2 and 3. We will at later points similarly make comparisons in connection with New Towns, metropolitan government, and other issues.

Very briefly, what this legislation contemplates is a:

> . . . total program . . . for rebuilding or restoring an entire section and neighborhoods in slum and blighted areas [in selected cities] . . . to improve the general welfare of the people living or working in the areas . . . provide a substantial increase in the supply of standard housing of low and moderate cost . . . with a view to reducing educational disadvantages, disease and enforced idleness. The rebuilding of sections or neighborhoods . . . with adequate public facilities [including those needed for transportation, education, and recreation], commercial facilities adequate to serve the residential areas, good access to industrial or other centers of employment. . . . program provides for educational and social services, widespread citizen participation . . . enlarged opportunity for work and training . . . administrative machinery on a consolidated basis . . . cooperation of the local governing body and its agencies, enlisting all available resources.[1]

It is proposed to select sixty or seventy demonstration cities on the basis of the relative excellence and completeness of their proposed attack. The sum included for funding the act is $900 million for a two-year period, which most of those who have given evidence at hearings consider a far too little amount.

There are tremendous pluses in this fresh approach. Here are some of them:

■ Massive concentration on what I have called the invisible parts of our cities, such concentration having been mainly confined until now to the visible central areas, ex-slums converted into glittering concentrations.

■ Emphasis on total and coordinated Federal and local government attack, such as we have hitherto seen in a very few cases only, such as New Haven and Boston.

■ Emphasis on social, educational, and employment factors and on needs of the whole man and whole life in addition to the mainly physical construction and rehabilitation.

■ "Creative federalism," as Secretary Weaver has called it, by which it is sought to make Federal resources available to the localities but which emphasizes decentralization and localization of initiative and decision.

What are the minuses?

The emphasis of the act is on "rebuilding" and "restoring" to better standards and better lives. But as the language reads, this still means slum clearance and replacement, rehabilitation in place. The same people will stay where they are, in better conditions. There is no conception of restructuring the city in the sense of living and work being more closely related to each other; in the sense of creatively minimizing the traffic flows within the city, particularly into and out of the heavily crowded center, by means of subcentralizations of major employment opportunities in districts and neighborhoods (just commercial facilities adequate for their residential local areas are contemplated in the bill); in the sense of thinning out population to make these ends possible.

Going a step further, the concept of reciprocal renewal outlined in Chapter 3, i.e., the concept of a number of dovetailing undertakings in *different* localities in the city to produce creative relocation, each being a piece of a new total city plan, is quite the opposite of the massive single undertaking for a whole district, which freezes the city pattern piece by piece even while upgrading in place. While a very serious and justified complaint against urban renewal has been excessive and almost lighthearted displacement of people, the present demonstration-cities bill goes excessively far in the other direction of freezing present geographical patterns. The creative dispersion of renewal which I have strongly urged, so that *every* section of a city can achieve palpable enhancement and upsurge of spirit even while awaiting its fully active involvement in the renewal program—this is not considered in the bill, and furthermore, because of the heavy and much-underestimated requirements of funds for the large single districts, it is probably out of the question.

[1] Excerpts from "Section-by-Section Summary of the Act of 1966," Department of Housing and Urban Development.

While the act makes a sporting and spectacular challenge, it is unrealistic and indeed unjust to select sixty or seventy cities for this demonstration out of the hundreds needing drastic help and re-creation, and then, within each chosen city, to select one area, say 5 to 10 per cent, while equally eager and dreadfully needy areas in that city go without. This possibly disastrous course can only be avoided by making available much larger funds for public housing and urban renewal than have been considered up to now.

But beyond this need, the only way it seems to me that the government can salvage the pluses underlying and animating the demonstration-cities act, those I have mentioned and others, is to make far greater funds available in *this* act and to tie them to new housing, on a much greater scale, which is the key to any major attack, to appurtenant community facilities, and to new area distribution, or subcentralization of varied employment. Such area distribution forms the large organic nuclei from which total areas can be created and can grow over the years in the whole sense the bill aims at. Simultaneously and reciprocally, the areas involved can be large centers of healthy infection, of important stirring, large enough to set a new course for the whole city. This process would be a far cry from saturating one great concentrated area with what might be called "static improvement" and waiting out the substantial time gap before there are funds for the next one.[2]

A final great plus about the 1966 act must be emphasized, in fairness and in enthusiasm. The act makes a fresh departure and formulates an opening synthesis that in public hearings unleashed tremendous positive response from almost all quarters. Also, this very major 1966 act follows hard on the heels of the important act of 1965 in the realm of housing and urban development. This is a splendid change from the norm of a gap of some years between important pieces of legislation in this field. Perhaps this marks an end to excessive gradualism, and the reorientation of, and changes in, the act which are indicated above need not wait long. Certainly, these improvements need to be made quickly and massively to justify and enhance the all-important atmosphere of fresh hope and high

expectation the bill has created. Thus we give it staying power and enhancement, not disillusion.

As a method of approach to the determined conclusion that we can attain the ends presented so far, as well as others that will be developed in later chapters, it is important to visualize a totality of goals and form some notion of their cost. Many witnesses at hearings on the demonstration cities bill pointed out both that its proposed funding at a total of $900 million over two years is absurdly small and that the amount for urban renewal is also absurdly small. Right they are. But nobody proposed a *total* program and a period of years in which to accomplish it and then examined what expenditure would be involved and whether we could afford it. After almost two decades of very fragmentary or specimen urban renewal, it's high time that we did.[3]

At the end of the public housing chapter, I set up a very nonrevolutionary but significant goal of twenty years for achieving an adequate home for every citizen and worked out the implications in public housing. A similar goal of twenty years for rebuilding our cities seems reasonable, and worth fighting for. Let us get some very rough idea of what this might involve.

John W. Dyckman and Reginald R. Isaacs did an exhaustive job on the cost of urban renewal.[4] They defined urban renewal as "the total of all the public and private actions which must be taken to provide for the continuous sound maintenance and development of the urban areas." They worked out the probable costs on a ten-year basis, concluding that they would be $100 billion a year and that to invest this much in urban renewal was mathematically possible. Doubling the period allowed for attainment, and particularly bearing in mind that many of the constituent undertakings, such as schools, hospitals, and roads, are going forward anyway, the annual sum arrived at will be very substantially less.

Without attempting to set any even tolerably accurate figure, varied comparisons indicate this could be readily possible. It would mean not over

[2] To speak of far greater funds is not to make the usual plea by every protagonist for more funds for his favorite purpose. The money tag attached by the administration to its 1966 bill is so ridiculously below what is required that there is practically no correspondence between the eloquently stated objectives and the funds requested. *Architectural Forum* has dryly and aptly referred to this as the oratory gap.

[3] It is also important to give priorities of allegiance to various goals all attainable or in large measure attainable. Indeed, this seems essential to a dynamic quest. For guidance toward a dynamic perspective and an order of magnitudes, I found most stimulating an article entitled "The Cost of Our National Goals," in *Looking Ahead*, monthly bulletin of the National Planning Association, June, 1965, issue. It summarizes a book by Leonard A. Lecht, *Goals, Priorities, and Dollars: The Next Decade*, to be published in 1966 by The Macmillan Company, New York.

[4] J. W. Dyckman and R. R. Isaacs, *Capital Requirements for Urban Development and Renewal*, McGraw-Hill Book Company, New York, 1961.

5 per cent of our national income, which too is constantly growing. The country should consider this proposition in competition with, and at a higher priority than, for example, the vast expenditures for space exploration and flight to the moon as well as some of the fancier items in the huge national annual research bill. But it is an even broader question than that. Urban renewal, city building, will not change from its present very demonstration or token character in any sort of natural or inevitable gradual way, but only by our determined choice and pressures. The principal point is that we must insist on vastly raising the levels of collective consumption and community well-being which have for so long lagged behind conspicuous individual consumption in our affluent society.

This is the first of two pivotal chapters. They are pivotal because they look backward and forward. In this chapter we shall consider the underlying dynamics that are now dominant in all social and physical development—dynamics that to a large extent depend on the previously discussed character of the development tools, including the weaknesses and the gaps in them. Chapter 5 deals with the new dynamics we must discern or conjure up, and strengthen.

Our present lines of activity insufficiently recognize or do not recognize at all that we must radically change our obsolete development forces and reallocate the levers of power, if we hope to move ahead. The bright new future will not be won by dressing in shinier colors the past and present forms of development. We still rely on development forces and machinery that in the apparently simpler nineteenth century and the early part of the twentieth were to a degree effective, but that have helped largely to pile up essentially anarchic conditions. These we must now resolve with quite different driving forces and transformed machinery.

Before we consider further how we can perform this task of travail as well as of high excitement, let us refresh our spirits and intentions by recognizing again what we seek, what makes the travail worthwhile and transforms it into a great mission. To explain what we want to, indeed *must*, get away from, I quote a compact statement by Artur Glikson. While I am not in full agreement with it factually, the tone is right:

> In the metropolitan concentrations, urbanization has come to mean the uniformization and mechanization of the processes of human interaction and the introduction of a giant incomprehensible scale in the environment, leading to the annihilation of social and environmental complexity. The contrast of the confusion in the metropolitan centers with the monotony of suburbia does not represent a valuable form of environmental diversification, but a bundle of environmental incompatibilities. The unsolved traffic problems are only a physical manifestation of the unsolved general problems of human communication and interaction in the focal regions of metropolitan civilization.[1]

And on the positive side, quoting from our introduction,

We should now be able to create for all a life with diminished tensions and more drama; a life of expanded understanding and vision and daily

[1] From *Humanisation du Milieu*, Le Carre bleu Feuille internationale d'Architecture, no. 4, 1963.

CHAPTER FOUR

UNDERLYING DYNAMICS OF SOCIAL AND PHYSICAL DEVELOPMENT: EXISTING, ENTRENCHED

experiences that reinforce them; a life in which drudgery is diminished and transformed into unforced creative activities; a life in which market place and community and the counterpoint of healing nature are easily interaccessible. . . . The purpose of this study is to explore the elements in the physical and social planning and development of our urban civilization and how these elements must be deployed in order to realize much more fully the promise of the new forces and minimize their wastes and menaces.

Now, let us set out again.

Three of the Master Factors

First, here are three master factors, from among the many factors that compose the existing and entrenched dynamics of development:

1. *Population Explosion, and More Homes.* The population explosion is well recognized, of course, and by almost everyone mentally pigeonholed. But listen to this hair-raising statement by Robert Weaver, Secretary of the Department of Housing and Urban Development:

> In the remaining 40 years of this century, our urban population is expected to more than double, from 125 million to 280 million by the year 2000 (some reliable sources say it will reach 340 million by then). This means that in the 40-year period we have now entered, we will have to provide homes and all of the facilities needed for urban employment and enjoyment *equal to all that has been built to date in the entire history of our country.* (Italics mine)

Let's just repeat that: Forty years in which to more than duplicate the total of existing living and work structures and their entire framework, in this entire country! Is there anything in the existing programs we have reviewed or in the visible performance of the industry to suggest that we can do or are preparing to do this stupendous work and at the same time to rebuild a large part of what is already here? Quantitatively, this job will require a sustained yearly output for the whole period higher than the maximum number we have *ever* reached. And it should evoke the imagination and the discipline to achieve a quality of habitability and an equitable cost range beyond any we have ever achieved or now have the machinery to achieve.

It is overwhelmingly important to have this stupendous prospect make a burning and ever-present impact, and not just be met with an intel-

lectual nod: we must have more homes—massively, more homes. Let us, for example, not follow in the footsteps of those leaders and citizens who are becoming confused by, and excessively preoccupied with, the appeal of rehabilitation and conservation. These do good, and they are important—*if* the limitations are recognized. But all the rehabilitation in the world does not add one cubit to the needed supply of housing. Indeed, in many situations it decreases supply because it involves elimination of overcrowding. In others, it effectively decreases the supply of low-rent housing because the improvements often price people out. *It is only new building* that increases supply and gives us the necessary leverage to realistically enforce building codes, etc. Let's not get lost in the fine byway of rehabilitation or think that byway is the highway.

And let us in this context again vividly remember that we will never get rid of slums through equivalent slum clearance—i.e., building only as many low-rent houses as we tear down slums—because this will always give an artificial scarcity value to the slums. It must be everlastingly clear that we must first cure the chronic shortage of good low-rental housing, and *then* we can readily get rid of slums.

2. *Urban Disarray versus Productive Efficiency.* We come to the second of these still submerged master points. It is this: that our effective leaders, our "men who get things done," are far from realizing the life-and-death importance of the quality, livability, viability economy of our cities in terms of national efficiency and productive economy. There is a certain amiable agreement that we ought to be improving things, and determination to revive our city centers. But beyond that, no sense of urgency, by no means a comprehensive understanding that total city conditions are getting so far out of hand that they affect not only amenity but efficient productivity and our competitive place in the world.

Lowdon Wingo has put this cogently:

> The national interest arises from the productivity of urban land, not the amount. Urban space represents substantially less than one per cent of the nation's area, but it houses three out of every four people in this nation and produces well over four-fifths of the total economic output. This massive concentration suggests the critical importance of urban efficiency to the national product: increasing inefficiency in the organization and functioning of our major urban areas will in short order militate against the effectiveness of our national economic establishment simply because

they will affect the bulk of our economic activities.[2]

Western European nations—in particular Great Britain, the Netherlands, the Scandinavian countries, and recently France—have actively recognized this connection. In the last two decades they have hammered out policy and have been taking effective measures. We, in our outstandingly productive preeminence and self-confidence, have been overlooking or underestimating the galloping human disarray that is reflected in mental-health costs, in traffic costs (most palpably), and in constantly rising local taxation that just cannot keep up with the need.

It is later than you think. I am always reminded of the possible similarity of our position to the industrial preeminence of Victorian England, with its overweening and static self-confidence. The sands of time were running out, and progress in the United States and Germany was silently but relentlessly undercutting the grimy obsolescence of Manchester and Glasgow and Durham. Suddenly came ultimate awareness, but by then competitive reality had caught up and outstripped England, which has painfully, but not yet fully, recovered from this luxury of unawareness and cocksureness.

The power men have to realize that the increasing costs of the lengthening daily journey to work, including the dissatisfactions and tensions it builds up, and the costs of massive highway systems and fanciful interchanges are all ultimately reflected in their production costs. The heavy direct and indirect costs are considered good business in that they provide work and sales of materials. The oil industry has a heavy budget to push road construction, for example. But surely we can find more socially useful employment than by further promoting expenditure of money, time, and energy through mutual centrifugality.

There are many people who are greatly worried by the silently ticking time bomb: planners, sociologists, researchers in many fields. But their statesmanlike worry hasn't penetrated to the power structure of business and its associations, whose worry and gratification in urban development are generally concentrated on the bothersome visible central slums and their conversion to prestige centers. How to transmute their delightful and each time satisfying activity of converting one to the other, a readily tangible enterprise, into more sweeping transforma-

tion, and how to do this now: this is the problem.[3]

3. *Social Process and Result.* In this probably arbitrary and personal choice of three factors as "first among equals" of the numerous crucial obscured factors to be discussed, the third is the thesis that *process* is fully as important as tangible *result* or physical *product,* and is essential to them. We tend in general to overvalue the visible physical product and underrate the electrifying potentials of positive involvement. If, for example, the psychological accompaniment of urban renewal is lasting or long bitterness and resentment on the part of many people, the tangible result, however handsome, is still a negative. Of course no historic change is ever accomplished painlessly; one simply tries to see that the pain is creatively minimized. To take a less drastic case, if the results are on balance beneficial but the people affected have merely acquiesced, the undertaking and the experience have still not had their maximum flowering. In fact, the process itself can best produce the growth, the met challenge, the conquest for once of the frustration that so permeates so many lives. It may be added, as an element in process, that the more the creators and the designers of the new environment have based themselves on contact with the people involved, the more aesthetically and ecologically satisfying and thrilling will be the product—the more handsome and the more deeply and fully appropriate.

Let me now discuss and analyze some other major underlying forces in development, existing and entrenched.

The Dog-wagging Developer

Previous chapters have touched sharply but briefly on the role, practices, and effects of "straight" private developers on our cities and countryside. We will now penetrate into this at some length.

Private enterprise, *in the form of the speculative land developer-cum-builder,* operates both in the

---

[2] "Urban Space in a Policy Perspective," in Lowdon Wingo, Jr. (ed.), *Cities and Space: The Future of Urban Land,* The Johns Hopkins Press, Baltimore, 1963, p. 7.

[3] There are some notable clear-sighted and farseeing exceptions in business circles, such as members of the National Planning Association, New York Regional Planning Association, and the Northeastern Illinois Metropolitan Area Planning Commission. But these are fringe organizations. The real muscle groups, such as the National Association of Manufacturers, the United States Chamber of Commerce and the local chambers of commerce, and the American Bankers Association, either are unaware altogether of the national economic importance of the urban structure or are bitterly opposed to positive efforts. The labor unions too are deaf to this music of the future.

expanding periphery of the city and outlying areas, and in the central areas of the city. In both cases, he thrives on change in kind of land use or intensity of land use, and on "different rates of obsolescence." He *follows* various trends, or he *forces* trend. The essence is to buy land at low cost, convert it into "higher" (denser) use, and make a profit on this differential. In the outlying situation, the major profit is in this land conversion rather than in the building construction; in the central situation, the building profit is often more important.

On the periphery and in the suburbs and beyond, the highway system and the superhighways permit and encourage the potential homeowner to go farther and farther out, even if his job is in the city; and ownership of a car permits him to go out *in any direction,* because with a car he need not be very close to the major highway and bus route. Thus the developer-builder has a wide range of distant former farm land which he can buy at very low prices, and he converts it into housing colonies. These, because they will then accommodate many times the number of families the land accommodated before—i.e., a suburban density instead of a farm density—produce that greater land value and sales price which make this operation worth his while. The fact that a single large operation of this character has been consummated attracts many others into this area or similar areas more distant from the city. This is now the characteristic type of outlying development.

This is not new in kind. This kind of operation has always characterized the suburban push and our land-development system. But the new mobility (the combination of widely expanded car ownership and the highways and superhighways), the population splurge, and the new kind of financing available have accelerated the process greatly. Many more gray areas and blighted areas are being left behind, and there is much more scatteration ahead.

How does the system of financing encourage and accelerate this process? In the building and development industry, the promoter-builder himself has only a minimum of investment, and that only catalytic and temporary if he guesses right. It is he who calls the shots and chooses the locations, while the lender or mortgage holder—the insurance company or the savings bank or the building and loan association—is very much the major and permanent but quite passive investor. It makes loans of so high a percentage of total cost that the builder has only a small and temporary investment. That investment is reduced to zero when the houses are sold. Thus the alert developer is the tail that wags the dog,

the passive mortgage-holding organization. The builder has made his profit or his loss, and goes on again to find new cheap land and another differential-obsolescence situation, leaving recently new neighborhoods behind.

Currently—and this is of great immediate importance—the peppering of such residential developments in so many locations and farther and farther out spoils the land and makes very difficult and very much limits rational development such as has been proposed, for example, for Baltimore's regional "Metro-Towns." And as at best any such development will take years to get well under way and to complete, this spoiling or interference becomes progressively more destructive of possibilities.

A similar dynamic is at work in the center of cities, with differences appropriate to the different locational circumstances and weight of factors. There, depending for its intensity on whether the city is a national metropolis or a middle-sized city, there is a similar finding or assembling single pieces of land, often occupied by older though by no means physically worn-out buildings; or there is property assembled by urban renewal. The entrepreneur (or, in the big cities, several, in various locations) sees a chance for promoting an operation of greater density and higher rentals, hence supporting considerably higher land price, and develops a tall office building or an apartment house. If this is an initial success, it immediately sends in an optimistic upward direction the values and prices of a whole belt or area of parcels of land located in adjacent or similar areas, makes it tempting to a number of other developers to follow suit, and, once there are several new buildings, makes it difficult for the owner of older buildings to carry on. In addition, his land taxes, based on the new denser use, have gone up severely. Thus this new cycle of building tends to empty out or thin out the tenancies of older buildings, their level of proper maintenance can no longer be afforded, and this becomes a contributing cause of new blight or slum, residential or commercial or whatever.

Here again the process is accelerated and aggravated by the financing system: the office building with substantial space leased to a big-name firm can borrow out 100 per cent of the cost of the operation or nearly so. In the case of apartment houses, cooperative purchasers take over the equity and leave the builder free to move on; in a substantial number of other cases, the FHA has insured the high mortgage loans of inlying apartments. Mostly these apartments are for upper-middle income and beyond; hence they do not increase the housing supply in the low price range and in the location where low-priced housing is most needed, and even diminish it by demolition. Again, there is constant change, a large part of whose end product is the deterioration of large areas of the city.

While there are a few estates and large development companies that intentionally keep their own properties over the long pull, this is not at all characteristic of the system. Characteristically, the builder-developer has no particular allegiance to his creation and sells it for a profit at the earliest possible moment. This very thin financial interest in his property, and its characteristically temporary nature, is underlined by the fact that there is a large group of men in this field whose main function is to buy and resell properties. Indeed, sometimes an operator makes a contract to buy a property, buys it, and resells it to another operator in a matter of months, before anyone actually "takes title," i.e., fully completes the purchase. There are innumerable cases and gradations. There happens to be one case we can follow over some ten months of varied activity.

In the New York *Times* of November 3, 1964, under the headline "Realty Equities in $8,827,115 Deal," we read that "the properties which will be held for resale" are in Albany and three other cities. In the *Times* of March 18, 1965, there is a note that two Albany properties of those purchased as announced in the previous November have already been resold. In the Philadelphia *Inquirer* of September 18, 1965, on the occasion of another, much larger purchase by this firm, we learn of the philosophy of this kind of operation. We quote from it, since some understanding of this philosophy is necessary to grasp what is constantly happening to us and our cities, and why the system has to be drastically changed for urban survival and for better things.

The headline "New Company Buys Land Like Supermart Buys Up Groceries." Then: "He [the president] said most persons do not understand R.E.C.'s [the company's] methods of operation because they think of real estate as a long-term investment. It is difficult for the man in the street or the big business man to think of property sitting on the shelf to be sold."

The temporariness of interest of the original developer and of those who succeed him as short-term owners establishes something crucial: their attitude, as far as a real sense of responsibility or commitment goes, toward an entity of property which strongly affects the lives and activities of the people who occupy it and the community of which

it should be a part. Bear in mind this kind of attitude (as well as the factual characteristics of the system) in appraising how fitted private enterprise in its present form may be to carry on the large-scale statesmanlike developments that must be contemplated and undertaken. Current private enterprise in building entrepreneurship is in this sense much more irresponsible in the United States than in England and Europe, and much more irresponsible than most other industry in the United States.

This account is an oversimplification, but does present a true picture of the role of the developer in the underlying dynamics of social and physical development. The purpose here is not to pick out the developer as the moral villain in the piece. The point is that his attitudes and practices are all part of a system essentially not geared to optimum development and maximum long-run civic and economic social value. What then follows from this? Clearly, speculative developers cannot continue to dominate the scene if we are to have or establish a rational urban civilization. There is a place for their drives and ingenuities, but covering a very much smaller portion of the total spectrum.[4] But there are emerging alternatives, governmental, quasi-governmental, and altogether nongovernmental—*private in a new sense*. These we must seek, foster, encourage. These alternatives constitute one of the most stimulating and realistically hopeful of the topics in Chapter 5, when we turn to the embryonic and potential dynamics of development.

Land Ownership and Policy as a Key Force

Public policy on land for housing in the city and in the metropolitan region is a key element in both existing and potential dynamics of development. The point is that land is going to have to be considered and regulated like a public utility and that policy on land in certain kinds of locations will have to go even further to embrace large-scale purchases and continuing ownership by government. To see where we stand now in this regard, we must take up a frequently unrecognized facet of the relation of the city, and especially the central city, to the metropolitan region.

A matter of the greatest seriousness in relation to land for housing is the failure of this country to develop "local public agencies established on a . . . regional or unified metropolitan basis . . .

[4] Compare Sweden. The two large public cooperative organizations build 25 per cent of the housing volume; government, 40 per cent; private enterprise, 35 per cent. This is real competition by different forms of enterprise.

to contribute toward the solution of community development or redevelopment problems on . . . a unified metropolitan basis," as envisioned in the recent housing acts. In the case of low-cost and low- and low-medium-rental housing, the effect is catastrophic. Vacant land in the central city is almost nonexistent, so expansion of the terribly tight housing supply is all but impossible there; and the cost of acquisition, because of the necessity of acquiring occupied buildings, is extremely high. In the suburbs and outlying areas there still is vacant land which could alleviate this supply situation and permit low-income workers to be nearer their jobs in the decentralizing industries. But the callous decision has almost everywhere been made to keep these groups out, by minimum-size zoning for large lots and by other devices. There are other reasons even more potent why the narrow atomization of metropolitan jurisdictions should be overcome—among them, the damage these outlying areas are doing to themselves. But how to convince them or overcome the preventers?

As a number of such outlying communities are already themselves seeking and applying urban renewal funds, it may well be possible and practicable for the Federal government, through the URA and others of its financial-aid dispensers, to make inducements or to practice withholding. The Business Committee of the National Planning Association notes in its 1963 report on urban renewal and redevelopment: "It is . . . necessary to integrate local initiative into a consistent regional pattern of urban renewal projects. . . . One way to reduce local reluctance to participate in a metropolitan or regional plan would involve the provision of financial inducement on the part of the Federal Government." This thinking should be followed through, and this association, an outstanding group of businessmen, researchers, and labor leaders, may be able to gain wide support for it.[5]

The Spiraling Cost of Housing and Community

The spiraling cost of producing community, in terms of land, finance, and construction, is another major aspect of the existing underlying dynamics of social and physical development.

[5] Just as this book is being completed, the act covering metropolitan development has been passed (1966). The section on grants to assist in planned metropolitan development is a significant step in the indicated direction, but too feeble for the high purpose. In Chapter 9 we will consider this matter closely.

One of the most relentless obstacles to our quest for good living in the twentieth century, desperately immediate for those of low and middle-low income and seriously so for almost all of us, is the constant rise of house costs and carrying charges or rental. There are three components operating here, aggravated by the steep population growth. They are:

Land prices, which have risen most steeply.

Financing costs and inefficient over-all administration of the development and building industry.

High cost of the building process itself, seemingly with us permanently, in spite of periodic predictions by Sunday newspaper magazines that spectacular reductions are just around the corner because of new methods.

Financing costs have been brought down for low- and lower-middle-income housing; this has been done by direct government subsidy, by lower interest rates, and by partial real estate tax exemption. Recently these measures have been largely negated by high interest rates as an anti-inflation measure. As for land prices, only that tiny part has been lowered that enters into urban renewal, through Federal grant, to produce a substantial write-down. As for costs of actual construction, two cost-reducing measures have been developed, both bad. Actual living space has been terribly crowded down both vertically, by oppresively low and lower headroom, and horizontally, by reducing area to the point where there simply isn't room for the various family functions—a great, indeed alarming social detriment. Children have no quiet place for study. Older children have no place for guests. Everybody in everybody else's hair. This harsh cutting down of actual livability, to say nothing of reasonable comfort, goes fairly far up the income line. The other cost-saving device is poor construction quality, also a function of the "get in and get out" character of developer private enterprise. There has been a limited genuine cost reduction in a few cases, notably that of the Levittowns, by volume, process standardization, preassembly, and year-round work.

Land costs have risen spectacularly because of population explosion, because of new accessibility, because of speculation, because of suburban zoning requirements for larger lots. Land, which used to represent a normal 10 per cent of total house price, is now over 20 per cent. Listen to the strong statements of *House and Home,* the most sophisticated and authoritative of the magazines that speak to the world of the speculative developer:

In the last decade average land prices have more than tripled, and some land has sky-rocketed as much as 2000%. . . . Land is a problem because it threatens to price housing right out of the market. In the next decade land cost could easily triple again while homebuyers' average real income will rise only 30% to 40%. . . . In the last decade increases in prices of raw, usable land have ranged from about 100% in slow-growing areas like Pittsburgh and Detroit to as much as 2000% for choice land in Los Angeles and Houston.

The estimated average price for new one-family homes varied from about $17,500 in 1962 to about $18,500 in 1963, clearly beyond the means of most U.S. families. Today the average family has an income of less than $6,600 a year. This means that the top price such a family can pay for housing is about $13,500. . . . Most experts agree that the average price of a house has risen $2,000 to $5,000 in the last decade, through land price alone.[6]

The matter of actual inherent construction costs has never yet been squarely faced in this country. The characteristically small-volume builder, the immobile craft unions, and the short work year and the attempt to compensate for it by constantly rising hourly wages—these combine and contribute to the constantly rising curve. Thus a large proportion of the low-income consumers are priced out of the market for good housing, except for the relative handful of units of heavily subsidized public housing. The resulting heavy unit subsidies stand in the way of a really significant total of satisfactory homes becoming available.

In other words, the only substantial reduction has been in cost of finance in a not very wide portion of the low and lower-middle income range. This must be done on a much larger scale to be really significant.

Traffic and Transportation: The Futile Chase

For this section, we will shift metaphors. Certainly, traffic and its problems cannot be thought of as a "submerged" underlying factor in the dynamics of development. It is obnoxiously well known. Also, it may be less an "underlying" factor than a result, though of course it is quite heavily both. The

metaphor in our first chapter is here more appropriate: we are shooting at the wrong target, and with the wrong ammunition.

In general our quests and studies and experiments in the field of traffic are concerned with such matters as individual car versus mass transit, adequate parking in optimum locations, and separation of pedestrians from vehicles and vehicles of different functions and speeds from each other by up to six different road levels. Even more sophisticatedly, we are considering the aesthetics of location and motion. All problems have clever and imaginative (and expensive, frightfully expensive) technological solutions. It is all based on two major assumptions: that the volume of cars and traffic must continue and accelerate its steep rise, and that technology can, naturally and of course, solve anything. In traffic, we always keep expecting that the next $100 billion will solve what the last $100 billion only made worse.

The guest of honor is in fact absent at this fancy dress party: The heart of the issue is urban and metropolitan development which will minimize the *need* for ever-increasing traffic, which will place living and working and recreation in such physical relation to each other that the up-trending curves will bend, somewhat or greatly. The fancy remedies will be used as needed—and of course they will be much needed—and improved or transformed rapid transit will need to play a much more important role to help solve a soluble problem, and will not be excessively relied on to solve the insoluble.

One may find a relevant evolution in the history of flood-control policies. The earliest remedies against floods were dikes or levees down river. Where a bigger flood breached or overflowed existing levees, stronger and higher ones were placed; and they were carried farther up the river. And so forth. Finally it dawned on those responsible that this wasn't getting us anywhere, and that indeed some of those remedies were actually increasing flood volumes and so causing bigger floods. So, for some decades now we have proceeded with main attention to *diminishing the flood volumes to be dealt with*. Gully plugging, small dams, afforestation near the headwaters and below, and large dams down river. Dikes and levees at the mouth, yes. But now they are only part of a full system, neither the only nor the major part.

The crux is diminution of volumes to be handled —whether water or automobiles. Under a different system of living, working, and recreational locations and relations, every vehicle need not reach the

[6] From *House and Home*, September, 1964, pp. 41–42. By 1966, the average cost of the home had risen from $18,500 to $22,000; average income to almost $7,300. This family can afford to pay $15,500 (*House and Home*, letter from the editor, Nov. 23, 1966). The gap between price and what the family can afford to pay has increased.

mouth (i.e., center) at the same time, and a large number not at all.

Traffic and Transportation: Flattening Out the Need

We must apply this lesson; we must drastically change our approach. Through our development policies and measures we must build in a lesser *need* for traffic, i.e., the proportionate increase can be much lower than the inevitably rising number of cars. And then we solve the problems presented by the *irreducible* volumes. In our naïve reliance on technological remedies, we pay little attention to the full cure.[7] In the city, urban renewal has missed the opportunity for being the first stage of the full cure. Indeed it often intensifies the sickness. Each urban renewal should provide its small increment of improvement in traffic as part of a whole ultimate plan. Beyond the city limits, and now in the city, the interstate highway system is not only anarchic and devil-take-the-hindmost in this regard, but by its seemingly virtuous cost-benefit ratio, it actually *increases* concentration.

This must again be raised as a major issue. Obviously, the best *immediate* cost-benefit ratio will obtain where traffic and need are already heaviest. So, we pile still more traffic into already concentrated situations, accentuating and accelerating trend instead of spreading and redirecting the load. We bask in these short-run, shortsighted economies and clevernesses. A striking illustration of this dominant viewpoint: In the case of the interstate highway system, which connects our most prosperous concentrated areas, the Federal government contrib-

---

[7] One technological resource will make its contribution to the cure: substitution of communication by message and direct voice for physical trips.

utes 90 per cent of the cost. In the case of the development of Appalachia, which can ill afford or not afford its contribution, Washington contributes only 70 per cent. Is this a creative development policy?

Again our new highways, our currently-being-widened throughways (widenings which had to be undertaken a very few years after to improve original major "solutions") and our three-, four-, five-level interchanges—these are sized to meet *peak* traffic loads (and again this increases costs). For the rest of the day and the week they have much more capacity than needed. A policy of integrating work and living locations and at the same time determinedly staggering working hours could importantly lighten this phenomenon. A major key is the relative self-containment of the New Town. In Chapter 6 on New Towns this subject will be developed not only critically, but creatively.

There is, however, a limit to what even this rationalization can accomplish as the population of metropolitan areas continues its rapid increase. It is to forestall the new peaks of population concentration, among other gargantuan effects of metropolitan growth, that we think in terms of new regions. Another visibly emerging crisis in traffic congestion is overcrowded airways around our major airports. This shows both in accident toll and in the now almost customary rush-hour delays which force planes to stack and circle before they receive permission to land, in such airports as those of Washington and New York. Los Angeles shows the combined effects of the excesses of air and ground traffic. When completed in 1959, the airport was provided with 9,000 parking spaces. They are now having to triple these, to provide for a total of 27,000 cars. These are among the problems to be dealt with in Chapter 10 on New Regions.

Solid American Experience for
the New Development Dynamics:
The Foundation

1, 2. Example from Pittsburgh: Chatham Village. Middle-income housing by Buhl Foundation completed thirty-three years ago, currently still flourishing

Lower Costs of Housing-Community, and Greater Freedom for Total Planning.
Sweden Speaks.
Public Ownership of Development Land

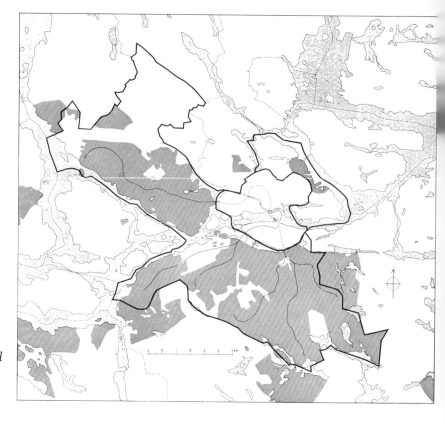

1. *Stockholm. Gray-colored areas municipally owned*

2. *Quality of Vallingby: new sub-city in Stockholm at low cost, made possible by municipal ownership*

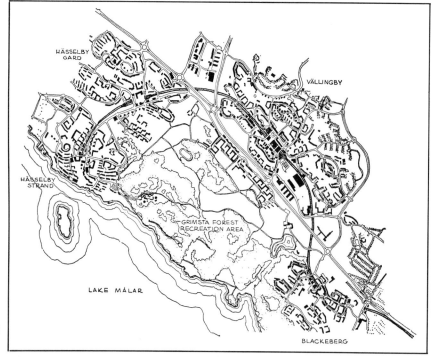

3. *Also made possible: the new communities surround a forested recreation area*

60

g Virginia Cafe Chain
pens Doors to Negroes

ork Times Service

RLINGTON, Va., June —Color barriers were ing today at eating ces in the northern Virnia community of Arling-n, a major suburb of Washington, D.C.

today by leading drug, variety and department stores to serve Negroes at their lunch counters in Arlington.

The end of segregation at the Hot Shoppes is considered especially significant

Moderate Wins Demo Race for N. C. Governor

RALEIGH, N. C., June 25 (Æ)—Lawyer Terry Sanford, ex-FBI agent, who espoused North Carolina's middle-of-the-road approach to the school integration issue, today won the Democratic nomination for governor from strong segregationist I. Beverly Lake in a runoff primary.

Sanford, who led a four-man field by more than 87,000 votes in the first primary May 28, campaigned for increased spending on education and to continue the state's moderate policy that has admitted a handful of Negroes to previously all-white public schools.

Winning the Democratic

Hundreds of Whites Attending Negro Colleges

Hundreds of white students are attending educational institutions that were once Negro, according to The Associated Press.

"Reverse integration," this development is called. It has happened at many colleges and universities across the country, North and South

State College in Wilberforce, Ohio. Once solidly Negro, the school now has about 450 whites in an enrollment of 2,300.

Charles H. Wesley, its president, declares: "Integration is a two-way street."

The shift has come largely since the United States Supreme

It now has a record enrollment of 2,502.

"We didn't recruit white students," says Dr. William J. L. Wallace, State's president, a Negro. "We felt it might be resented. However, we knew many persons were interested, and when white students showed up we accepted them."

Such hospitality has marked

and three white men in a student body that previously was all Negro.

"They participate in all activities quite normally," the spokesman said. "There is no social strain." The college is operated by the Disciples of Christ and the United Church (Congregationalist and Reformed)

Integration. Barriers Falling All Over:
Selection from Many Examples Across-the-Board

INTEGRATED T. LOUIS HOTEL

ogists' Group Forces Chase-Plaza to Act

By DONALD JANSON
Special to The New York Times

LOUIS, Aug. 30—The rican Sociological Association forced one of the largest els in St. Louis to open its ls to Negroes today.

he pool, previously open to guests of the hotel except groes, is at the Chase-Park aza. The hotel is the head-arters for the fifty-sixth anual meeting of the association national organization of ociologists.

INTEGRATION PLAN WINS IN TEANECK

School System Proponents Victors in Record Vote

By WALTER WAGGONER
Special to The New York Times

TEANECK, N. J., Feb. 9—The advocates of integration won a decisive victory tonight over the supporters of a neighborhood school system.

BAR GROUPS OPEN DOORS TO NEGROES

Integration of Lawyers in South Gathers Momentum

By FRED P. GRAHAM
Special to The New York Times

WASHINGTON, Jan. 15—Negroes are being accepted in increasing numbers into the traditional bastions of Southern conservatism—its bar associations.

The process is uneven, and it lags behind the Negroes'

700 IGNORE RAC AT JERSEY DANG

Interracial Group Wants to Show 'People Are People'

By WILLIAM BORDERS
Special to The New York Times

MORRISTOWN, N. J., March 13—In what it described as an attempt at "genuine social integration," a civil-rights group here held an interracial dance last night at one of the area's most elegant ballrooms.

With 700 guests—about half of them white and half of them Negro—dancing to the jazz beat of Count Basie and his 16-piece band, the party was unlike anything this fashionable suburban community had ever seen

1, 2. *Dixwell Area: In this previously all-Negro slum, now Florence Virtue Homes, an integrated cooperative development*

Integration. In Both Directions: New Haven's Urban Renewal Housing

3, 4. *Wooster Square Area: In the previously all-white slum, now Columbus Mall, an integrated cooperative*

In this second of the pivot chapters, we shall explore how we can counter or replace some of the obsolete but still potent factors in this powerful realm of underlying dynamics by energizing embryonic forces that are emerging here. And we shall see by recently past and current experience how this is being accomplished in capitalist Western Europe.[1] Again we do not cover anything like the whole spectrum, but select those elements for discussion and emphasis that most closely bear on future progress and its quality.

Replacing the Dog-wagging Developer

Massively involving other sectors of private enterprise in direct development operation on a new basis could eliminate a good deal of the dog-wagging developer's irresponsibility and its wanton result.

Insurance companies and savings banks, with their enormously large aggregations of capital, and pension funds of big companies and labor unions— these now generally play the supine role of mortgage lender and make the fantastic current operations possible. The capital these institutions need to invest should be invested in major part in direct equity development. Then the *actual* investor would weigh his policy in terms of income over many years, not look forward to the hoped-for killing and moving on. Some insurance companies have made some very substantial equity (common stock) investments which have produced steady income and which have sometimes contributed to positive social development. They have of late years given this up because of public relations considerations, such as tensions of racial integration, unpopularity resulting from raising rents, etc. As one of their executives has put it, they prefer not to have investments of "high visibility." Perhaps it is understandable business policy not to assume what is considered a special risk that competitors avoid. The way to get over this hurdle is by legislation to require direct capital investment in development of a definite percentage of assets by all these institutions—the insurance companies and the others—so that any real or imagined competitive disadvantage would be removed because all would be involved.[2]

---

[1] In this chapter, we shall mostly consider the case of Sweden. Later we shall take up stirring current solutions from England, France, and the Netherlands. These countries used to be almost as ultra-private enterprise as we. But decades ago they began to see that in the difficult sphere of building community, the methods and ingrained outlook of private enterprise were simply not adequate.

[2] There are already similar statutory requirements governing other parts of their investment portfolios.

CHAPTER FIVE

UNDERLYING DYNAMICS OF SOCIAL AND PHYSICAL DEVELOPMENT: EMBRYONIC, POTENTIAL

Philanthropic foundations should be required to invest some of their huge funds similarly. Indeed, such foundations are peculiarly fitted for this social-economic-explorational function. Decades back we had foundation enterprise. Examples are the Rosenwald Foundation in Chicago, and the Buhl Foundation in Pittsburgh, which developed Chatham Village, one of our handsomest developments and a most consistently satisfactory investment for well over thirty years. The Lavanburg Foundation is now creatively active in New York (see page 27).

In the last decade particularly, the truly nonprofit cooperative has attained considerable skill, stature, and quantity in the field of middle-income housing. The Foundation for Cooperative Housing, the United Housing Foundation, and the Association for Middle-income Housing are making a dent in the market and in the motivations of development enterprises, as well as fostering alert participation by the citizens who are their members. Here is a dynamic sector of private enterprise that is rapidly acquiring experience and know-how.

There are some excellent current examples of pension-fund activity in direct investment. The fine example of St. Francis Square in a San Francisco urban renewal area by the fund of the International Longshoremen's and Warehousemen's Union and the Pacific Maritime Association has already been described. Some American labor unions have with uniform success built middle-income cooperatives. We find this very much more prevalent in Sweden. The Svenska Riksbyggen, the cooperative housing agency of the building-trades unions, together with the famous HSB, a cooperative building and loan association, handles 25 per cent of all home building. In England there are the nonprofit associations and trusts.

Such enterprises (all are private but motivated quite differently from those of the normal private developer) are by no means cure-alls. For one thing, they don't get down to really low incomes; for that, public subsidy is required, and the housing-authority form. But they do eliminate the anarchy, the differential-obsolescence motivation, the initial inflation of land costs, and the sales and resales of the normal developer sector of private enterprise. Certainly we should not lose the drive and initiative of our customary private developer. He can handle the actual building operations, can bring his ingenuity and drive to bear, as part of a quite differently oriented system of private enterprise. And he can take on *sections* of large undertakings such as New

Towns, once the ground rules have been sensitively established and are being vigilantly administered.

I have noted the enhanced opportunity for positive continuing social participation that being a cooperative owner-member in a development gives the citizen. In an even more dynamic capacity, he can help form a public interest group to work toward the design and building of a new development. Often these groups are church-based; examples cited were in Chapter 3 and on a national level. Another, is the Methodist Church group for middle- and low-income families formed in January, 1966. The potential has already been proved, in a number of instances. Strong positive moves are urgently needed to multiply such groups vastly and speedily. The Ford Foundation in 1965 made a large fund available, through the Local Development Services Division of Urban America–Action Council, to advise them technically and financially. But I must regretfully note a strong caveat here in two respects. Often a public interest group is guided by a member who is a speculative builder, whose experience is therefore respected, and who with possibly the best intentions injects his ingrained speculator outlook. The upshot is frequently that while a development is done under the auspices of a public interest group, the process and result are little different from those of the speculative developer on his own. The second part of this caveat is broader and more subtle. Even where there is no such speculative outlook, the public interest groups and the development funds that aid them generally have the quite limited outlook of the business power structure, which then dominates both over-all policy and much in the specific undertakings.

This is partly the result of stepping into a vacuum. Labor unions, for one example, could and should develop quite a different planning and development viewpoint. But even though the development fund or public interest group may have a representative of labor, he generally is purely a symbol.[3] Except for some very fine activity in promoting cooperative housing, labor has not seriously worked out sophisticated urban development poli-

[3] A typical example is Washington, D.C. There Downtown Progress, Inc., has forty-four members, of whom forty are bankers or businessmen, three are newspaper publishers, and one is an acting university president. This is referred to as a committee of "business and civic leaders." The development plan they have presented for a very large downtown residential area contains nothing in the way of low-rental housing, except for a small number of units for the elderly.

cies and plans to challenge or seriously modify those of the business power structure.

Reducing the Cost of Housing and Community. Swedish Experience as a Beacon

In Sweden, they have grappled with the complex of factors involved in development and have worked out answers which cry out for analysis and creative study by us. In the United States, land prices continue to spiral; in Sweden, early and continuing large-scale public purchase and retention of land give to the consumer and to the public weal the benefit of reasonable land costs, in perpetuity. Stockholm has been purchasing large areas of land for over sixty years, and most of it has now been carefully developed, on leasehold. During this period, over 500,000 acres have been acquired. (In about the same period, the city of Copenhagen has likewise acquired large amounts of vacant land inside and outside the city. This land has now reached the large value of some 40 million Danish crowns. Copenhagen has a carefully circumscribed policy of disposition and development.)[4]

A note here about Stockholm's understanding and cumulative action on the land problem and other metropolitan problems:

> In 1961 the international union of architects awarded to Stockholm the prize bearing the name of Sir Patrick Abercrombie citing "the organic growth and the internal reconstruction of Stockholm and its region." . . .
>
> An important condition for the planned execution of urban development has been the municipal land policy: the city acquired large tracts of land at an early stage and therefore it has been able to lead building development along rational lines, in accordance with its general planning policy. . . .
>
> The City of Stockholm is cooperating with the neighboring municipalities in planning increased housing production within the framework of the regional plan. This plan, adopted by an association of 47 municipalities belonging to the greater Stockholm region, was approved by the national government in 1960. . . .
>
> Co-operating with other municipalities of the Greater Stockholm area, the city thus tries to program its housing production, for example, in five-year terms. . . .
>
> Inside Stockholm proper, the implementation of

the plans has been fully protected by municipal ownership of the land. Even when municipal properties are developed by private enterprise, the land is leased and not sold. . . .[5]

Here, on the other hand, speculation is uncurbed. In urban renewal, government makes grants of billions to write down land costs after buying out current owners at a stiff price; then it sells the land at a low price to new speculative builders without even nailing down the resale price. So the upward cycle of land prices starts all over again. Does this make sense, or is it weird? We must once and for all begin to take hold and keep hold of this land situation.

Let us turn to the matter of housing. I quote from a striking article by Jerome Liblit in the New York *Herald Tribune* of December 22, 1963:

> This country has not established the kind of housing institutions which are able to plan long-range programs or assume responsibility for continuing development. In this respect, the Scandinavian countries seem to have done a much better job. . . .
>
> These advances have been in the organization of the housing industry itself. Sweden has one-twentieth of our population, yet one housing organization produces more than twice as many residential units each year as our largest private developer. The organizations [Svenska Riksbyggen and H.S.B.] are private-cooperative, nonprofit in character.[6]
>
> The 25,000 relatively small building contractors in the housing field at this count [in the United States] are in no position to conduct meaningful research or exercise real leadership. Certainly, this has contributed to a steady rise in building costs and the continuing shortage of housing of low- and moderate-income families.
>
> A long-term continuing housing program might go a long way toward persuading labor to cooperate in a program of wage stabilization and to increase productivity.
>
> In Sweden, where construction workers can count on sustained employment, the Building Trades Union itself encourages mechanization.

[4] Even in France, with all its financial conservatism and ingrained individualism, there is now a law, to be applied in connection with the Paris plan for the year 2000, to freeze land prices in key areas so as not to hamstring proposed development.

[5] From article by Yngve Larsson, formerly commissioner for traffic and planning, in *Stockholm: Regional and City Planning,* Planning Commission, City of Stockholm, 1964, pp. 8–10, and 21.

[6] It is also to be noted that in the decades when building costs were being lowered relative to other costs in the economy, the volume being handled by cooperatives and other public and public interest groups had sharply risen, while the proportion handled by private enterprise had diminished.

The unions boast that due to automation the income of their members has more than doubled in the past ten years. . . .

H.S.B. was the first society to be organized on a permanent basis with plans for a continuous building program. H.S.B. started with one society in Stockholm; today it has 1400 affiliated societies in 188 communities throughout the country. . . . The national association maintains a technical research department and has discovered and promoted significant innovation in the housing field. . . . Any savings it is able to achieve are passed on to the consumer. Yet H.S.B. is not a public agency. . . .[7]

What We Can Learn from It: Research and Action. This is exciting reading, and again, it is later than you think. With this Swedish experience as a starting point, why in heaven's name do we not move with some imagination and with utmost determination? Is it not absolutely imperative and long overdue that organized authoritative studies be made which might, through perfectly rational and non-revolutionary methods, revolutionize *our* productivity and production of housing?

Now as to construction costs themselves, a prime factor in housing productivity and costs: Some research is under way in the United States on the construction operation and on combinations of materials and techniques.[8] The administration's legislation of 1966 asks for a large sum to cover much more of it, and actual demonstrations are under way. But research on construction techniques and organization rationalization, however heavily financed and however cogent the indicated results, will not get anywhere unless some leaders of the building-trades unions are willing to help initiate it, and can be involved by being convinced that the possible answers can so increase the volume of effective demand that their constituents will gain, not lose. This is the Swedish claim, and in Sweden the second largest nongovernment entrepreneur, the Svenska Riksbyggen, was originally founded by the labor unions as a response to unemployment, and is still

a union operation. A well-laid plan for research in this field should have as part of it a totally uncommitted study trip to Scandinavia by a team including labor leaders to see what the Swedish building revolution has accomplished and how, and what its implications are for us.[9]

With spiraling costs of construction and of almost every other factor in the housing equation having such a serious direct effect on the well-being of all people and cities and on national production, it perpetually amazes me that urgent discussion is so lacking, and that foundations or a foundation is not mounting a massive attack on all the factors that enter into costs. Trend or mastery? Oh, for a touch of the questing psychology of the underdeveloped countries, to lead us to study what is accomplished elsewhere, to leaven our complacent self-confidence!

Racial Integration

In contrast to the absence of worry and discussion in this grievous matter of housing costs, the matter of racial integration is arousing endless discussion and emotional involvement. But in spite of the turmoil and the tumult, the violence and the non-violence, the crisis in conscience throughout this country, in spite of the Presidential order barring discrimination in any government-aided undertaking, in spite of the tremendous Civil Rights Acts of 1964 and 1965—in spite of all this churning up, I know of no large-scale development plan or urban renewal plan of any city or urban-metropolitan area except the small city of New Haven that deals with the matter of color equality and residential discrimination and stratification as the very major issue that it is and interweaves it in a major way with physical planning and development. As a basis for a broad-scale action plan, it is ignored.

The issue is major and painfully visible, and much dealt with in books and pamphlets on civil rights, and in that sense is not a submerged or only underlying issue. But in urban development, where it is dealt with at all on the plane of program and action, it is dealt with in only fragmentary ways. It is very secondary in comparison with the goals of primary importance such as slum clearance and urban renewal sponsorship mainly privately for profit. Just enough is done to make those activities possible without too much hell breaking loose—although sometimes it does anyway. Inevitably, the

[7] Dramatic illustrations of major prefabrication—of structure, of bathroom assemblies, etc., are quite common in Swedish housing construction. Both construction cost and time have been reduced, hence also interest accumulating during construction. A nine-story building takes three months to build, from excavation to occupancy! Of course, such methods are *known* here, but because of various vested interests, they are not being used on any appreciable scale in the cities.

[8] This does not refer to the many millions being spent on researching individual products—e.g., flooring, acoustical treatments, electric plugs—which have comparatively little effect on total construction cost.

[9] The fact is, indeed, that advanced money-saving techniques are available and in use here, including the "mobile home," but are generally not allowed within city limits due to the opposition of labor and other interests.

action is tokenism or less. It is certainly far, far, from anything like movement into the new era.

The time is here when we must and *can* put this whole matter of integration among our clearest visualizations and top priorities. We must build up an over-all goal picture of what kind of city and metropolitan area we would then have and go ahead and carry it out as a major element in each development of any size. We cannot continue in the present tempo of only the most minor single positive actions in already segregated areas; we must propose, debate, and activate major answers. If we fail to do these things, we will continue to pile up and worsen mutual tensions, particularly in view of present Negro overcrowding and population increase. There is massive and encouraging evidence of a new burgeoning positive trend toward full acceptance of the Negro, over an unexpectedly wide spectrum of citizen action and opinion in many places, that we can foster and multiply and intensify. The great exclusionist power could well be on the down curve in the face of new attitudes and forces *and* determined policy. What are some signs?

On the legislative front, the Civil Rights Acts, passed by huge congressional majorities, involved the sensitive area of personal contact in schools and in eating and other public places. Thirty-seven powerful national organizations form the National Committee against Discrimination in Housing. In New York City there is an exclusively white group called EQUAL, consisting of thirty-eight chapters, whose members *advocate* school busing and educational integration as a positive good for their own white children. In a number of middle-upper-class communities, white congregations now have Negro pastors. These are nonbusiness and nongovernment areas; in the latter, of course, the progress is much faster. In Great Neck and other upper-middle-class suburbs around New York, a large group has formed to welcome and to seek nonwhite families. There are similar groups in Washington, in San Francisco. There are over 1,000 volunteer fair-housing committees around the country. The constitution of the National Association of Housing Cooperatives, composed of cooperatives with 60,000 families, pledges open occupancy, and I am told this is generally lived up to. In Berkeley, California, a drastic integration ordinance lost by only a very close vote. Berkeley has since done an excellent job in school integration.

There are many other examples, in housing and in diverse pervasive fields. Another great factor in our favor: studies show that the *experience* of interracial housing and of other daily relationships much reduces negative attitudes. One among them: in the European theater of war a survey showed 64 per cent of enlisted men in mixed companies approving mixed units, as compared with 18 per cent in segregated white companies. The Washington *Post* of May 28, 1965, headlined the Gallup poll: "Opposition to Negroes as Neighbors Decreases." And then: "On a survey in May, 1963, 45% of whites across the nation said they would move if a Negro family moved next door. Today the comparable figure is 35%."

In a speech delivered on June 29, 1965, at the conference of the National Committee against Discrimination in Housing, Frank S. Horne noted:

> Public opinion may well be way ahead of us. As reported in *Look* Magazine for June 29, 1965, a Gallup poll, in sampling national opinion on a number of questions reports:
>
> "One question produced the greatest surprise of the survey. It was this: 'Suppose a Negro family moved next door to you. What would you do?' *Eight in ten white Americans* said they would not move. Incredibly, only 23 percent of Southerners said they would move.
>
> "The willingness to accept Negroes as neighbors was even more emphatic among teenagers. Only 11 percent said they would want their parents to move or to sell their homes."

Time does march on, despite defeat in Congress.

The first thing is to see what the picture would look like. Here is a program:

1. *The Goal.* Freedom of residential movement and settlement for all, in the city, in the suburbs, in the New Town, wherever. This means that there should be no very large residential area anywhere without range of housing supply that is geared to different incomes and open to whoever can pay. This does not mean a homogenized result where every ethnic strain and every income level have their proportionate representation in every building and every block. It means providing the unfettered possibility for mixing. The actual result will be accepted presence of minorities in *any* area. But it is likely that the largest percentage of minorities will stay put where they are. A fairly minor percentage would embrace the opportunity to move. A builder of open communities in the suburbs of New York City, each of which has some Negro families, tells me he is disappointed in the small number of Negroes who apply. The incomes are undoubtedly there in the New York area, but not the inclination or the drive. The general preference and comfort of minorities (as one can see all over

1. *Guided self-help. Backfilling foundations for a neighborhood common, Washington, D. C.*

People's Initiative and Involvement

2. *Pouring concrete for the amphitheater, Washington, D. C.*

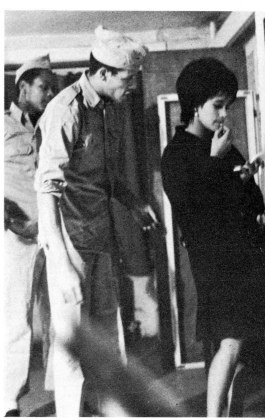

3. *East Harlem: A play authored, presented, and acted by "The Miracles"*

GRASS ROOTS

VOL. 1 NO. 7

LA VOZ DEL HARLEM DEL ESTE

25 enero 1965

EDITORIAL

En circulos comunales de Harlem de Este se comenta con inusitado interes el biaje gratis a Puerto Rico de que gozo un grupo de Harlem Este. Este viaje era proyectado para los lideres locales de arraigo entre la masa popular. Sin embargo la lista de viajeros incluyo un director de una de las agencias locales ademas de cinco otros personajes cuya reputacion como lideres es muy cuestionable, entre los cuales viajo un matrimonio bajo nombres incognitos. El Rev. Lon Dring nosinformo que el Gobierno de Puerto Rico auspiciaba este viaje. Corroborando esta informacion con la oficina del gobierno de Puerto Rico en Nueva York, nos sorprendio saber que dicha oficina no tenia conocimiento de esto arreglos.

De fuentes fidedignas del mas entero credito, supimos que el coordinador de esta caravana a Puerto Rico era el sincero y buenazo David Borden quien en otros tiempos fueramiembro del personal del East Harlem Project y quien parece ostentar una maravillosa posicion con el gobierno de Puerto Rico. De acuerdo con informes en nuestro poder, David Borden ha recibido una donacion preliminar de fondos para establecer un proyecto suyo basado en organizacion de manzanas de calle. Tenemos entendido que al radicar la solicitud de fondos, el nombre East Harlem Committee, Inc. fue utilizado. No sabemos cuanta influencia ejercio el uso de dicho nombre. Cu-- hecho que ningun miem-- del Action Com -- torizar

Observadores En Puerto Rico

En enero 8, en el vuelo 837 de la Eastern Airlines, salieron de la ciudad de Nueva York a las 10:45 P.M. un grupo de 18 personas de la comunidad del Harlem Este. Los observadores fueron llevados al centro Investigacion sobre Adiccion a Drogas, Clinica de Siquiatria de Rio Piedras, dirigidos por el Dr. Effren Ramirez. Encloido el Programa de Desarrollo de la Comunidad Rural, dirigido por el Sr. Fred Wale. El grupo fue recibido en el aeropuerto de San Juan por el Sr. David Borden y fueron llevados a La Clinica de Siquiatria donde el grupo estuvo hospedado durante su estadia en Puerto Rico. El Dr. Ramirez estuvo a cargo del seminario de orientacion sobre el programa de narcoticos. Estuvieron cinco dias en la clinica obsevando el procedimiento terapeutico aplicado los adictos, tambien visitando y hablando con los adictos en la clinica.

El programa tambien incluia salidas con trabajadores de la comunidad, (adictos rehabilitados)hablando con adictos en las calles, reuniendose con los familiares de los adictos que estan en la clinica.

AREA RURAL

El grupo estuvo un dia en el departamento de Instruccion con el Sr. Wale. La orientacion fue dada en relacion con el Programa de -- llo de la Comunidad Ru-- fue dividio en pa-- dos a ciertas de la --

Comunidad Se Une Al Piquete

La ciudad de Nueva York a sido afectaida por la huelga de los empleados del Bienestar Publico. Muchas organizaciones de la comunidad han estado activamente soportando la huelga. Los huelguistas, miembros de la Union de Empleados del Estado y la Ciudad demandan aumento en los salarios y numero limitado de casos para trabajar con mejor eficiencia.

La ciudad a revsado discutir negociaciones con los lideres de la Union Los decididos empleados no solamente estan tratando que se les aumenten los sueldos, sino tambien corregir muchas de las indignidades del Bienestar Publico. En otras palabras, mejor eficiencia en la administracion y real proveco de la ayuda.

El Bienestar Publico del 309 de la calle 108, del Harlem Este, fue uno de los primeros centros en la ciudad en soportar la huelga varios dias despues de haber empezado.

Piquetes, Marchan

La actitud de los manifestantes es reminicencia de las demostraciones de los Derechos Civiles, hace algun tiempo atras. Un punto de significacion en la huelga, es las muchas caras nuevas y voces que se han unido a los huelguistas, en la linea de piquetes. Entre ellos ministros y clerigos del Harlem y otros

ESCUELA DE LA LIBERTAD

El Sr. Allan Robbins, Profesor, y Presidente del capitulo de la Federacion Unida de Maestros en la escuela 83 por sugerencia de Doris Theiler, ayudante del principal, sugirio -- -doptar una escuela -- En un san -- de que el Negro conozca su poder politico. Cada escuela sigue su propio pat ron. Una de ellas ofrece clases de kindergarten, juegos atleticos supervisados, para los primarios. Varias veces en semana, ofrece clases de discusion por las noch -- para adultos y jovenes.

---

4. East Harlem News Sheet. In Spanish and English. Now defunct

---

GRASS ROOTS

VOL. 1 NO. 7

THE VOICE OF EAST HARLEM

January 25,1965

EDITORIAL

In certain quarters of East Harlem Rev. Lon Dring generated much excitment with FREE trips to Puerto Rico. Rev. Dring,(who chose the people) reported the trip was for grass roots leaders and was being sponsored by the Office of the Commonwealth of Puerto Rico. However, a director of a social agency went, along with six people of questionable leadership background, this included a married couple traveling incognito. A phone call to that office showed that NO ONE KNEW ANYTHING about the trip. Further inquiry turned up the following information: the trip was being coordinated from Puerto Rico by the well meaning and sincere David Borden (formally of East Harlem Project), who has a unique position with the Government of Puerto Rico. Mr. Borden reports say, has received an initial grant for a pet project centering around block organizations. The proposal for the grant mentions East Harlem Action Committee Inc. Whether this played a part in the grant being approved is not known. What is known NONE OF THE OFFICERS OF THE ACTION COMMITTEE KNEW WHAT WAS GOING ON.

NOTHING NEW

In this old concept of block organizations, Mr. Borden has hired three persons as block workers at $100 a wee-- -- -- -- been consid-- -- on the

Observers In Puerto Rico

On January 8th, flight 837 departed from New York City at 10:45 p.m., bound for San Juan, Puerto Rico Tickets for the trip to Puerto Rico were issued to eighteen residents of the East Harlem community. The group was picked to observe the addiction program at the Addiction Research Center,Psychiatric Clinic Rio Piedras Puerto Rico. Which is directed by Dr. Efren Ramirez.The group also observed the Community Rural Development Program, directed by Mr. Fred Wale.

The group was met at the San Juan airport by Mr. David Borden and taken to the Psychiatric Clinic where the group stayed while in Puerto Rico. Dr. Ramirez opened the seminar with an orientation session in relation to the narcotics program. Five days were spent at the clinic sitting in on group therapy sessions. The program included field work with community workers (a rehabilitated addict)which centered around addicts in the street and the wives and families of addicts interned at the clinic.

RURAL AREA

The group spent a day at the Department of Instruction in the office with Mr. Wales. A briefing was given on the Community Rural Development Area Program.The group was split into pairs, after which they were sent to rural areas throughout the island to spend two days with community organizers.The group returned to th- clinic and met with Dr. R-- -ff

Community Join Pickets

The New York City Dept. of Welfare has been crippled by a strike of it's Welfare investigators. Many local church and community organizations have all ready taken sides and are actively supporting the strikers.

The strikers,members of the State, City and Municipal Workers Union are demanding an increase in salaries, smaller case loads to enable them to render better and efficient service to Welfare recipients.

To date the City refuses to sit down and negotiate with Union leaders The dissident workers are not only seeking to improve their career wage scales but to correct many of the indignities that Welfare recipients must suffer. In short, a more efficient administration and a realistic approach to Welfare aid.

The East End Welfare Center at 309 East 108 Street,was one of the first Welfare centers in the city where community support blossomed within a

Pickets at East End Welfare center

few days after the strike had started the militant attitude of the pickets is reminiscent of the Civil Rights demonstrations of a few short months ago. Especially significant are the many new faces and voices that have joined the strikers on the picket lines—Welfare recipients, clergymen and other concerned East Harlemites.

FREEDOM SCHOOL ADOPTED

Mr. Allen Robbins, teacher and Chapter Chairman of the United Federation of Teachers, at P.S. 83, with a suggestion byMiss Doris Theiler, Assistant Principal, sponsored for the adoption of a Free- in Mississippi. On a moment drive the -- -ollected $52 -- to enable the Negro to know his political power. Of the schools there are no two alike. This is a day at one of these schools: Kindergarten class -ools have none) sup-rvised for grade schoolers in Several tires o -cussion periods -ng people at

this country, whether of Polish, Swedish, Italian, or whatever extraction) is to live and to socialize with each other, *provided* the conditions are made humane.[10] The difference between the ghetto and normally related living with one's natural fellows is that the former is an enforced humiliation, the latter is a free choice. As for actual numbers living in the ghetto, before and after it is transformed, there won't be a violent difference. There will be enough diminution of numbers to eliminate the inhuman and profitable overcrowding and to attract white people to move in.

As of now, with the iron chain around it, every inevitable burst out of the ghetto and into a new area causes a new ghetto and new white insecurity, because only the one area has yielded. Everyone must move into it because there is nowhere else. And this is repeated. Repeated too are the "block busting," the planned and fostered panic. But what if there is general freedom? Then there are no new incipient ghettos with frightened whites packing up and fleeing, and the old ones become places to live with self-respect.

There are enough of these areas of general freedom everywhere now to demonstrate this point: the large-scale Prairie Shores and Lake Meadows in Chicago; Park Forest, one of Chicago's middle-class suburbs; Eichler's operations in California; Modern Home Builders in the East; and dozens of others. In Cleveland, a number of communities in the exclusive Shaker Heights suburb have absorbed Negro families in a positive spirit in a number of sections. In other suburbs there: Morland ($12,000 to $25,000 houses) now has a large minority of Negroes; in Ludlow ($35,000 to $50,000) ditto; also Lomond and Sussex. This goes back eight years, and the suitation is quite stable. In New Jersey, a volunteer group called CHOICE has reported that in a period of a few months in 1965, it placed 200 Negro families in a number of previously all-white neighborhoods in suburban towns. Salesmen in a large open-occupancy suburb in New Jersey reported in 1963 that just 11 per cent of all prospects indicated any concern about this question; less than 2 per cent were uncompromisingly opposed to open occupancy.[11] The Greater St. Louis Committee for Freedom of Residence noted in 1965 that in three years Negro families had satisfactorily moved into

thirty-one previously all-white suburban communities. In that citadel of suburbia, Westchester, a number of upper-middle-class developments have been opened to Negro families without fanfare.[12]

It is also now well documented that real estate values are not depreciated except where there is unscrupulously planned or fanned panic. Thus complete residential freedom means massive psychological release for *all* elements, minority and majority, and remarkably less moving around than fear has conjured up. The seeming paradox is documented that the proposed and embryonic freedom of movement and of settlement leads to stability, which replaces the familiar patterns of resistance and deterioration and of precipitous flight.

2. *Means for Achieving.* Such a natural freedom will be attained only if every sizable development operation is creatively, and as high priority, *seeking* this over-all state of well-being.

New Towns should have a comprehensive range of industrial, service, and commercial jobs, and not just jobs in the "in" types of electronics firms and laboratories that are coming to ring our cities. And public housing for really low-income workers. This is of the first importance, because population is increasing, of all colors, and it is a principal function of the New Town to take the increase, across the board. The New Town, certainly, must be a locus for new habits both of mind and of living.

Urban renewal in cities cannot continue to be of the opportunistic type, locations chosen with an eye to the two considerations of slumminess and appeal to private sponsors of middle- and high-income apartments and of office buildings. These characteristically displace existing mixed residence areas and minorities, thus *increasing* segregation. Lately there is some emphasis on rehabilitation and conservation. Both by and large leave the racial composition of an area relatively unchanged. Urban

---

[10] This is not just an easy generalization. I match it with a specific remark in conversation which I vividly recall: "I want to see East Harlem improve itself. This is my home. I will not move. I will keep on living here. I want to live in a better neighborhood, here."

[11] *A Series of Case Studies,* Housing and Home Finance Agency, June, 1964, p. 8.

[12] The phrase "without fanfare" is significant: the instances of integration are so increasing as not to arouse surprise or great attention. Moreover, the freedom from fanfare is not altogether new. Few have heard of the Barrett Construction Company's operations in Richmond, California, but over the last ten years Barrett has sold three separate well (not tokenly) integrated developments totaling 700 homes, and is soon starting a 357-unit rental apartment house. And contrary to the widely accepted axiom that stability over time requires establishment of a maximum quota for the minority, this firm has disregarded quotas. But proportions of races have stayed stable. . . . The case of Kansas City is likewise little known. The Kansas City *Star* reports that since 1962 Negro families have moved into 26 widely dispersed areas of blue-collar workers. This experience counters the widely held view that harmonious integration occurs only in middle- and upper-class areas.

renewal must seize the opportunity to deliberately select nonsegregated areas, provide the range of accommodation for adequate freedom of movement and of settlement in them, and program nonsegregated schools of excellence to serve them, as in New Haven.

In no form of development will it be enough to have the negative virtue of no discrimination. We must have positive high priority for selection of areas suitable to free integration, we must have this objective high in the planning and design program, and we must positively seek the range of occupants we want. The proposed Demonstration Cities Act does not contribute any positive element. True, it specifies nondiscrimination, but the injunction is as usual mild, and will be inadequate unless it is placed high among objectives. And the stated purpose being to rebuild and to rehouse those now living in each district touched by the act, the racial status quo seems destined to be frozen.

There is a twofold strategic role for public housing. First, the low rentals that its subsidies make possible must be made available in quantity both in New Towns and in the new kind of urban renewal. Second, in its locations in the existing city, while it will undoubtedly need to continue building massively in presently segregated areas with a view to upgrading the people where they are, thereby attracting outsiders, as can happen and actually has happened, there must be insistence too on choosing and building in nonenclave locations sufficiently magnetic in layout and price that there will be natural intergrouping.

3. *The Thinned-out Ex-ghetto.* Widespread freedom of residence can be achieved only by a combination of imagination, determination, and dovetailed timing. One of the very first steps must be to create housing and an environment in the ghetto, so desirable that people wanting to live with their most comfortably congenial friends will have full chance quite early in the cycle to see what has been created, judge its quality, and cheerfully decide, "this is for me." Our present tools permit this result. Consider the large-scale instance of Franklin Plaza in East Harlem. It is a middle-income co-op development of 1,600 families built by the housing authority in such a way that it not only held local residents but attracted outsiders and developed a desirable mix whose proportions have remained stable in the three years since completion. Q.E.D. On an even larger scale, the Rochdale Village Co-op of 6,000 units was built by the United Housing Foundation in the solid Negro area of South Jamaica. White people occupy 4,800

of the units. The 20 per cent of Negroes are not in clumps, but well distributed throughout the development. These are massive examples, not oddities. On a more intimate but more pervasive scale, from New Haven's urban renewal: An integrated cooperative has flourished stably since it was built two years ago in the hitherto solidly Negro Dixwell Avenue area. In the hitherto all-white Wooster Square area, there are Negroes in the Columbus Mall Cooperative. We need more such situations, and we need them intertwined with our cities' total fabric of housing supply. Then the thinned-out ex-ghetto will be on its way, with a *range* of income and social and racial groups, a stimulating place to live in and to visit, by choice.[13]

In presenting this program for integration and for transforming the ghetto, I have mainly discussed housing, schools, and environmental elements. In Chapter 7, which deals with restructuring the city, I advocate and cite examples (foreign) of decentralization and subcentralization—moving business and public institutions from the gargantuan center into the districts so as to achieve various economic and social advantages. Here let me simply note that this is a very strategic thing to do in an integrating policy. It is particularly appropriate where we have a key location, as at the convenient confluence of bridges, subways, and commuter railroad in New York's Harlem. In this specific location, we also have the city planning opportunity of making a substantial contribution to unraveling the total traffic problem by diminishing the volume flooding into the impossibly traffic-inundated major centers.

4. *And Can It Really Be Done?* I am convinced it can. Not yet, in Southern areas. And not quite yet in some other areas. But in many, it can. The instances cited and others not cited show that when housing is made available that is attractive

[13] New Haven, a great exception among our cities, is well on the road to achieving all this. I quote from a letter to me of Feb. 21, 1966, from Joel Cogen, deputy director and general counsel:

"Every single one of our housing developments (including those built by private developers or regular builders) is substantially integrated, and has reversed the previous pattern dominant in the neighborhood, largely due to the efforts of the Redevelopment Agency and the Commission on Equal Opportunities together with the cooperation of the sponsors and builders. In addition, all of our public housing projects are integrated.

"Thus, you can see that non-profit sponsors are building the equivalents of Florence Virtue and Columbus Mall not only in the same urban renewal areas (Dixwell and Wooster Square) but in other renewal and redevelopment areas as well. Many other organizations—churches, unions, foundations, etc.—have expressed interest in sponsoring similar developments."

and *a really good buy,* families of both colors just naturally take advantage of it and move in, without special motivation or self-consciousness.

Required, too, are city and county executives who have placed the goal of integration in housing adequately high on their list of priorities, and who resourcefully utilize and foster all the formative elements. They should be able to, and should, call on the Federal government to use the leverage it has in fund allocation and withholding, as it is doing in other fields where this integration issue is involved—for example, in the case of the Office of Economic Opportunity. When possible this program should be pushed in areas where new towns, those reservoirs of the future, are built by government authorities or public interest groups, not by essentially private investors, so timid in social innovation. *And* with the emerging and building up of forces of conscience and personal conviction, with the focused pressures in action that are increasing, with all churches deeply committed, with a host of examples of successful integration, this is the poised moment. Where such conditions obtain, as they do in some areas and will do in more and more areas, the symphony of freedom can be performed *now.*

In all such path finding enterprises of great moment, these are the required ingredients, to be molded with care and determination. With them, we succeed. In New Haven's imaginative and successful urban renewal, there is splendid evidence of an important breakthrough. The Florence Virtue co-op has 55 per cent Negro and 45 per cent white in a previously all-Negro slum, and *in previously white neighborhoods,* the occupancy of two new low-middle-income housing developments is 20 to 25 per cent Negro. The city of Louisville smoothly integrated its whole school system even before the Federal laws of 1964 and 1965, by the combination of thorough preparation and determination; others floundered and met violence. And as long ago as 1950, a study in another field concluded that whenever industrial management takes a firm stand in hiring members of minority groups, the workers are likely to accept, while indecisive management encourages protest, picketing.

I have heavily drawn on the positive, favorable experience of integration in many places and over a very wide gamut of human relations in addition to housing. I am, of course, aware that there is a preponderance still of the negative, possibly the most jolting recent example of which was passage of the infamous proposition 14 in California. I have concentrated on the growing mass of creative expe-

rience of integration because it is generally much less known, and because true integration will come about, not by endless gradualism but by the strong wills of informed and devoted men.

Energizing the Social Base. The Role of Social Science. Infusion into Architecture

One of our most underdeveloped resources for the creation of urban human wholeness and its ultimate fulfillment in architectural design is the insight of social science. A great deal is known by the social scientists. But they have by and large not done much in taking direct action on what they know, nor have they developed skill in transmitting and transmuting it. Nor, in general, are those social scientists who are involved in active community design yet ready to absorb deeply the fact that their contribution is a strand of creative formulation that must be woven into a whole design.

The need and still not activated opportunity exist on several planes. The first is that of observation and diagnosis of social facts and attitudes, aspirations and cultural harmonies, and family and individual needs and desires and functions, all as the raw material to be transmuted into physical designs. This is the first step in producing maximum suitability of what is designed, in minimizing mistakes and negative reactions, in becoming able to predict and promote positive responses. Until now, the practical application of social science, where it has occurred, has been largely in the realm of managing and operating the already existing, correcting or modifying the past. Now, we greatly need permeating help and participation in forward projection, in planning and design.

Some beginnings can be cited:

The San Antonio Housing Authority in 1964 brought together the architects and landscape architects for its new developments, key members of its own staff, relevant personnel of other city agencies such as the Community Welfare Council, and Dr. Ozzie Simmons, director of the Institute of Behavioral Science of the University of Colorado. The discussion was mutually enlightening, and it was expansive: the record of the meeting filled 98 pages. In Chicago, Paul Mundy, professor of sociology at Loyola University, worked closely and effectively with the architects and sponsors of the South Commons urban renewal development of the church-sponsored Community Renewal Foundation.

A fascinating example lies in the planning of the projected New Town of Columbia in Maryland. There the developer, James W. Rouse, through

Donald L. Michael of the Institute of Policy Studies in Washington, arranged a series of preplanning studies and repeated conferences involving an interacting galaxy of advisers, including specialists in human relations, social structure, adult education, and related areas. Their interplay influenced the development plans and produced new interrelationships. In this case the social-science group also continued as critics of the early planning and architectural stages, strengthening the understanding of the architects.

The emphasis here has been on *transmission* and *infusion* of social-research findings now available. The accumulating research itself must keep questing, must not only contribute to initial design and creation but currently observe the resulting reactions and continue to improve in order to become part of the creative process and product and feedback.

Another dimension of research is the business of all of us who are actively concerned with the creation of community: "homemade" research. Practically every facet of our work should be researched by us ourselves. Without formal and formidable research, we should be our own personal researchers. The fact is that we let a lot of important and significant raw material go unobserved and lose its projective value. How many architects or officials later visit their finished developments at regular intervals to see how social and recreational spaces that were designed with specific creative intent are really used? How many have circulated around *any* projects to get a firsthand impression for their guidance? How many architects or social workers or *anybodies* have been interested to see whether rooms were furnished at all the way the blueprints or the model apartments showed, and whether it might have been better to plan for other sizes and shapes? Another thing: With the huge volume of construction that has taken place over the last twenty-five years, many "accidental alternatives" for space use have developed, many different arrangements and subdivisions for more or less the same total space. There have been virtually no systematic observations and comparisons of these in actual use, to serve as pragmatic guides.[14]

These are simple illustrations, but they point up the fact that we ought to get into the habit of cultivating "homemade" research so that we can get the vivid personal feel of things which we cannot adequately distill from formal statistical research. Personal judgment is constantly stimulated and renewed by warm direct field contacts; they equip one with a kind of corrective, sixth sense. One doesn't want either an obscurantist disregard of research or, because of the availability of research, a secondhand watered-down contact with the problem.

We also very much need continuous, built-in organizational evaluation-research and feedback. Incredibly, organizations like the Urban Renewal Administration, Public Housing Administration, and Federal Housing Administration, with their vast "laboratories" of accumulating developments, do not yet have any commensurate scale of social-scientist observer-evaluators—only, occasionally, analysts for this evaluating purpose. This is part of a situation which I have experienced in work in the United States and in working for other governments abroad. Huge project budgets in hundreds of millions are voted and implemented, with absurdly inadequate staff in the programming and operating agency, qualitatively and quantitatively. The wastes of this habit so satisfying to law-making bodies, of effecting small economies by slashing the administrative payroll, are incalculably more than the miserable little savings.

Process and People's Involvement. Now, fully shifting gears, let us see how participation in the social process of development can cause and has caused the growth that has usually been expected from just the physical product.

This participation should take two different but equally powerful forms:

■ Individual and social self-help, in the local community and small in scale.

■ Local groups mustering strength and self-discipline and exercising influence on large-scale matters in the local community and more indirectly on decisions in city hall—sometimes for, sometimes against, sometimes making new proposals, sometimes modifying, sometimes failing, but almost always gaining cohesiveness and self-confidence.

In Chapter 3 on urban renewal, we considered the case of Washington Park in Boston, where action originated in the local urge for self-change and renewal. In the same chapter, we considered Woodlawn in Chicago, where the local strength born of outside-imposed crisis—found itself in order to oppose remotely conceived renewal plans which would bring about excessive displacement and relocation. Both of these powerfully positive instances are from underprivileged communities.

---

[14] One result has been endlessly repeated poor division of a given amount of space between living room and kitchen. How many plans I have examined for low-income housing which out of this provide minimum kitchen dimensions without even minimal sitting and table space. Thus all meals, even kids' snacks, must be in the living room. A miserable situation for most low-income families. At the least, let us have some choice.

Such cases of strength through experience, of growth through process, are not by any means confined to urban renewal situations. A brief typical instance of another character: The Board of Education of Syracuse, bedeviled by delays, finally selected an 8-acre site for a junior high school, to be bitten out of Onondaga Park. In reaction, a local group formed itself into the Onondaga Park Protective Association and bombarded the board with cards, letters, phone calls, visits. The protesters enlisted professionals—architects, landscapers, educators, a lawyer—to make technical studies. A 40-page report was issued, exposing the inadequacy of the site and analyzing and proposing alternate sites. The proposal was dropped. The total cost was $400 plus countless unpaid man-hours. One of the admirable elements: the thoroughness and resourcefulness of people who at the start were novices.

In other ways, too, we need and are beginning to get cross-fertilization between local people and the design professions. Take the case of the Neighborhood Commons, in Washington and Philadelphia. Architects and landscape architects designed these neighborhood improvements right on the ground with the people, relying largely on the people's own resources in skills and eagerness. Prof. Karl Linn's name is associated with the initiation of these efforts. A hopeful beginning along another line is the New York architects' current effort called ARCH: Architects' Renewal Committee in Harlem. There are four large areas in Harlem into which urban renewal is moving. A number of volunteer architects and planners have divided themselves into teams—to study on the ground, to elicit people's views, to inform them of potentials and limitations, to interpret between groups, to try in many ways to make urban renewal culminate in locally based and locally understood design. They are working also with local organizations, social observers, social-action people, educators. For architects, these interactions feed the roots of design.[15]

The Component of Creative Employment. The core of participation in the kinds of significant locality-based movements just reviewed should be voluntary; this bolsters up the strength and animation and resourcefulness of such movements. But for full effectiveness and permanent drive, these movements must also involve paid organizers and staff at a number of levels. This is particularly the case where the amount of voluntary work is restricted by economic necessity, i.e., in the poor neighborhoods.

Many of these paid workers should be grass-roots —or asphalt-pavement—social workers, people who live in the locality and are part of it and who do not necessarily or even preferably have the M.A. that conventional practice still usually requires a social worker to have. Such people combine tough local experience with some sense of mission, and there are potentially many of them available. And once we expand our views beyond the customary into such fruitful fresh fields, we discern how varied and manifold are the needs and opportunities for their work. Yet it is hard for them to arrange to be paid.

Personal experience: At twenty-two, a quite successful and prestigeful gangster had had enough; in fact, he had become anxious to take on a positive role in society. He attracted several cohorts away from his previous group, as well as some others. He had managed to get a basement and yard as meeting place; he produced locally written and acted plays which made a little money, and he organized a trip each summer to a crude summer camp. In short, he became an unsung grass-roots leader, a channeler of youthful impulses and needs into nonlethal challenging activities and competitions.

As well as a doer and a subleader, he can be a valuable consultant. But at the moment, and in the last several years since I've known him, he has not been able to find outside support or to command an even modest wage for his important grass-roots social work In another case, someone edits a paper *Grass Roots,* in English and Spanish. He scrounges around to get a little support for this undertaking, which likewise has no recognized niche, no subprofessional label that is recognized as job-worthy or wage-worthy. Michael Harrington has generalized: ". . . the [unemployment] figures suggest that if these young people are to have meaningful lives, perhaps the nation will have to make some new definitions of work." [16] Are not even the full-time officers of a nonbopping club in the slums social workers of a sort?

In another context, a discussion of the connection of mental health and city planning, E. James Lieberman and Leonard J. Duhl have this to say: "Mental health programs should also have a neigh-

---

[15] These two are examples of important beginnings. But one cannot be too dewy-eyed: there are always formidable real-life limitations, and one must be aware of both the great promise and the spotted actuality. For an excellent perspective on both, from actual experience, see James G. Stockard, Jr., *Designing Neighborhood Commons,* mimeograph with illustrations, Washington Center for Metropolitan Studies, Washington, 1964.

[16] From Michael Harrington, "The New Lost Generation: Jobless Youth," *The New York Times Magazine,* May 24, 1964. Harrington is the author of *The Other America.*

borhood orientation. . . . Mental health manpower will be bolstered from the ground up with recruitment of persons with human relations aptitudes from the increasing roster of unemployed workers." [17]

Another crucial need and opportunity: persons in the community who, with some training, can inform the local ordinary persons or families of what a galaxy of municipal and other services are available and tell them where and how to get at them. Another still: a multipurpose worker or urban agent to bring the consumer and the services together, practitioners of "urban extension work."

In summary and exhortation, participation in the social process of development not only constitutes an indispensable element in physical-economic development and design but also has the vital and timely component of great employment potential. On the total scale of the whole country with its myriad local communities, a vast number of workers could be paid for performing hitherto scarcely recognized or quite unrecognized functions of a useful and vitalizing nature. This could both raise community morale and add to positive employment, automation or no automation, because the functions proposed are not displaceable by any automation. The meaning and impact of process and its effects are highlighted by the current temporary employment of such people in the antipoverty program.

[17] "Physical and Mental Health in the City," *The Annals* of the American Academy of Political & Social Science, March, 1964, p. 20.

But that program needs to be made permanent, expanded, augmented by imaginative training for the kind of new work proposed here if it is to begin to reach the real needs and potentials of our communities.

In connection with these fresh programs and operations, the great thing to bear in mind is that though help, especially initially, may or must come from outside, local control is essential for making them mean much in terms of process and growth. We must work out efficient administrative and political arrangements to achieve this. At the same time, we must build a physical frame and process of design that will evoke identification of the people with their environment and its design. In this chapter there have been outlined the needed social base and process. In other places (as in the chapter on the district or sub-city, and in presenting the concept of decentralization of excellence), I shall deal with these other essentials, tie all the elements together and show them reinforcing each other.

There is no doubt, as will next be seen, that New Towns and new regions must play a very major role in urban development. The skills and habits and social and design developments that have been emphasized here in the context of the communities we already have will be urgently needed there too. More urgently needed, indeed, for these new settlements both present maximum opportunity for, and make maximum demand on, social experience, imagination, self-reliance, and adaptability.

CHAPTER SIX

NEW TOWNS AND FRESH IN-CITY COMMUNITIES

Now we are ready to embark on the truly adventurous part of our presentation, in which we shall see how we can truly *win our way into the new integration of living*.

In this chapter we shall deal with the creation of New Towns and fresh in-city communities. Then we shall turn to reorganization of the large-city complex—*any* large city's metropolitan area. Then comes region, and consideration of how to effectuate this physical-social process in an appropriate matrix in *and beyond* the existing metropolitan areas, as well as consideration of quite different possibilities in other, new locations for the vastly increasing populations. And then the finale: we shall explore the great opportunity for the architects and architecture to participate integrally with the planners and the people in crystallizing and enhancing a continuum of many scales of integrated living, from nucleus to region.

From the start it has been emphasized that we must be in CREATIVE CONTROL, that TREND is not DESTINY. But if we are to play a statesmanlike role in development, not just be wishful thinkers, we must recognize that certain trends are truly irresistible for our time, are truly the wave of our foreseeable future. We must then make a statesmanlike distinction between them and what we can, with determination and tenacity, change, and should change. In this we must always recognize and deal with one subtle but pervasively influential tendency. The wrong needs are commonly and almost automatically imputed from irresistible trend. For example, with rising incomes and more leisure, the curve of car ownership will rise steeply. The automatic reflex is to say this creates an equally steep need for ever more roads and more carrying capacities, more and wider superhighways. This is not at all a necessary corollary. Indeed, cars will be more of a positive asset and pleasure under a different road hypothesis and system.

So we formulate goals based on our conception of the good life, test them against the real realities, exorcise the pseudo-realities, and, our goals thus refined and strengthened, proceed with our program. And we bear in mind that we do not want to find any one rigorous pattern in a pluralistic society, that in our materially dynamic civilization, *any* solution should be flexible enough to absorb unforeseen developments.

The Real Trends and Others

We must deal with these real trends:

■ Increasing population, increasing leisure, increasing automobile ownership.[1]

■ Spread, both to take additional population and to make existing cities less dense and thus more acceptable, habitable, and re-creatable. Spread is inevitable and not undesirable. The question is whether we shall have spread by planned formation of organic communities or by undifferentiated despoilment at the city fringes (in legally zoned 2-acre hunks or catch-as-catch-can smaller hunks) and scatteration beyond.

■ Technological advance. We must recognize it and use it, and we will. We certainly don't want to attempt to turn our backs on it, in the nineteenth-century, nostalgic sense of William Morris and his sentimental reversion to the hand press, the vine-clad cottage. Nor do we want to be infatuated by our great technology and be tempted to place so much confidence in it that we feel basic decisions and basic self-discipline don't much matter because our technical inventiveness can solve anything and everything, no matter how anarchic. Uncontrolled, technology piles up increasingly complicated headaches. Subtly and powerfully directed toward conscious goals, it permits greatness in our lives.

In the fields of motion communication (auto and bus, subway, train, plane) and message communication (telephone, television, electronic computer) modern technology has conjured up two distorted visions, both extrapolations from presently dominating trends. A sort of inverted latter-day equivalent of William Morris envisions and advocates the ever-greater city, because of its grand culture of museums, concerts, theaters, art galleries. To this sophisticate, the larger the city, the vaster and deeper can be these excellences. How few of the people in the city really imbibe them, and at what costs in money and in energy spent just going and coming! The other vision: that with improvements in the technology of communication, anyone can live almost anywhere, however far away from anywhere and anyone else, and can still manage to get where he needs to or can stay home and do all his communications by message. Again, for almost anyone the vision is false. And both of these visions are ultimate horrors.

The apparent feasibility of these visions stems from reliance on technology to solve anything. Their

psychological appeal stems from mechanistic willingness or even compulsive eagerness to discern trend and follow it or accelerate it, and a willingness to ignore basic sociological and ecological needs, such as both social structure and the warmth of human propinquity tempered by the counterpoint of solitude and access to nature. We do have virtually unlimited materials and techniques that have taken us out of the old enforced discipline of scarce necessities and lack of choice, and we must use them. But we must temper this new excess by sensitive choice and by self-discipline. Let us see how we can harness our technological powers to gain the best possible twentieth-century world.

There are two major kinds of enterprise potentially at our command that can satisfy the various planes of our human need, more or less where we are. One is to build New Towns that can both make a fresh start at community and provide an indispensable large net increase in our housing supply for added urban population. The other is to reorganize our cities into constituent communities that are more economical to operate and better in general physical and social amenity. We shall take up the two in order.

What Are New Towns?

What are New Towns—functionally, physically, socially, economically? What are we trying to create? And what do New Towns offer uniquely for better living? And let it be strongly noted here that not everything *called* a "New Town" is a real New Town in our sense.[2]

New Towns are planned crystallized communities to take up the pressing metropolitan population increase, to organize dispersal in order to create

---

[1] The upward curve of population may, of course, be bent by birth control. But the population increase and the in-migration from rural areas will be still sharply upward for several decades. So they have to be one basis of our goals and measures.

[2] Familiarity with some of the probably over one hundred American "New Towns" in various stages of development by private enterprise leads to this statement. In this context, one finds relevant a dry and wry comment on p. 65 of Frederic J. Osborn and Arnold Whittick, *The New Towns: The Answer to Megalopolis,* a rewarding account of the New Towns created in England since 1946:

"Commercial builders, public-utility societies . . . appropriated [Ebenezer] Howard's carefully defined term of art, 'Garden City,' and used it indiscriminately as a label of prestige for any kind of residential development. . . . And so the suburban flood went on, often despite the expostulations of Howard's followers, under the stolen banner, 'Garden City.' "

This book, published by Leonard Hill, London, in 1963, is a moving and comprehensive account of a stirring nationwide enterprise. As noted earlier, there are now 28 New Towns in England.

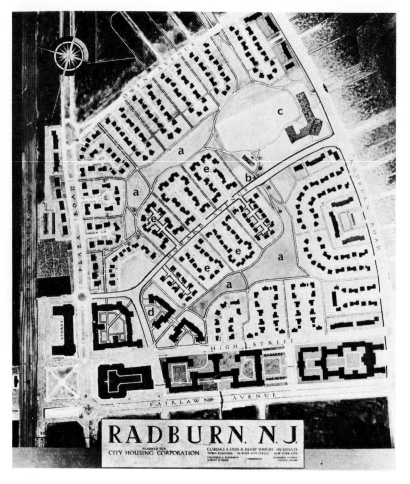

Radburn

The social-industrial-regional philosophy of the New Town had been laid down by Ebenezer Howard and the British at the turn of the century. The next major contribution was (in 1929) Radburn, rightly called "the town for the motor age." The concept developed by Clarence S. Stein and Henry Wright introduced the superblock unpierced by through-traffic; complete separation of pedestrian and motorcar; the internal social-recreational park on land gained by the cluster-principle. It was made possible by the vision of Alexander Bing, a large-scale private builder. Due to the Depression of 1929, he had to give it up, and it remained only the fragment of a New Town. But its technical, land use, and social conceptions have had world-wide impact.

1. *The Super-block neighborhood*
   A. *Internal block parks in each superblock*
   B. *Pedestrian underpass between blocks (see photo)*
   C. *Elementary school and playground*
   D. *Community center, management, shops*
   E. *Typical cul-de-sacs or deadend streets*

2. *Underpass between blocks, completing separation of pedestrians from vehicles . . . freedom and safety for children*

1. *Stevenage: Festiveness, gaiety*

New Towns: Town Centers

This and the three pages of illustrations which follow are from New Towns in England, which has been the forerunner and gone the furthest in theory and actuality; and from elsewhere. There is no stereotype. New Towns, in fact, give maximum freedom in variety of scale, of architecture, of character, and of choice of living; and adventurously varying character both between towns and in the same town.

2. *Cumbernauld: Sophistication: compact, urbane, multilevel separating traffic, shopping, promenades. (Now under construction—1966)*

3. *Basildon: One of the Towns with early, substantial office employment*

1. *Crawley*

Sub-Centers and Neighborhood Centers

2. *Hemel Hempstead*

3. *Harlow*

elbow room within the cities. They are communities of residence and of employment, of culture and of recreation, in convenient relation to each other and within each new community; closely accessible to re-creative nature. They can be within the metropolitan orbit, or beyond, or in "New" regions.

They are conceived internally as integrated or balanced in terms of:

Jobs and workers in varied occupations
Economic and social and racial groups
Developed areas and open space

By intelligently relating homes, employment, recreation, and nature, we can make automobile use pleasurable and economical even though there are increased numbers of automobiles. By improving relative location of homes, work, and recreation areas, we can cause cars to be used for shorter distances, cutting down the long and sweaty journeys to and from work and recreation. By proper and actually attainable time-of-use relationships, we can reduce both work travel in peak hours and recreational travel on peak weekends. And of course, the two kinds of changes will work together, enhance each other. In short, it is no paradox but simply common sense and imagination to proclaim boldly: more cars, fewer jams, less sweat, far simpler road systems—proportionately fewer road lanes and fewer routing complications for cars and trucks—far fewer mileage hours.

If we are as successful as the British New Towns, the tedious workday suburb-to-city and city-to-suburb journeys will be all but eliminated, mainly by employment in one's own town; to a lesser extent, by employment in peripheral belt-road—connected towns. Only to a minor extent will New Town residents work in the central city. In the case of the eight New Towns around London, Wyndham Thomas states:

> About 44% of the inhabitants are in employment—for instance, 28,000 of Hemel Hempstead's 66,000 people are in insured employment. About 85 to 90% of those who are employed work in the town—for example, 25,000 out of Hemel Hempstead's 28,000. There seems to be a rough balance between numbers going outside the towns to work and those coming in—for instance, again, 3,000 or so each way at Hemel Hempstead.
>
> In brief, as far as employment is concerned the London new towns are almost fully self-sufficient. Of the 15% of local people who work outside the new towns, only about one in three (5% of the total) travels to London. In all cases there is a slowly increasing interchange with

neighboring towns, while the commuting rate to London remains steady.[3]

As this suggests, there is a variety of employment available in the British New Towns, and for employers, there is a labor market equivalent in size and variety to the central-city labor market. Peak traffic to and from London is avoided for most individuals, and total traffic is heavily slashed.

Our New Towns will not be of any standard population; they may well vary from 50,000 to several hundred thousand. But each will be of a *predetermined* size appropriate to its individual location, function, and regional outlook, because only so can utilities and city structure be economically provided and maintained, only so can we forestall the fringe creation that plagues our cities now, only so can we keep open green between towns or between town and city and avoid their oozing together in a no man's land of honky-tonk and shanty. The effective implementation of such limits also depends on the surrounding land purchased as greenbelt. These greenbelts are not to be pretty but sterile spaces; they are to be kept always essentially open for agriculture, forests, sports and recreation, ventilation, children's education by intimate contact with nature and biological processes, adventure close at hand. Land for the greenbelt must be acquired integrally with that for the built-up area.

It is vitally essential that a public government-backed body with ample finance acquire and *retain* the land—or, for planned comparison, a massive source of private capital operating on the same principles. In the first place, normal private developers cannot afford to acquire the very large acreage, including that for the greenbelt; and, as experience shows, they certainly cannot afford to keep heavy capital tied up and to pay taxes over the long period required for development. The build-up of pressure to reduce such involvement and to become liquid is usually irresistible.[4] Land must be sold off,

[3] Wyndham Thomas, director of the British Town and Country Planning Association, personal letter, Jan. 25, 1966.

[4] Consider the case of Alexander M. Bing. A man of very considerable wealth, he was the developer-statesman of the twenties who gave a free experimental hand to Henry Wright and Clarence Stein to develop the epoch-making enterprises of Sunnyside and Radburn, physical and social landmarks of the greatest significance. But Radburn remained only a two-superblock suburban fragment because Bing could not hold on to the large amount of land he acquired in the face of declining values in the Depression, and inexorable taxes. His name, little known now, is one to which our generation owes a great deal.

whether or not the uses are optimum for the city, or prematurely forced into building; or too little land is acquired at the start, so that there is practically built-in fringe development and deterioration. Also, one of the major advantages of the New Town is the initial low cost of land. As we have seen, land cost has otherwise become a major factor in increased cost of homes. Unless this price continues to be kept down, a major benefit is lost; the rat race of land price increase starts all over again, and the consumer is again priced out of the market. Or the land spiral is partially met by smaller and skimped living quarters.[5]

Unlimited Variety and Fresh New Worlds

Consider the great and practically untrammeled opportunities which New Towns offer for varied living and for the application of modern principles of planning:

■ Street planning and community layout for safety, efficiency, and amenity, largely separating the pedestrian from the tensions of competition with vehicles, and separating through and local automobile movement without land-devouring multi-level interchanges.

■ Green spaces close at hand, schools and community facilities within walking distance in the neighborhood.

■ Industry close enough to the residential areas to eliminate the long, tiring journey to work.

■ Decreased cost and maintenance of roads, utilities, and parking areas, as in the Radburn prototype and as since applied in many places in many countries.

This is the core of essentials. But there is no standardized package. There is room for many solutions and for many preferences, for individuality and privacy as well as community. The wooded romanticism of Finland's Tapiola, the low-density garden-city character of Harlow in England, the close-knit urban quality of Cumbernauld in Scotland, the peripheral density and the central green heart of the theoretic Alcan: these offer some illustrations of the wide variety of these new creations.

[5] In "Fitting Cities to the Future," *Engineering News Record,* Jan. 28, 1965, p. 54, the writer says of Reston, the New Town in Virginia: "Land purchased at an average cost of $1,900 per acre is now selling at prices up to 15 times as much for fully serviced lake-front or golf course sites. Local builders have been paying from $4,200 to $10,000 for lots ranging from one-fifth to one-half acre." R. E. Simon, the developer of Reston, is quoted in *House and Home* for February, 1964, p. 126: "More profit can be made in real estate than in anything else."

Note in this connection the invalidity of some clichés. The towns should to a maximum extent be self-contained as far as daily life is concerned, with work near at hand and easily accessible cultural and recreational opportunities. But I don't see that any of this need promote parochialism or enforced local fellowship as contrasted with desirable community *esprit.* Nor does this mean separation from a major city's greater cultural opportunities and stimulating cultural flavor. Each town should certainly have its own characteristic layout and special flavor and special attractions, real reasons for inter-town interchange. And indeed the character of each town will vary between neighborhoods and within neighborhoods, as in the plans for varied "villages" for Reston, Virginia. And the simpler and less bumper-to-bumper road system leading to the major city will put the New Town dweller in an excellent time position for meeting face to face a major city's outstanding cultural and entertainment opportunities as compared with many of the in-city dwellers.

On the social side and on the side of the citizen's political stake and alertness, the New Town offers a whole gamut of advantages. It is on a total scale— also in the crystallized communities composing it —that will allow the citizen to feel some degree of significance, identification, and influence instead of the frustration and loneliness that often characterize big-city social and political life. The very fact of its starting freshly and building up can be a strong stimulus. The essential drama inherent in the conception and creation of the New Town can give life there a tremendous dimension of excitement—*if* we don't just slide into the act of building it, but fully create it.

Finally, on the side of building a functional physical environment, we can more fully create and experiment in the fresh situation of the New Town, and then feed back the lessons we have learned into the inner city.

The Wrong Way to Create New Towns

So much for what New Towns are and can be. How to bring them into being, and on something like an adequate scale? What kind of legislation, effectuating organization, land policy should be set up? More immediately, how much promise is there in the administration's program for New Towns proposed to Congress in 1964 and again in 1965 (and 1966)? For the Housing Bills of 1964 and 1965 included provisions for New Towns, to be created entirely by way of loan help to private developers. The government agency through which

1. *Cwmbran: Hillside row houses*

2. *Basildon: Public housing*

Housing Variety

3. *Harlow: 13-story apartments*

4. *Crawley: Free-standing houses for sale*

5. *Harlow: "A Close"*

this would be done is the Federal Housing Administration.

Prima facie, the fact that the administration is making *any* serious proposal to aid New Towns may be important and gratifying. However, the route it contemplates essentially fails to reach the kind of goal that is worth attaining. Private enterprise in its developer form is, with very few discernible exceptions, not the agency by which to attain our objectives. Its efforts will go ahead in very considerable numbers in any event. But to encourage these efforts, to give extraordinary help to private developers, to use them as the chosen instrument—to do these things is to take us on a costly detour.

What can be expected under the proposed setup? For the purposes of this discussion let us confine ourselves to the development of a given town, assuming for the moment that the specific location and the regional configuration can be satisfactorily created, by some regional organization that is in real control. This will in itself be plenty difficult, but that is a metropolitan-regional matter with which we will grapple in a later chapter. For now, let us assume that the location is determined and can be made to stick, and also that the size of the community has been set within certain tolerances and can be made to stick.

The problem is the composition and quality—physical, social, ethnic, and economic—of the town itself, and what the setup under the proposed legislation will do to the real New Town objectives and potential in these areas. Essentially the driving force is the private developer-entrepreneur. It is he who calls the shots, makes the primary decisions, finds and disposes of the large funds energized by his thin-edge investment, on which he plans to get high and essentially quick returns. True, the Federal Housing Administration will scrutinize, and a scrutinizer can modify, adjust, make improvements. But a scrutinizer cannot substitute a philosophy, approach, and emphasis different from those that basically characterize the central figure. Let us see what this must result in.

We do not want a single-class suburb or a thin-social-economic-stratum suburb or town. We have plenty of those now. Though we may grant that under the proposed setup they would be rather more orderly, somewhat more self-contained, that is not enough. We hope to create a community that is economically and racially integrated. While it is true that by Presidential order any housing aided by government may not practice discrimination or segregation, a private developer may live up to this

requirement and yet have only a very small sprinkling of minority and low-income families. He may passively, even willingly, accept anyone who turns up and who qualifies. But we know that unless a quite special effort is made to interest them, minority families will not apply in serious numbers, for reasons of diffidence, habit, and inadequate income, and we know that without subsidized public housing the income range of those who can be accommodated is pretty thin, even with 221(d) (3).[6]

Normal private enterprise is eager to build and sell houses quickly at a profit. It is basically not socially or administratively or motivationally geared, or financially in a position, to make a paramount and realistic commitment to a well-integrated community on any large scale. It just isn't in the cards. This is not to say that there are no private developers who will try to do this. But certainly there are not enough to justify relying on them in this matter which is so central for the future of our country. Even in the few individual promising cases—e.g., Robert Simon's Reston near Washington and James Rouse's New Town near Baltimore—we will not achieve this. In spite of declared good intentions about ultimately accommodating those of low income, note the observable upper-class flavor of these two developments. Reston has been described in the *Engineering News Record* as "a totally planned community where fishermen will cast from their lakefront lawns, golfers will live on fairway-bordering home sites, and horsemen living in their own equestrian village will ride to a main street complete with hitching posts."[7] Columbia, the New Town by Rouse, anticipates a median income of $9,200, very much higher than the median income of the Washington metropolitan area.[8]

Lacking a reasonably full economic cross section, such setups are also not going to be able to make a serious contribution to diminution of traffic and commuter miles. With industry massively moving out of the central city to get more land for elbow room and 1-story assembly lines, with private builders creating new middle- and upper-class communities, and with more office buildings in the central city for prestige and other semicompelling reasons,

[6] English New Towns have a substantial proportion of public subsidized housing.

[7] "Fitting Cities to the Future," *Engineering News Record,* Jan. 28, 1965.

[8] Another instance: Sterling Forest near New York, also one of the more reputed current private-developer New Towns, is totally planned for education, scientific research, and residence. Homes are priced from $35,000 (*New York Times,* Nov. 20, 1965).

1. *Waterlow and Sons. Factory, East Kilbride*

Local Employment: Industry (now, much office employment also)

2. *British Visqueen Factory, Stevenage*

3. *"Standard" Factories. Built by the Crawley Development Corporation in 7,000 square foot units for small firms, who can subsequently enlarge*

the two-directional commuting will continue to rise and will create new traffic peaks.

The large American new communities of recent years—the Levittowns and Park Forest, near Chicago, are leading examples—demonstrate another inadequacy of the private entrepreneur: his failure to combine industry and housing. Park Forest did start out by earmarking an area for industry, but it did not bear fruit. There was no particular leverage available to the builders with which to attract industry, and the profitable creation of housing absorbed their attention and energies. A generic reason for such failures may be that characteristically open-planned industry cannot compete for land at the prices that privately produced houses can command, particularly with the bait of resale at a profit. Thus again we are back to the proposition that as long as land is a freely disposable private commodity and speculative profit is a basic factor, large-scale logically related development is not going to take place, though the volume of development may prove large.[9]

The Wrong Center of Gravity

The center of gravity of the legislation is wrong. The kind of private enterprise it will help so massively just is not, in any serious numbers, fundamentally interested in a fully fruitful New Town program, though it will, no doubt, manage to inclulde elements of such a program to satisfy the Federal Housing Administration. The job in its real social-civic-ecological form is essentially much too complex and time-consuming and long-run in character to fit into the private developer's characteristics and needs. His three characteristic out-of-city operations are and have been separate and single-purpose:

Narrow-stratum suburban residential developments

Regional shopping centers

Industrial parks

These quick operations, pinpointed on markets in which there is *a quick profitable turnover* of property ownership, have a limited rationale that satisfactorily meets definite needs. The developments, which are particularly attractive to the larger-scale

[9] The act of 1966 now provides, as an alternative to loans directly to private builders, that loans can be made to municipal or other land development agencies. At appropriate times the land would be sold to private developers, with no subsequent control of price. Thus, the upward spiral begins again, the original advantage of low land cost is rapidly lost.

development entrepreneur, are certainly more orderly than haphazard roadside spot peppering of their elements. And they have other merits as well—for example, some handsome architectural and landscaping work, and a gala atmosphere in the shopping centers (once you are in them, past the sea of parking). But essentially they do not meet the kind of larger positive needs that we have set out, and as far as the suburban belt is concerned, they have very likely worsened the internal-traffic situation.

The New Towns effort represents a conception of living and work and social relationships drastically different from the present prevailing modes of life which the private developer sets up. To try to attain real New Towns by a mild and painless adaptation of his laissez-faire attitudes and methods, as the government proposes to do, is to underestimate the real magnitude and nature of the issues. Placing New Towns under the FHA, the most custom-bound and developer-bound of all the agencies, perhaps epitomizes this underestimation.

A Realistic and Creative Setup

Consider the kind of setup that could be equal to the situation and its challenges. In doing so we will draw to a considerable and varying extent on the British, Finnish, and Swedish examples. They have elements suitable to the American situation, and they have worked successfully. And while we are on the British, let us bear in mind that preceding the New Towns legislation of 1946, there had been long national debate and a series of remarkably thorough and imaginative official and unofficial reports. The reports were both the outgrowth of the discussions and the forerunner of new pinpointed purposeful debate which culminated in action. There had been real focus on the subject in all its facets. Here, there has been no rigorous sustained full-dress discussion, before the Federal bills were introduced or since. Scarcely the way to launch a great policy, and, again, a case of serious underestimation of importance.

We must completely change our proposed center of gravity; and in place of just agency checkup and control, we should have a top-quality and high-prestige study by an initiating and continuingly participating group: a New Town committee or commission. It should study incisively every important element of policy and proposed practice and make recommendations—for example, as to the tough problem of getting the synchronous coopera-

**Contrast Within
the Same Town.
Tapiola Garden City,
near Helsinki, Finland**

1. *Romantic wooded area*

2. *High-rise apartments in close
ranks*

tion of industry in decentralizing into New Towns instead of quite independently and haphazardly. This would not be just check control, but the setting out of a creative program by a highly competent and well-respected group with the ability and determination to crystallize, to outline, and to get action.[10]

No matter how determined and effective such a committee is, and no matter how many allies are acquired along the way, this is going to take time. And so it should. The trouble with the short cut is that it probably in most cases leads to the wrong place and that the steps taken while we are on it may for years postpone the realization of what it is we really must have. It must be noted here again that the big developers or consortia of developers doing the 100 "New Towns," and no doubt more, are going ahead anyway. So one isn't stopping the wheels of the temporarily inevitable while tooling up for a glittering optimum and expediting the real solutions that are possible.

What kind of organization could formulate and do the actual individual undertakings? What kind of groups have succeeded in this in other essentially private-enterprise countries? In England, these bodies have been governmentally appointed development corporations, one for each New Town. They are composed of qualified important citizens, who, in general, function independently, but substantially less arbitrarily independent than we have seen many authorities to be. They are subject to elected government for budgets, and for periodic reports to the government. This setup was intended to provide, and in practice does provide, flexibility and directness of action, combined with the primary purpose of public service. In this and other ways, such a group is similar to what is called an authority in this country, such as a port authority.

This would be a major mechanism. Another has been suggested earlier: equity investments of large amounts of the private capital of insurance companies, pension funds, and large foundations, by legislative requirement. The Humble Oil Company illustrates another kind of case, involving very large capital and long-range-return considerations, in its

New Town Clear Lake City and port, a synchronous development of varied industries and a port now being built twenty-five miles outside of Houston, planned for an ultimate population of 180,000. In Stockholm, in the case of Farsta, there is an interesting combination of methods which should produce interesting possibilities for comparisons: one-third built by the municipality; one-third by the big cooperative association HSB; one-third by groups of private builders.

In the case of Tapiola, the Finnish New Town, the sponsoring group is a housing foundation called Asunosaatio. It was formed by the combined efforts of the:

Finnish Family Welfare League
Mannerheim League
Confederation of Finnish Trade Unions
Society of Civil Servants
Central Association of Tenants
Association of Disabled Civilian and Ex-Service Men

We have, then, a number of tried methods for achieving genuine New Towns, with all their glittering possibilities, rather than the generally inadequate "New Towns" which the administration's legislation would offer and foster.

I have referred a good deal to the English experience and called it successful. English New Towns and New Town policy have been much cited because England has been the pioneer country and has had the most experience and a constantly expanding experience. It is the fashion here to discount this: England's conditions are too different, it is alleged. Note, however, that France, with its quite different conditions, tradition of noncentralization, conservative and certainly non-Anglophile, recently announced in its Paris plan for the year 2000 that eight New Towns are to be built to absorb excessive population growth in Paris itself.

What are some of the additional criteria of success in the English case?

After a somewhat slow start, industry became convinced of the advantages of New Town locations. Now there is also office-building construction; i.e., an even more essentially noncommuting town is emerging. A good and dynamic balance has been maintained between quantities of residence and of employment. Up to the end of 1964, some 750 factories of most variegated character had been built; i.e., the New Towns are not one-industry towns. A large number of new ones are abuilding.

What about financial results? The British New

---

[10] Membership of a New Towns committee might, for example, include a couple of farsighted developers; "New Town thinkers" including architect-planners; an economist and an industrial-location specialist; a communications specialist and a roads specialist; a representative each from a pension fund, an insurance company (capital aggregations), and a cooperative organization; and an ecologist-sociologist—adding up to perhaps ten or a dozen people.

The "Circuit Linear Town"

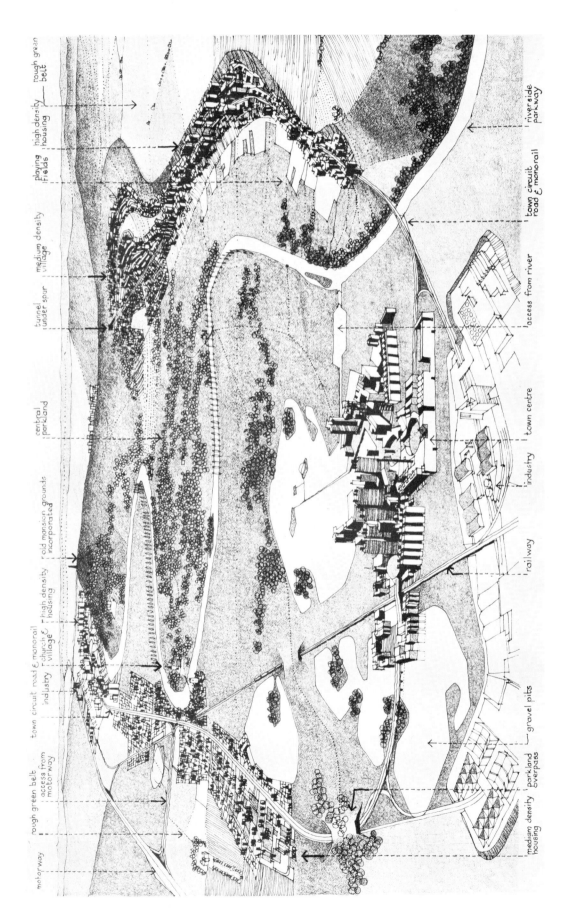

Labels (from image):
rough green belt • high density housing • playing fields • medium density village • tunnel under spur • central parkland • old mansion grounds incorporated • high density housing • church & village • industry • town circuit road & monorail • rough green belt • access from motorway • motorway • medium density housing • parkland overpass • gravel pits • railway • industry • town centre • access from river • town circuit road & monorail • riverside parkway

Still another variation of New Town. Theoretical town called ALCAN, adjacent to major highway, off the main highway. Principle is a green heart; peripheral loop or circuit road; combines short walks and easy motor or bus transportation linking all elements.

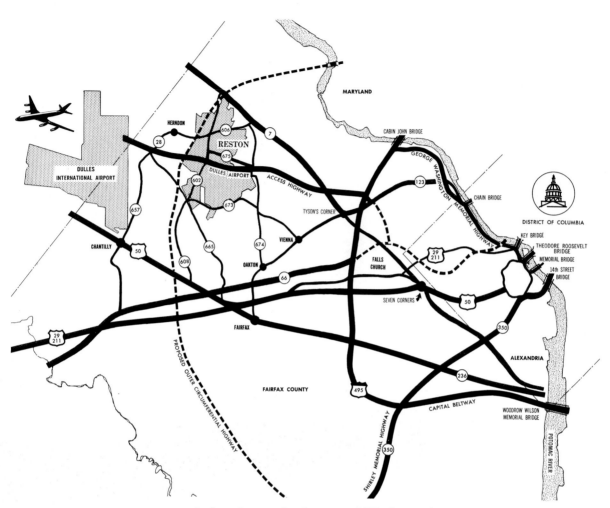

1. *Location to absorb some of Washington's metropolitan increase. Conforms to proposed Washington Plan of the Year 2000.*

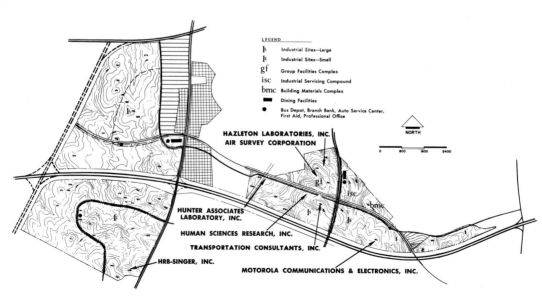

2. *Well-planned industrial area, attracting the "in" type of industry. Will there be an economic cross section of employment?*

Towns since 1962 have begun to show substantial surplus over interest and amortization.[11]

How about people's satisfaction as evidenced by figures of population turnover? "Population turnover is of the order of 4% to 5% per annum. It is much higher (10-12%) among professional, highly skilled technical and administrative staffs, but this is true also for the country as a whole."[12]

How about an economic cross section of residents, as against the danger of one-class towns? The New Towns have not become one-class towns. Consider these approximate figures comparing two of them with the entire country:

Classification	Hemel-Hempstead *	Crawley *	England *
Managerial-Professional-Executive	26%	27%	19%
Skilled workers	54.5	50	51
Semiskilled	14.5	17.5	16
Unskilled	5	5.5	13

* Figures from Wyndham Thomas, personal letter, Sept. 24, 1965.

In the case of Tapiola, Finland, the figures in May, 1964, were:

Professionals and executives....................36%
Small businessmen, foremen, etc.................26
White-collar and blue-collar
   laborers, service workers.....................38

New Towns as an Instrument for Twentieth-century Democracy

New Towns in this country and this century *can and must* perform another function, and a very primary one, though not yet at all adequately realized. They can and must be a major instrument for recharging our democracy. Everyone knows that the recent and present unchecked trend is for middle-class and wealthy families to move out of the city

[11] In the course of presenting development objectives for public housing and urban renewal, crude figures were worked out to see whether government could manage to do what needs to be done, and in what period. In the case of New Towns, the British experience indicates that this is not necessary, because they pay off, even with some subsidized housing. A major reason is the low land cost, *which stays low*, so that it is generally not necessary, as it is in the case of urban renewal or other in-city land, to buy and subsidize high-cost land. Also, to reach the rentals that people can pay, a very considerably smaller portion of the housing needs to be subsidized. Again, government purchase and retention of land at its initial low cost is essential.

[12] Wyndham Thomas, personal letter, Jan. 25, 1966.

and for in-migrants from the South and from rural areas to move in on the city. If these twin moves are unchecked for even a little while longer, we will have an irreversible national schism between the city of the poor and the old and the very rich; and the beyond-the-city of the middle and upper classes.

With the fresh start that is in our grasp by way of New Towns, and by a determined and sustained effort to have them absorb a true economic, social, and ethnic cross section of our society, we can initiate a massive countermove to the disastrous cleavage now developing between city on the one hand and suburb-exurb on the other. But the presently emerging "New Towns" of private enterprise are not accomplishing and cannot be expected to accomplish this. In fact, they accentuate the cleavage. Even in the case of the relatively few private developers of "New Towns," who claim they will seek to take in a true cross section of society, we note that the homes being offered are in the $25,000-and-up class, and that the industries being introduced are the electronic and research industries that employ relatively few low-echelon and moderately paid workers. Later, these developers plan to come down the ladder, after they have established a cachet, a fashionable tone. But the fact is that even the best-intentioned of the private-developer "New Towns" will not have and by their very nature cannot have a true cross section, such as the British figures quoted above represent. They will only achieve a sprinkling of variety.

One word more on this matter of a true cross section. In plain words, will the advantaged move to our New Towns, or will we plan for them and not attract them? I believe we can attract them. We have seen that where values are outstanding, integrated housing developments fill up and are stable. We have seen the excellent opportunities for living that our New Towns present. We have seen, especially, that homes in our New Towns, with their permanently very low land costs, can be substantially cheaper to produce than comparable housing elsewhere. These factors will produce the same acceptance of integration.

So real New Towns, as contrasted with "New Towns," not only are a physical breakthrough, but *could* constitute the new world and the new balance that our democracy so urgently needs.

New and Reborn In-city Communities

The fresh in-city communities that can be created by reorganizing our cities into more economically

Columbia.
New Town
Between Washington
and Baltimore

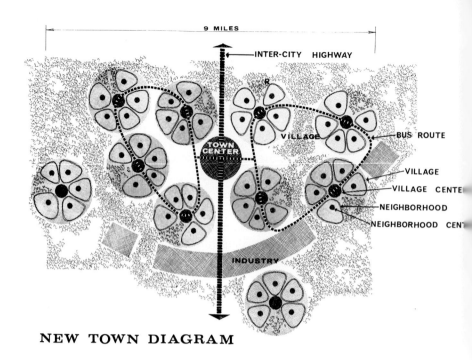

NEW TOWN DIAGRAM

1. Diagram of Town Plan, showing "villages," neighborhoods, circulation plan. A rigorous application of the neighborhood theory; perhaps too self-contained, here and in Reston

2. "Village one" path and sidewalk system. Pedestrian underpasses under major roads

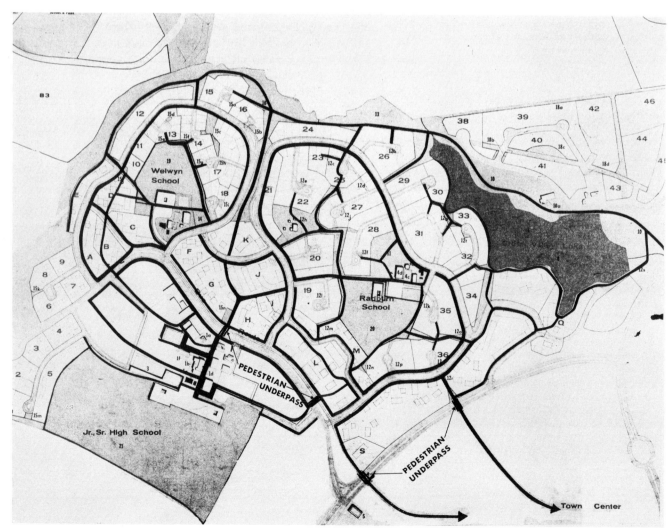

feasible and more amenable parts are of two types.

The New type can be built for those cities, generally middle-sized or under where they can be found at all, which have unspoiled or relatively unspoiled adjacent land and can acquire it. As previously discussed, the city of Stockholm has been accumulating such land over a long period. Stockholm has used a large part of this land to create three fine integrated new communities. Substantial employment in industry and office employment have been built in, and majestic nature is part of the scene. More will be said of this in the later discussion of regions, where I shall also discuss the superior potential of the middle-sized city to absorb population consciously channeled from the great metropolitan sprawl, and the potentially superior quality of culture and stimulation which we can create as compared with the surfeited large metropolis.

The Reborn type of fresh in-city community offers a very important and ubiquitous challenge. Our cities are largely amorphous, not crystallized in viable, identifiable, or self-identified subentities. With us, decisions are made remotely in remote city halls. The original separate settlements which coalesced into the city have in most cases all but disappeared. The traffic movements within the city are even more confused and more time-consuming than in the metropolitan area as a whole; commuting within the city is as long and exhausting as commuting to it. Living conditions, as we all know, are generally congested, economically and racially segregated. The slum has made such great demands on our indignation and emotional energy that not enough has been left over for dealing with the unfruitful, overtense, and wasteful conditions that characterize all parts of the city's formless mass.

We must address ourselves to reorganization, to structuring the city, to recognizing the vestiges of,

and helping to re-create and create, an organic cellular structure with much more local employment and local opportunity generally. Our big cities should be multicentered. We usually think of decentralization as a beyond-the-city concept. It should be applied within the city also. In this connection, there is a notable gain waiting to be achieved, in our bigger cities, in bringing a unified set of city services to each such district. This would give the services greater actual effectiveness, would have a happy social-psychological effect on the people, and would create the nucleus for a future district civic center. This idea for transforming the in-city situation is closely akin to New Town objectives.

The mayors of existing cities have by and large opposed a New Towns program and New Town ideas. This seems to me shortsighted. Cities are *now* and have been losing and continue to lose population to the fringes and beyond *without* improving their quality in this oozing process. The outside New Towns, the inside new districts, the greenbelt between: these total moves can produce the city resurgent, not the constant outward movement of the middle and upper classes.

Urban renewal must operate on two levels. It must have as its large aim to produce significant city districts. And each of its single operations must be visualized and planned to produce local communities, each of which makes sense in itself and all of which in their interrelation constitute the kind of vital district whose corporate life has a lively validity, is not just a fragment or part of a total viscous magma.

Together, the two programs of New Town and restructured city offer a stirring outlook. We must find the way and create the effective and insistent and clear-sighted public opinion and demand that can move us along to creative achievement in each of these needed related enterprises.

CHAPTER SEVEN

RESTRUCTURING THE CITY. SUB-CITY OR DISTRICT. NEIGHBORHOOD RECONSIDERED. DECENTRALIZATION OF EXCELLENCE

As has just been suggested, the physical and social configurations which we are able to create and prove out in the New Towns can be reflected back into the reanimated city. To a considerable extent the city can become a galaxy of New Towns, as it were—a galaxy of interlinked subcities, or districts, each of which will have an animation and magnetism of its own. At the same time these districts will be satellite to their common sun, the city's major center.

This is an exhilarating subject because it is a dramatic illustration of the major continuing message of this book: that we must grasp, demonstrate, and fulfill the inextricable interaction, in our urban civilization, of the physical, the economic, the social, the architectural, and even the political and administrative. Each meshes into, and depends on and enhances, the others, and this creates a new totality.

The New Towns have the same challenging ingredients and opportunities as the cities. But difficult as New Towns are to achieve, or as any great adventure is to achieve, they are not quite so heroic an undertaking. They are in the fresh air, on largely virgin land. Our in-city re-creation is a determined and sustained act of crystallizing community out of a dense, stubborn, viscous mass.

Decentralization and Subcentralization: Sub-city: The New Ensemble

Administratively and politically there is decentralization of a number of kinds of decisions and operations. Those that are purely local in character and impact come down from city hall, down to the subcity level, and are subcentralized there. The big decisions stay in city hall where they belong. City hall is decluttered. This localization animates and reactivates citizen interest and citizen validity, so it requires physical housing for activities, and a physical setting for this housing. Meeting this necessity means an architectural act of creation—a physical crystallization of a subcity center, a new ensemble of meaningful structures to replace the nothingness or the typical confusion of local drugstore, movie house, gasoline station, traffic junction. There is now something to express in architectural terms, to evoke architecture, because at the social base are new vital functions and purpose. And the architecture in turn arouses a new animation. Action, reaction, interaction.

The new local town hall and the administrative action headquarters in the center bring out a flow of persons to make complaints or appear at meetings for joint complaints and/or recommendations, or just to meet and discuss. Soon meeting rooms are provided for private and public groups of various kinds. In short, the center grows with need. That it is not too very far from anyone's home means that people can and will spend time there. So a social center is created, with a promenade, sitting areas, cafés. A theater becomes part of the ensemble, and a local band shell as well.

This new center has added to the district a local scaled world of new dimensions: social, political, administrative, physical, and emotional. Emotional, because for the first time there is a local focus of activity and allegiance, near enough to be visited, on a scale that has local meaning, a galvanizing and symbolic local element. But it isn't down to the small neighborhood scale. Its initial function is at the district level, and from there it takes its start. From there on it develops an intimately suited and therefore compelling architecture. For example, the subcity is large enough to command a higher level of cultural performance than the neighborhood. Establishments that express this spontaneously grow up in the center: a library-museum of specifically local character, exhibit space for the artists who live in the district, maybe a community college.

No more need be said at this point as to exact content or scope. Enough has been said to evoke the essence and the interplay of our glittering local center in its various planes and facets. The surrounding matrix of the subcity, or district, is leavened by the kinds of commercial office activities which can advantageously disperse from the main center of the city. Thus there is less traffic to and from the main center, less friction of space, greater human leaven with managerial and submanagerial personnel, and sparkling physical variety of interesting nonresidential structures. For buildings, not just hand-me-down commercial "taxpayers," but important architectural statements. Note the two illustrations of this kind of development on page 97. Note the handsome Folksam office building in South Stockholm, and particularly its glitter at night: just exactly what we need to animate, physically and spiritually, our dim residential areas. Also, with the much less outrageous land prices than in the major downtown center, we can create the humane and distinctively local form of office building with serene re-creative interior garden court that we so happily encounter in Europe, and in suburbs here.

The underlying purpose of the administration's 1966 Demonstration Cities provisions is to upgrade massive areas in place, one at a time, without chang-ing their essential composition—to up-stabilize the present composition, as it were. This is also the act's basic, perhaps fatal defect. Precisely what we need is to restructure the city and to restructure its major components. By creating a new and versatile vitality within these components, we at the very same time rationalize and simplify the total operation, and in particular we damp down the ever-rising peaks of centripetal and centrifugal travel. A major tool in this is the concept of reciprocal urban renewal.

The Underlying Rationale

Now, having become acquainted with this stimulating ensemble, let us examine the rationale underlying it, the rationale that will get us there. There are two major potent elements in this rationale, the one local, the other the present normal state of that massive monolith in our middle-large and major cities, city hall. The essence of city hall is remoteness, in two senses. First, there is the impossibility or very great difficulty of creatively influencing or even penetrating it in the case of problems of the individual locality. This relates both to the adoption of policy and to its application in specific localities, e.g., school location and order of priority. Second, there is the actual distance remoteness. This concerns quality of daily services, street cleaning and garbage collection, for example; condition of local roads (generally, bad) and state of repair of living places. Satisfactory communication requires responsible and responsive municipal personnel near at hand. But the current actuality entails a long trip to the department at the center, an impersonal reception by preoccupied staff, maybe reference to another department, vague result. We will see examples of change-over from this double remoteness to local immediacy. They have to be embodied in both local government and in physical structure, in specifically suited and rooted design.

The second powerful element in the rationale of restructuring our cities is that we must create local cultural and social animation, cultural and social development, cultural-social centers with a galvanizing quality meeting or evoking submerged and visible cultural-social needs and, by the very fact of meeting them, creating self-expansiveness. I have deliberately used the term "cultural-social," because at our district and neighborhood levels the cultural and the social are much less separate from each other than in the great center, where all the world's a stage. In the act of decentralizing excellence, we create close-at-hand animation and pride in excellence, and we create more individualized and varied excellence, because each locality is individually different. I know a good deal about such new excellences, because I have created some.

The Case of London; and America's Need

Now as to the remoteness of city hall, and creative experience in remedying that remoteness. London has had good and long experience in localization of initiative and action. There, each of the local boroughs, which are in fact subcities or districts varying in population from 100,000 to 300,000 (the size of middle-sized cities), elects and for many years has elected its own council, responsible to the local citizenry, with extensive local functions and "subjects," over which it has jurisdiction. The over-all London County Council, which was replaced by expansion in area and population to become part of the Greater London Council, is in charge of over-all aspects, such as master development plan, population distribution, major housing and renewal policy, main highways, traffic control, fire services, and sewage disposal. The local borough has its own officials responsible to its own elected council, which has jurisdiction over extensive local activities, possibly more local power than would be appropriate here.[1] In London, the boroughs take charge of welfare services, public libraries, primary and secondary education, regulatory services, and housing conditions. Greater London thus has a two-tier federated government—the over-all GLC and the borough councils. Paris, with its arrondisements, and Berlin, with its Bezirke, have such subcity localization of functions, though to a considerably lesser degree.[2]

The essence of the London system is local animation and responsibility. There is true unquestioned representation, based on local votes. In New York City there is a very pale effort at localization by way of "community advisory boards" which have no power and, since they are appointive, represent nobody in particular; i.e., each is just one added committee. This is another example of the ineffectuality of painfully extended gradualism. This idea of community advisory board has been floating around in one form or another for well

over a quarter of a century, and is still about where it was. Like so many other ideas for civic action in American cities, it has suffered by our preoccupation with national affairs, which have actually seemed nearer, more affected by our vote action, than city hall.

The time to go to the roots is *now*, now that we have started to see inside the *anomie* of the slums (*and most other urban areas*), have started to grasp that urban renewal must be rebirth, or birth, of a local corporate spirit, not just physical upheaval. Moreover, this subcity concept is part of a current *Zeitgeist,* as highlighted by recent action in Philadelphia (1965) in connection with the war on poverty. After considerable agitation, the City-wide Anti-Poverty Action Committee has been constituted of twelve members appointed by the mayor plus twelve members *elected* by each of twelve designated poverty districts. Each of these districts elects *its own council* of twelve, and each of these twelve elects a member to the mayor's committee. This replaced the originally conceived committee, constituted purely of persons named by the mayor. The pattern Philadelphia has exists also in San Francisco and in Kansas City, Missouri. In Waterbury, Connecticut, the *majority* of members are directly elected by the localities. Thus, by a different route the concept of democratic localization is being adopted officially.[3]

The District in the Middle-sized City: City Representatives and District Deputy Mayors

The subcity, fully articulated form of subcentralization within a central frame, is essential for the vitalization of the large city, say the city of over 500,000. In the middle-sized city, it is important to work out a version suited to it, a substantial part of the total subcity concept, to be more properly called a district. Indeed the middle-sized city similarly

---

[1] We would need to be careful not to localize power excessively, which conceivably might be to repeat the anarchy we now have on the metropolitan scale because of the almost unbridled independence of each local entity. The danger may be slight, but it must be kept in mind.

[2] In Berlin as in London, the borough council (Bezirksverordneten Versammlung) is elected locally. It supervises local administrations and has a chairman, borough mayor, and staff. West Berlin has twelve Bezirke.

[3] Of course the total implication of this new weighting is potentially much more fundamental in the equations of power than this locational facet; but this aspect is most important nonetheless. A caveat here. These exhilarating new shifts of power toward the people themselves involve not only initial struggles with city hall and its power structure, but complex dealing with two inherently troubling basic facts. First, the indifference or complete alienation of local people has produced disappointingly small voter turnouts for local elections. Second, where there are no elections, there are rival claims at the local level to be the real people's voice, such as the recent and ongoing disputes in East Harlem between MEND and the East Harlem Tenants Council. Thus the road to these new balances of power is by no means smooth, but vastly important.

1,2. *Sub-City Centers. Stockholm: Farsta and Vallingby*

The Sub-City or District

5, 6. *The sub-city as local government unit. London. Town Halls in Borough of Greenwich, Hornsey: local sub-city legislative and administrative headquarters. (Obviously not shown for architectural excellence, but as the physical-functional-symbolic evidence of the durability and vitality of the subcity.)*

3,4. *De-Centralization and sub-Centralization. Stockholm. Major office buildings in the sub-cities: Farsta and Racksta*

cries out for attention. There, city hall is still remote, still compartmentalized into municipal departments, still responsive only to the strident organized protest, which only occasionally reaches the necessary pitch of fury and less often has the necessary sustained insistence to accomplish anything.

Consider this new proposal for such a setup. City departments should establish locality-based, district subcenters, and a competent local representative should be empowered to handle promptly a host of the local problems, with a substantial degree of responsibility and of final authority. This representative would acquire local identification, could locally establish some bridge of relationship to the central municipal government. This would apply to a number of departments. The building department, fire department, health department, social welfare department, and recreation department are examples.[4] A new nearness, new local colloquy between citizens and government, would develop. In addition, we badly need a submunicipal coordinator at this level, so as to pull together the current departmental fragmentation and to correlate responses and the work of the city at this district level: a sort of "district deputy mayor," or deputy coordinator-administrator.

Right now there is evidence as to how useful this sort of thing is. In several cities, when it was decided to rehabilitate certain residential areas, to the point of at least meeting legal standards, exactly this localization and coordination were found necessary and were created in an ad hoc way. Representatives of the concerned departments were placed on the spot to produce really effective action; and a local voluntary social agency, whose pleas had finally produced the confrontation, was called upon to act as ad hoc coordinator.

Let us now learn these lessons in a city-wide way, and permanently set up such district political and administrative entities.[5]

For the medium city, this district concept signifies what the full-blown subcity concept signifies for the major city. It supplies a rallying point for the citizen's resumption or assumption of interest in his living environment, and a functional-social nucleus for crystallizing local communication. To do this fully, of course, it should also, as in the large city, result in the creation of the local-scale center, the meeting place of the locality, the local architectural sublimation of new local significances and aspirations.

This book is not a treatise on political science. Its mission is to present urgently the holistic view of urban living, and to show that true urban architecture and ambient urban beauty will not just be created in White House conferences or ugliness seminars, but will emerge as a crystallizing final expression of our own and our cities' inner growth into revitalized conceptions of function, of cellular validity. And we will not achieve a diffusion of either alert participation or of beauty while all our attention is sucked up to the center, all authority and decision and major disposable wealth devoted to central aggrandizement, while the local scene is simply a gelatinous mass and we are inarticulate within it.

Fresh Cultural-Social Excellence, Decentralized

Cultural-social excellence of the subcity or district will be stimulated by this contemplated new vitalization of the local scene, a simple result of the ferment from significant local discussions leading to decisions. Also, such excellence is a current widespread response to the emerging cultural-social needs and impulses of our era; it is being catalyzed everywhere by increasing leisure time and educational diffusion. It is evidenced by the existence and excellence of myriad little theaters and numberless spontaneous local authors and actors and presenters of plays, often on local matters, that one doesn't even hear about unless one is a frequenter of their

[4] Evidence of the appropriateness and feasibility of this localization and of the subcity idea. On May 14, 1965, the newspapers announced that Bernard Donovan, acting superintendent of schools in New York City, had proposed to his board of education the transfer of administrative power from central headquarters to local districts. The district superintendent is to have complete responsibility and authority for all the schools in his district. There are to be thirty districts, each of which will have a school population of about 35,000 children. The New York *Times* noted that a "parent, teacher or principal will be able to deal with a nearby school official whose powers resemble those of a town superintendent, instead of trying to get a hearing at Board Headquarters in Brooklyn."

[5] In the New York City mayoralty election of 1965, John V. Lindsay's campaign included a number of intimate local "store-fronts" to keep the campaign close to the voters. He announced that as mayor he would keep thirty to thirty-five of these open and operating as official municipal locality centers: a start toward such structuring as I am advocating here. Unfortunately, few have yet been set up due to lack of funds. In Detroit, Mayor Cavanagh has in operation six centers in run-down areas, which he calls miniature city halls. Here people can come for a variety of social, health, and building-improvement services. While these instances known to me have come from larger cities, they are cited here because they are available examples—in-being, of what I am strongly advocating for the middle-sized city also.

locales. There are local orchestras of great verve and considerable merit. And it is not only the Greenwich Villages that have shows by indigenous artists. Forty-two local artists came forward to exhibit at the first show held at the East Harlem Plaza.

As of now, the cultural-social ferment is centered in neighborhoods (and by no means in many), and has not found what might be called a higher outlet. There is absolutely no bridge connecting it to any higher point, challenging the neighborhood locale to higher excellence. The excellence of the main city center is elegant and cosmopolitan (or pseudo-cosmopolitan), and comes largely from national or international sources, with no upward gush whatever from the locales.

The subcity or district must become a significant intermediate focus for our presently humble indigenous wellsprings. The subcity or district must take form and substance to supply recognition, sharper criticism, animation, challenge; it must become a competitive arena, as it were.

As a social-cultural focus, the subcity or district will be altogether valid in itself. It will not be a miniature or watered-down or derivative version of the main center. It will be a different *kind* of center, gathering together, encouraging, strengthening neighborhood indigenous impulses and expressions just as, in its political aspects, it is beginning to supply opportunity for creative, recognized, disciplined expression and action.

Neighborhood: Persistent, Perennial, Resurgent

But the "raw material" and the beginnings and the life satisfactions would for most people be in the neighborhoods, for which the subcity is the sublimating identification.

The subcity has been given seriously major attention here, because it is a new and overdue concept in this country. And in the fully vibrant form in which it is here offered, it probably doesn't yet exist anywhere. The neighborhoods *within* such subcities are of course *potentially* basic germinating cells in any case.

The neighborhood will not be given as extensive treatment here. There is a vast literature available on the neighborhood. At the same time, one simply cannot overrate the importance of vital neighborhood. In one form or another, neighborhood is quite universally recognized as the basis of healthy personal, social, and physical development. The job is to transform it out of its frequently invertebrate character, to end the too frequent absence of prideful self-identification (except where there is snobbish self-identification) and absence of facilities.

The cohesive, self-recognized neighborhood, which existed centuries before the modern large city, began to be obliterated in the industrial revolution, and its decline accelerated in latter-day migrations of people and expansions of cities. Reaction against this decline set in, however, culminating in Clarence Arthur Perry's famous monograph *The Neighborhood Unit*, published in 1929. He presented a social, geographical, functional, physical form of rather rigorous character. He was undertaking the job of both rediscovering the early values and grappling with the modern phenomenon of the automobile, by scaling the geographical size of the neighborhood to put varied facilities within walking distances, within a perimeter surrounded by traffic but not internally crossed by the automobile. Thus the neighborhood was to be safe for children, free of the tensions induced by the crisscrossing automobile, and internal distances were to be scaled to easy walking. He found the coincidence of all these requirements in an area which had the elementary school as its focus, with a constituency of about 1,000 to 1,500 families, an area also able to support daily-shopping facilities and other amenities. Its traffic-free form was called the superblock. A relatively large neighborhood might be composed of several superblocks.

Though somewhat overrigorous, this proved a compelling concept, and it held intellectual sway for twenty years or so. It did not, however, appeal to the private developer, except to the extent that it suited his exclusionist purposes. Like some other American planning concepts, it has been much more widely adopted abroad than here. And in the last fifteen years Perry's concept has been increasingly attacked here, on three bases:

First, the issue is raised that the geographical neighborhood has lost its compelling social validity because of the fractionated interests of modern urban man. He and his family are less likely, so the argument runs, to be intimate with his next-door neighbor than with the man next to whom he works in a distant factory.[6] He is less likely to go to meetings of some neighborhood group than to meetings of the bar association in the center of town or the labor-union meeting. And widespread automobile ownership furthers this dispersion of intimacy.

The second point is that the neighborhood in

---

[6] And other members of his family work in still other places.

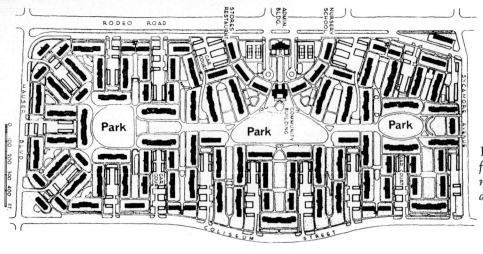

1. *Baldwin Hills: Prototype of traffic-free in-city adaptation of Radburn neighborhood. Note the Central Park and greenway.*

The Neighborhood: Three Variants

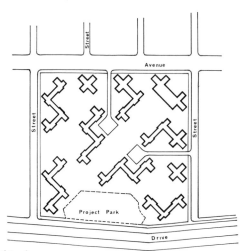

2. *Super-block: Rigidity and detachment. Too often, developments since have taken the course of strangeness, of arbitrary geometric patterns, of excessive discontinuity from the surrounding world*

3. *Franklin Plaza: Modulation with distinction. In-city neighborhood super-blocks. Self-identification, but social and physical continuity with surrounding patterns; enhancement of their character*

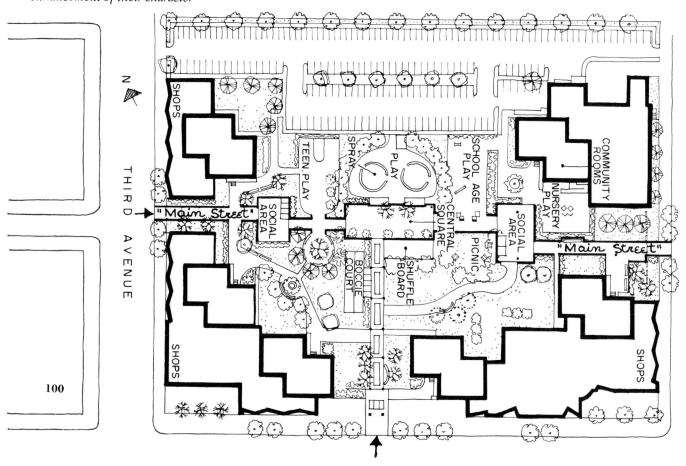

4. *Franklin Plaza's pedestrian "Main Street" by day*

5. *and by night*

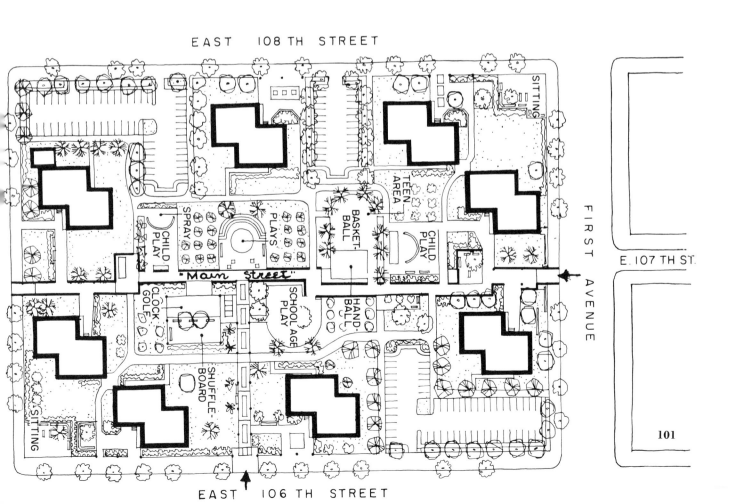

EAST 108 TH STREET

SITTING

TEEN AREA

CHILD PLAY

SPRAY

CHILD PLAY

PLAYS

BASKET-BALL

"Main Street"

CLOCK GOLF

SCHOOL AGE PLAY

HAND-BALL

SHUFFLE-BOARD

SITTING

FIRST AVENUE

E. 107 TH ST.

101

EAST 106 TH STREET

1. *East Harlem Plaza: daytime local recreation*

2. *A performance*

Neighborhood or Intermediate Center

3. *Local band*

4. *Some of the Audience*

5. *More of the Audience*

its rigorous Perry form brings about or accentuates social insularity and tends toward a one-class situation, perpetuating or intensifying present stratifications and segregations which we should get rid of.

And finally, it is held that education, and elementary school education in particular, is undergoing such drastic changes that the elementary school as neighborhood focus is not valid. The self-sufficient local elementary school, one element of the Perry neighborhood concept that is in widespread existence, is rejected for two reasons:

With discoveries both of existing educational lags and of enormous new educational potentials at hand, higher skills and quick access to multiple resources are called for. These are not flexibly available to the self-sufficient elementary school as we have known it.

The single elementary school has so small an orbit of attendance that it is bound to be substantially segregated racially and economically.

Both these contentions lead to the idea of concentration of a number of elementary schools and their association with the high school, with such possible additions as a vocational training center and an adult education center drawing from a much larger geographical orbit. One name for this kind of concentration is "educational park."

These criticisms all have enough validity to be taken creatively into account in forming or improving neighborhood. But the insistence of the sophisticated that geographical neighborhood is obsolete is in considerable measure a reflection of the habits of the critics themselves, who are a quite narrow segment of the city's life. They are writers, professionals of various kinds, cultural elite generally, who are essentially foot-loose, having interchangeable habitats corresponding to professional assignment and other upper-class phenomena.

Neighborhood: The New Positives

My own conviction is that neighborhood is a permanent positive attribute of human living, that its form and content are subject to change over time, and that it can and should assume varied forms in different places at any one time. In fact, its small and intimate scale demands individuality and diversity, within some overriding principles. Modern resources promote the neighborhood concept, rather than destroy it. Modern forms of communication, such as the telephone and the automobile, offer escape valves against the possible oppressiveness of undiluted propinquity. They can make the positive values of a sense of place, a sense

of current security, a sense of the familiar and the familial much more purely positive, for they temper these with much less sense of compulsion, of being immured as it were. Thus the degree to which one cares to belong to the local community is fairly optional. But the community is *there*, physically and potentially socially, with opportunity to participate; and it is reassuring to know that it is available and that its scale is sufficiently small so that one counts or can count, even without the overscaled competitive skill that it takes to be noticed in the larger arenas. Thus the neighborhood is a theater for local contribution and performance, a chance to show, a good chance for merited recognition. And at its minimum, it can provide a convenient and satisfying physical environment for those whose social and professional contacts are scattered through the city.[7]

It seems to me that the obliteration of neighborhood and the unsatisfactory nature of neighborhood are generally much less due to its being outmoded for reasons of irresistible modern change than to failure to create evocative substance and environment. Perhaps a larger part in the well-known phenomenon of American mobility is played by unsatisfactory environment than by the more commonly recognized causes. Let us consider further the major criticisms of neighborhood in this regard.

In the first place, the concept of geographical traffic boundaries not to be crossed by speeding automobiles is just updated common sense and self-protection under modern conditions. And an incalculable boon to mothers is the safe play of kids without constant adult bother. But this is not the situation of moat and drawn-up drawbridge. You cross when you have occasion to.

It is also true that in a number of actual cases the creation of the neighborhood haven has been handled in a way that to an extent justifies the charge of artificial enclave. The large-scale superblock unpierced by traffic is a first-class idea. But it is a poor idea when, as too often has been the case, its layout ignores the surrounding areas and streets, so that even pedestrians do not feel invited into

---

[7] The finding of ornithologists and animal biologists as to the life-and-death importance among some animals and birds of the sense of territoriality, of areas which have been recognized as theirs, have been extrapolated into a strong supposition that man has this strongly developed sense also. I am no judge as to whether this is science or pseudo science, but if true, it may have a good deal to say about the persistence of neighborhood. At any rate, it is worth considering as part of a general caveat: that roots may go down much further and be much more persistent than the latest *dernier cri* has any notion of.

Anatomical Profile of the City

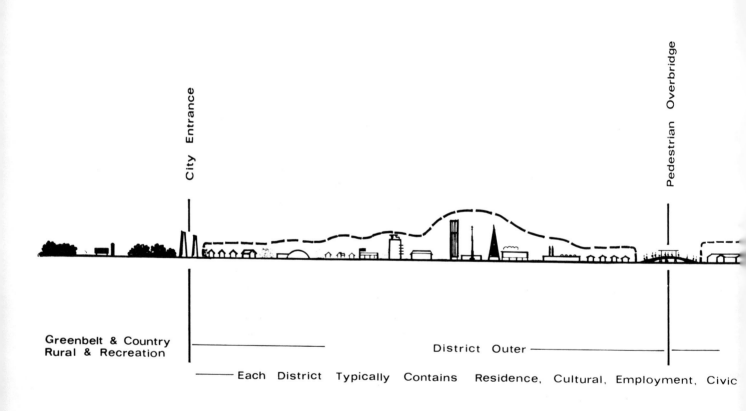

City Entrance

Pedestrian Overbridge

Greenbelt & Country
Rural & Recreation

District Outer

Each District Typically Contains Residence, Cultural, Employment, Civic

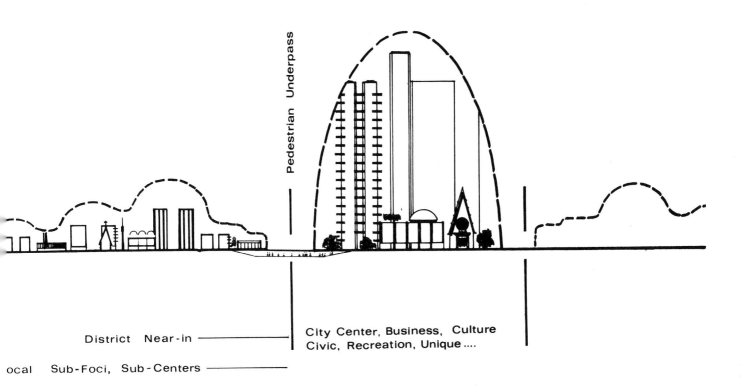

Pedestrian Underpass

District   Near-in ——————⌐ City Center, Business, Culture
                             | Civic, Recreation, Unique ....
ocal   Sub-Foci, Sub-Centers ——————

Beacons Visible from Afar

The City and Its Districts: Each district or community has its own civic-local-cultural center: physical, social, symbolic. It has industrial and office employment, parks. There is thus an important degree of local allegiance and identification, and of physical daily self-containment. Traffic to the center is less peak-intense; there is less friction of space and of daily tensions. But there is, as a result, a maximum degree of pleasurable intercourse with the center and with other communities. For, the local foci are sufficiently self-distinctive so that intercommunity visiting is in the nature of an adventure. The differing dotted "envelopes" mark off differences in characteristic height and spacing development, within three-dimensional planning.

the neighborhood, or get across it easily. But in recent cases, some of us have designed lively internal *pedestrian* Main Streets, which enter from, and exit onto, the continuity of surrounding city streets. In later inspecting such designs, I have found that our landscaped and eventful Main Streets have actually attracted adjacent families to share them in preference to their own shambles. We have enhanced the whole locality, not ignored it. This is part of the mosaic of the future and makes its vital contribution to it.

Another design and functional principle we have evolved is to make each neighborhood reasonably self-contained for daily purposes, as per the classical doctrine, but not to have each fully complete on this standard. Rather, we have sought to give to each neighborhood some special elements that others do not have, to promote cross communication, to counter the tendency toward isolation. For example, of two adjacent neighborhoods we designed, only one had a little amphitheater for local performances, and only the other had *boccie* courts. Both were popular. Both gave a feeling of identity and promoted cross visiting and visiting from beyond the two neighborhoods. But note that each asset was not of a constant-use nature like a children's playground, and thus did not mean constant or frequent running back and forth across the heavy-traffic street. What might be called the "fully complete" neighborhood is not sought. But the "reasonably complete" makes complete sense.

Neighborhood and Intermediate Foci and Symbols

This kind of thinking also has sometimes produced specific neighborhood architecture in its flowering, though we must definitely not think in terms of deliberate eclectic answers for just the sake of difference. Note also the unvarying basic content and idiom, of which one element must be the local park, verdure, and recreation to provide the sense of relief and release so sadly lacking for city dwellers now.

Present and future design of neighborhood must take creative account of the possible impending change in the classical focal character of the elementary school that has already been outlined. Experimenting will have to be done by actual examples. One form is clearly visible now. In the neighborhood itself, there will be the prekindergarten, kindergarten, and first four grades. Thus the children up to nine or ten years old will still be in walking distance, still be in the pedestrian do-

main unmolested by cars. Various considerations determine neighborhood size, and there may be two such schools in the neighborhood. The more distant concentration of educational resource, the educational park, can begin at the middle level of the four-four-four sequence [8] and continue through high school and possibly upward. Where there is this configuration, the educational park will become the focus of a center intermediate in scale and resource between the neighborhood and the subcity or district.

The neighborhood, conceived in flexible terms, remains the nucleus. Many or possibly most neighborhoods will be fashioned from existing situations by rehabilitation (drastic, we may hope), rather than completely *de novo*. But in every case and at every scale, neighborhood and beyond, there must be new focal as well as dispersed creative design. For instance, it is widely believed—and studies generally support this view—that the early patch-up, paint-up, fix-up approach to residential renewal of Detroit's Mack-Concord area has produced far less than had been hoped for in such matters as improved community morale and stabilized residential patterns. No strong community cohesiveness has resulted. Significant physical changes, among other things, appear necessary to create the symbolism for a personal sense of identification with an area and a feeling of satisfaction with the living space.

Possible Action Sequence

Our concept of city restructuring and re-creation consists, then, of an urgent program for vitally interrelated subcities or districts, and neighborhoods. What is a feasible action sequence to attain them? The steps could be these (not purely successive steps, but overlapping in time, indeed to a great degree simultaneous):

1. Delineating the subcities or districts in geographical boundaries, in functional content, in definition and in location of foci and subfoci, in layout of major roads.

2. Spotting the network of neighborhoods, with the most intense regard for the very local factors, sizes, and relations, and with some regard for the place of each neighborhood in the larger subentity. But this ubiquitous operation of neighborhood building can go forward intelligently and organically quite early in the first stage, without waiting for full detailed answers on the larger geography.

---

[8] The first four years of elementary school, the last four years of elementary school, and high school.

And so much building is now wildly going on that it needs to be steered into this emerging pattern. Especially is this true of urban renewal enterprises, each of which must be a stone intelligently placed in this city mosaic and building up toward it: reciprocal renewal.

3. Programming and design and actual building of foci and subfoci.

4. The decentralization of administration and its subcentralization under the district deputy mayors comprise an undertaking involving processes quite different from those of steps 1 and 2; this step can be studied fully and made ready for enactment while step 1 is going on.

5. The political side, the working out of subcity elective processes and procedures and of the "subjects," or functions, to be assigned to the subcity level, likewise goes forward from the beginning of step 1. In the case of London, the new Greater London setup was put into full action on April 30, 1965, 7½ years after the Royal Commission to study and make recommendations had been appointed (December, 1957). A long time indeed. But not so long, considering the issues and the stakes.

From this, two things flow:

The time to start is *at once*.

Each step can start and go forward according to its own character and nature. With determination, systematic analysis, ingenuity, there need be remarkably little cross-waiting.

The current prolonged building volume can carry us along headlong, as it is doing, into more frozen irrevocable misshapings and nonshapings; or it can —it must—be the vehicle for the city's true reshaping and restructuring.

CHAPTER EIGHT

THE CENTRAL CITY CENTER: THE PHENOMENON OF GIANTISM. COMPETITION WITH HOUSING-COMMUNITY

We have traced out the creation of New Towns and the re-creation of the existing city as an anatomy of lively constituent localities around a central heart. This heart, the major city center (or centers), is now dealt with.

Restructuring the city's elements generally into vibrant localities was considered first and most emphatically for two reasons. First, this area is the most seriously diseased tissue in our cities. And secondly, not being physically visible to our power structure, or being at least avoidable or conveniently invisible, it can be ignored or given a once-over-lightly treatment—treatment of a few specimens. The real effort currently, as we have seen, the real surgery, is devoted to removing the highly visible central slums and the people in them, and building large glittering centers in their place.

Major centers are needed, and each must not only be the epitome and illuminator of its city, but must sum up and concentrate the image of *city,* so as to illumine the region in which the city lies. There is no question, then, that our city centers have to be re-created, or created in modern terms; and there is no question that something is being done to them, and on a tremendous scale. But just what is this? Does it give promise or evidence of being sound and inspiring renascence or creation, or is it in many or most cases just an outsized set of undertakings? And, more worrisomely, do they interfere with the healthy development of the less powerful entities and subentities, both in the city and in other areas?

Let us now consider these center undertakings as they *are,* with a view to evolving the most fruitful total program. Let us see what typical present ones consist of, and what the alternatives may be or should be. Let us see whether the total urban picture cannot point us toward a more urbane and creative and productive *combination* of central concentration with decentralization and subcentralization, and toward a new intensity of attention to, and expenditure on, the residential matrix.

Size as Goal in Itself

In the matter of city centers there are some similarities between the large cities and the middle-sized cities. In both cases, the center is the cynosure not only of the city but of its metropolitan region. In both cases, it can and should aim to supply a more diverse range of animating elements than the outlying cities and towns, with their smaller publics, can encompass—a wide range that in our affluent civilization both the middle-sized regions

108

and the great metropolitan regions are entitled to. There are, also, some basic differences which make it worthwhile to consider them separately.

What we see now taking place in both situations is an almost unquestioning doctrine of size as an essential of excellence and brilliance. Size appears to be a goal in itself, an unquestioned motivation, an absolute good of our business-competitive civilization applied to the city dynamic by the power structure. This is manifest in the overblown standard new city and government center itself: the city-state-Federal aggregation with a large injection of courts of law and commercial buildings.

Other forms of oversize are to be found in still other categories: the Detroit Medical Center of 250 acres and culture center of 200 acres. Cleveland's 488-acre complex of two universities, museums, hospitals, School of Podiatry, Garden Center, Natural Science Museum, Automobile Museum, Music Center; New York's Lincoln Center for the Performing Arts; and New York's Columbia University, insistent that its continuing major expansion must be all in one vast university-sterilized location. I shall give detailed consideration to two current situations chosen as fairly typical, and use them to bring out the general issues in the metropolis. In the case of the large concentrated government-business-civic center, I know a good deal about those in Boston, New York, and Sacramento. I discuss in some detail Sacramento's planned Capitol Center.[1] To illustrate giantism in a nongovernmental and nonbusiness center, we have Cleveland's University Circle. After that we shall consider more briefly some of the other centers mentioned above.

Sacramento's Capitol Center

In Sacramento, there is a state and Federal government and handsome park complex of 138 acres.[2] As planned for the year 1980, it is to have about 27,000 workers and 11,400 parking spaces for them and the people who have business in the area. Just think: 11,400 parking spaces! But the planners believe (I don't) that this sea of parking spaces and garages will still be adequate twenty years later in the year 2000, even though by then there are expected to be some 50 per cent more workers, a final total of 40,000. The highly optimistic theory is that

---

[1] Sacramento is not, technically, a metropolis, but as a fast-growing state capital it has a center with similar characteristics, and the case is the simplest to analyze and present clearly.

[2] Plus abutting convention auditorium and city government area with their additional parking.

more people will use mass transportation and that the private automobile will occupy less space per passenger than today's models!

The major rationale for concentration is the importance of having those state employees close together who are required to have face-to-face contacts more than daily with each other or with the legislature or the governor's office. A survey turned up the fact that the employees in a number of departments in the center have such contacts only occasionally (less than one a day)—e.g., those in the department of employment, the department of motor vehicles, the water resources board, and the franchise tax board. For the employees surveyed, who total about one-third of all employees, the rationale of time saving has almost no meaning. Moreover, their agencies draw more than half the visitors to the center, and thus are an important congestion factor.

Now let us see what would happen if an alternative were adopted, of placing these latter agencies in "satellite groupings" in several other districts in the city. In the first place, the remaining concentrated Capitol Center would still be amply large (let us say 100 acres) and an amply prominent and monumental cynosure, including the imposing capitol itself, the Supreme Court, the governor's mansion, and 25,000 or so employees. But the amount of dispersion and subcentralization in several other centers would give to the city's areas in which they would be placed a dynamic and vitalizing push, an animation, a sense of importance, of counting, as it were, that the generally anonymous areas of our cities so badly need.

By this kind of balance, we lose nothing in central glamour or efficiency, but gain a great deal locally in identity and in animated urban texture and distinction. There are other important gains. We diminish the convergence of peak traffic loads into the center, the peaks being always the bane of traffic, no matter how clever and imaginative we are as engineers and inventors. The oceans of parking are substantially diminished into smaller concentrations. Land in the district centers is less costly, and more economical nonskyscraper construction becomes feasible.

In the large-scale metropolis, the alternative of subcentralization is even more attractive, for the city government's own buildings occupy a much larger part of the total. Also, as already explained, localization of many city government functions has multiple advantages in terms of functional availability where needed, financial economy, responsiveness to local requirements. But rather than rationalize reasonably and freshly consider fresh relationships, we extrapolate upward and inward in geometric ratio. Observe, in this connection, New York's complex of city, state, and Federal courts and office buildings. It adds millions of new square feet to an already tremendous center of concentration and traffic focus.[3]

Cleveland's University Circle

This is an area of 488 acres, an enclave of almost a square mile. The University Circle Development Foundation had an original membership of nineteen institutions in this location, and notes with pride that in 1962, five years after formation, it consisted of twenty-nine institutions and already had eighty buildings completed. Many Cleveland institutions, that were originally in other locations, such as the Institute of Music, the Automobile Museum, and the Natural Science Museum, have now located in this same area, as has the large Veterans' Hospital.

Some of the facts and dominant viewpoints are seen in typical quotations from *The First Five Years,* a brochure issued by the University Circle Development Foundation in 1962:

> University Circle is the cultural, educational and medical center of the Cleveland metropolitan area. Comprising 29 institutions it is one of the largest and most diversified centers of its kind in the world. Located there are the city's largest higher-educational complex, its museums of art and natural history, several of its major hospitals, its symphony orchestra, its institutes of art and music and several of its largest churches. The Circle covers 488 acres of parks, buildings, streets, parking space and playgrounds about four miles from downtown Cleveland. . . .
>
> The goal of University Circle and the Development Foundation is a cultural center for Cleveland *that rivals any in the world,* where the interplay of diverse ideas and skills represented by the remarkable cluster of scientific, religious and educational institutions enhances the environment for learning, and where people can go for the enjoyment of beautiful surroundings as well as for intellectual nourishment. . . .
>
> As a physical entity in which people "enjoy" the city, it can fulfill a function similar to the cathedral square of medieval times or the village

greens of eighteenth-century New England. . . .

> The proposal was ambitious. It carried a total price tag of $174,500,000. But the stakes were too high and *the potential rewards too great to consider anything less.*
>
> In the area of parking and traffic control, the Foundation with the cooperation of the City of Cleveland has constructed 422,000 square feet of new parking facilities, including the Foundation's 350-car $670,000 garage on Abington Road. This has eased *what had threatened to be an impossible automobile congestion problem.*
>
> Last year a fleet of four Circle-operated nine-passenger buses started shuttle service between points within the circle, further easing the pressure of automobile traffic.[4]

These quotations give an eminently fair idea of the thinking, the goals, and the actualities of this enterprise. A first reading, especially by a layman, and especially by one engulfed in the idiom of our time in America, could make it appear to be an unqualifiedly admirable undertaking, which in some respects indeed it is. Let us probe. But first, let us just reconsider, next to each other, a few of the quotations. This will reveal the contradictions in the thinking.

> . . . one of the largest and most diversified centers of its kind in the world. . . . a function similar to the cathedral square of medieval times or the village greens of eighteenth-century New England [but 488 acres!] . . . nine-passenger buses . . . shuttle service . . . easing the pressure of automobile traffic.

One can see the irreconcilability of the statements.

Let it be clear once again that I am not advocating atomized dispersal, that I advocate the concept of major center, but that there is in this locational realm a law of diminishing spiritual and functional returns; beyond a certain point, in our field, the advantages diminish or even turn into disadvantages.

We are in this ambitious enterprise confusing words, levels, and meanings. The "interplay of diverse ideas," at its highest creative levels, takes place in an atmosphere of stimulating quietude, as, for example, at the Institute for the Behavioral Sciences at Stanford or the Institute for Advanced Studies in Princeton. These may be ideal cases. But the Cleveland thesis of attracting the public in large numbers into one area for the excitements of an absorptive-entertainment-cultural set of experiences

---

[3] And in noting this outsize chunk of giantism, please remember from Chapter 1 the World Trade Center, that pending project of New York Port Authority (it will have 2–110-story buildings) a little way south. Both the concentrations depend on pretty much the same subways and other trafficways, already a desperate twice-daily experience for workers.

[4] These quotations are from the inside cover and pp. 1, 2, 3, 4, and 6. Italics mine.

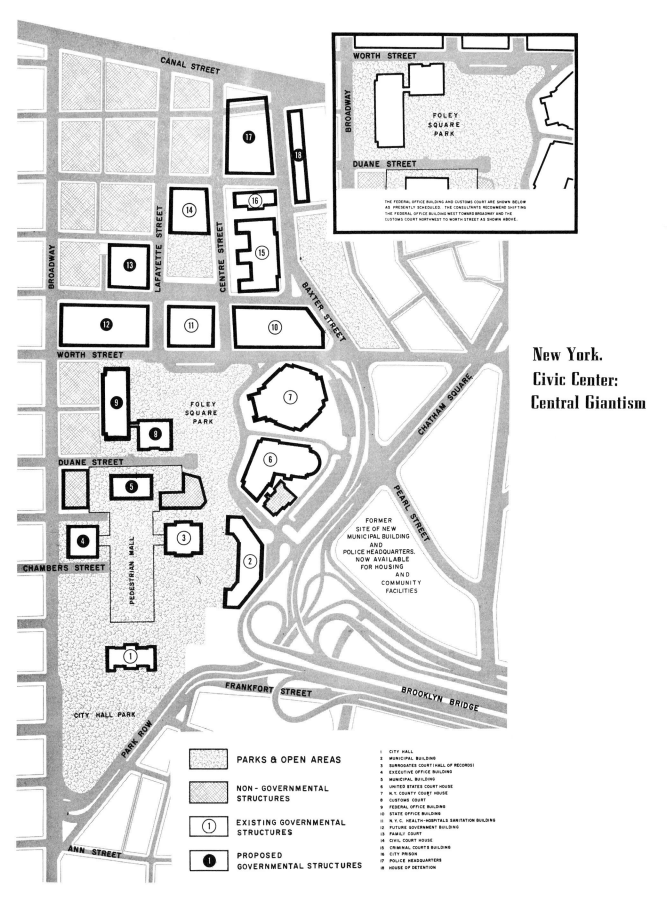

THE FEDERAL OFFICE BUILDING AND CUSTOMS COURT ARE SHOWN BELOW
AS PRESENTLY SCHEDULED. THE CONSULTANTS RECOMMEND SHIFTING
THE FEDERAL OFFICE BUILDING WEST TOWARD BROADWAY AND THE
CUSTOMS COURT NORTHWEST TO WORTH STREET AS SHOWN ABOVE.

**New York.
Civic Center:
Central Giantism**

FORMER
SITE OF NEW
MUNICIPAL BUILDING
AND
POLICE HEADQUARTERS.
NOW AVAILABLE
FOR HOUSING
AND
COMMUNITY
FACILITIES

PARKS & OPEN AREAS

NON-GOVERNMENTAL
STRUCTURES

EXISTING GOVERNMENTAL
STRUCTURES

PROPOSED
GOVERNMENTAL STRUCTURES

1   CITY HALL
2   MUNICIPAL BUILDING
3   SURROGATES COURT (HALL OF RECORDS)
4   EXECUTIVE OFFICE BUILDING
5   MUNICIPAL BUILDING
6   UNITED STATES COURT HOUSE
7   N.Y. COUNTY COURT HOUSE
8   CUSTOMS COURT
9   FEDERAL OFFICE BUILDING
10 STATE OFFICE BUILDING
11 N.Y.C. HEALTH-HOSPITALS SANITATION BUILDING
12 FUTURE GOVERNMENT BUILDING
13 FAMILY COURT
14 CIVIL COURT HOUSE
15 CRIMINAL COURTS BUILDING
16 CITY PRISON
17 POLICE HEADQUARTERS
18 HOUSE OF DETENTION

1: *City Hall.*   2, 4, 5, 9, 10, 12: *Municipal, State, Federal office buildings: present Municipal building plus new Municipal 40-story building of over 1,000,000 square feet. New Federal building of 673,000 square feet just announced, in addition to 41-story building under construction. These figures include hundreds of thousands of square feet for archives. These other uses could of course be anywhere; in some cases more advantageously.   3, 6, 7, 8, 13, 14, 15: Courts, Courts, Courts. (Surrogate's Court, County Court, Customs Court, U.S. Court, Family Court, Civil Court House, Criminal Courts).   11, 16, 17, 18: Miscellaneous*

necessarily interferes with the atmosphere needed for creativity. Certainly this is not fatal. Certainly one isn't seeking isolation. But the least that can be said is that this large-scale diverse operation does less well the job of stimulating the creative mind than a less-catchall setup would do.

Viewpoint of the "Consumer." How beneficial is it to the "consumer" and his family to be deposited in a world's fair of culture, ranging from the Automobile Museum to the Institute of Music to the Garden Center to the Historical Society to the Natural Science Museum? It seems to me that cultural or even entertainment experience is not most sensitively absorbed in such an exposition atmosphere, that exposure and sensitive absorption thrive in a more selective ambience.

Here again, as we have seen at the shopping center, traffic convergence and the world of parking must be faced. "This [outdoor parking and, of course, garages] has eased what had threatened to be an impossible automobile congestion problem." Even this cautious optimism is likely to be disproved as the construction program continues and the spectacular increases in numbers of visitors go on, which the 1962 report already cited with satisfaction.

Effect on the City at Large. So large and diverse a center is, then, at a scale beyond the optimum benefit to those directly involved in it. "The proposal was ambitious. It carried a total price tag of $174,500,000. But the stakes were too high and the potential rewards were too great to consider anything less." But that is just what we ought to do, consider alternatives—alternatives that might be superior even if less single-locationally ambitious.[5]

The area would be more happily served by retention of the major really related elements. The splitting off of some into other centers, or their remain-

[5] In an ambitious vein similar to Cleveland's, Mayor Cavanagh of Detroit has said of Detroit's proposed 200-acre cultural center that it will be "greater than New York City's Lincoln Center or any other cultural development." From *Architectural Forum*, June, 1965, p. 49.

Fort Worth, Texas, offers a prime instance of the appeal of the quantitative concept of giantism. The New York *Times* of Jan. 25, 1966, reporting on the opening night of the new civic theater in the burgeoning Fort Worth entertainment center, noted that the center is known locally as "Fort Worth's square mile of culture."

This quantitative measure of "culture" characterizes not only the provinces. See it in action, too, in *the* metropolis. On the death of James Rorimer, director of New York's Metropolitan Museum of Art, the New York *Times* of May 12, 1966, wrote, in praise of him and it, "The exhibition area [during his incumbency] increased to 17½ acres, a 40% addition."

ing at previously occupied sites to become nuclei of smaller centers of stimulation at other points in the city—this would mean a new leavening of life in the city. Such a combination would more truly deliver and distribute the qualities and advantages and stimulating aura which the promotion brochure notes. The totality of effect would be greater: dignity and worth and animation more pervasively in the city, with subpeaks and with *a few* stirring peaks. The distribution of cultural elements in different places with different atmospheres has always, in my experience, enhanced the quality of experience and sense of adventure in Paris, London, Rome.

The problem in the major city, then, is less one of finding and exploiting attractions and uniquenesses than of subduing the temptation to promote and assemble everything in sight, to overdo the collecting and the massing. It is a problem that must be solved if the major city is to have an electric quality and elegance, a high urbanity.

Miscellaneous Cases of Giantism

This driving force of giantism that underlies the creation of the supercenters not only dampens the possibility of vital content and texture of the remainder of the city, as in Cleveland and Sacramento, but dries up the potentials of cities of the outlying region and of other regions.

The Lincoln Center for the Performing Arts in New York, for instance, has done damage within and outside New York. As for its effect on the city itself, it has concentrated a number of crowd-attracting major cultural-entertainment resources in one area. This, mind you, is an area where traffic problems are peculiarly difficult already, because it is west of Central Park and only two narrow cross routes through the Park are available from the East Side, whence much of Lincoln Center's patronage comes. One of its constituent enterprises is the Metropolitan Opera, whose previous location was ideally reachable by subway, motor car, and bus, because it was *not* in the middle of a number of other simultaneous attractions. Getting there so readily and without struggle I always felt to be one of the pleasurable accompaniments of going there. *Now,* in its new location, it is filled with the hurly-burly of many thousands of people all trying to get into and out of the same place at the same time.

As to its own city: The total cost of Lincoln Center is of the order of $170 million. Suppose the prestige and power group who put this together

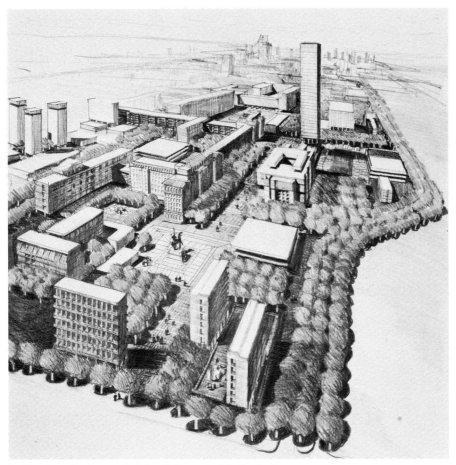

Detroit's Great Concentrations

1. *Portion (only one-half) of Detroit Medical Center*

2. *Portion (only one-half) of Detroit Cultural Center*

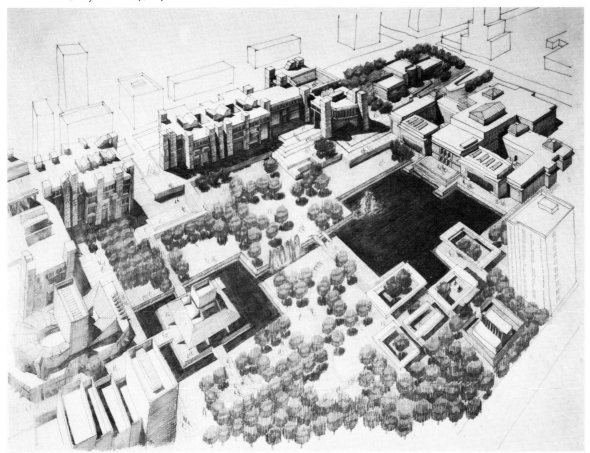

had allocated only $70 million to the single Lincoln Center and had taken the remaining $100 million and made $2 million available to each of fifty culture-drama centers in the districts of the city. What a leavening effect on the life of the city! What cultural effervescence! Lincoln Center is a dramatic epitome of the sucking up of resources into the gargantuan center, to the mutual self-satisfaction of the prestige interdispensers, at the expense of the voiceless citizens.[6]

Lincoln Center furnishes an illustration, too, of harming the potentials of another city. After prolonged difficulties culminating in resignations from its repertory-theater *regie,* and abortive attempts at replacement, the management finally, in 1965, reached across the continent to the San Francisco Actor's Workshop to take away (one quite sober newspaper article used the word "raided") the two founder-directors who had finally made a go there after thirteen struggling years. No doubt San Francisco's comparative neglect laid it open to this loss. At last reports, a year later, the San Francisco enterprise had not yet managed a recovery.

The famous $2.3 million acquisition of a Rembrandt by the Metropolitan Museum of Art illustrates another facet of what I have called other-regional desiccation by the drive for giantism. For such up-pricing of this masterpiece inflates the whole art market, sets a price level which makes it most difficult for cities of less prodigious wealth concentrations to equip themselves.

One other illustration of the prevailing impulse of giantism. In the New York *Times,* under the heading "Hotels Here Seek Convention Hall," we read:

> New York has the Coliseum and a large exhibition hall in the New York Hilton, as well as smaller exposition rooms in other hotels. In addition, a new Madison Square Garden is under construction atop Penn Station.
> None of these rooms, however, can satisfy the demands of such groups as the American Medical Association, the National Association of Home Builders, and other large national groups that can draw as many as 70,000 delegates to a convention.[7]

Douglas Leigh, a prominent creator of Broadway spectaculars, had proposed a convention hall for

[6] I have previously in this chapter remarked on the overscale concentration of the 200-acre Detroit cultural center. Charles Blessing, their city planner, informs me (in a letter of Apr. 5, 1966) that they do propose to have sixteen locality cultural and activity centers there also.
[7] New York *Times* Real Estate Section, Oct. 4, 1964.

80,000 people in the heart of the Broadway area, which the article goes on to say the hotel men liked. And with the dynamic pressures of these giantists and their formidable trade associations, they will no doubt promote this monster into actuality. Anyone who knows the already sardine-can nature of the Broadway area, and the tense and clogged surface and subsurface arteries surrounding and leading into it, can only shudder.

It is pressingly appropriate to point out that decisions on the nature and size or oversize of these centers often are basically not planning decisions, but pressure decisions, prestige decisions, which the technicians do not make but which they accept and whose execution they make possible in one way or another. These are basically spiritual decisions, value-judgment decisions. The citizen should know that if he cares enough about them, he *can* qualify himself to take a decisive part, that he need not just have the role of He Who Gets Slapped.

The Middle-sized City: Dilemma of Present Practice

The opportunities and the means are different in the middle-sized city—much more restricted of course. But considered in the light of the local and national picture, the need and the desirability of rich centers of potent attraction in the middle-sized city are desperately pressing. Why? Because in this era of mobility and fast communications, in this era of revolutionarily more leisure and education, these cities must offer to themselves and to their regions such attractions and such stimulation that the drift and rush from them into the great megalopolises will not further pile up irresistibly, to the further detriment of megalopolis and the further denuding of the more human-scaled polis and its region.

On the other hand, the very same factors of mobility and communications, dispersed affluence and cultural potential, can regenerate, can indeed beget a transfiguration of the middle-sized city—another instance of the two-headed nature, the possibilities for good or evil, of our twentieth-century social and technological instruments.

The characteristic setup for, and limitations of, central rebuilding in such a city are roughly as follows:

The core and spark is government-sponsored urban renewal with its accompanying powers and advantages. Large acreages of land can be acquired by the right of eminent domain, and the cost of write-down of acquisition price is borne almost entirely by Federal government. The purpose of this drastic write-down is to make redevelopment of the center attractive in profit possibilities to private enterprise. And the dominant mystique of renewal or redevelopment is that it must be overwhelmingly by private enterprise. This is a major boost, indeed, the sales basis, for the authorizing congressional legislation and its repeated renewals. We will see the severe limitations inherent in the actuality and even more in this powerful psychology which constitutes the atmosphere of formulation and operation of the central-city program, particularly in the middle-sized city.

We find from experience with this private-enterprise orientation that there is a very small range of acceptable types of standard bread-and-butter undertakings which the private entrepreneur feels hold a secure profit prospect and which the middle-sized city can help him to engage in, once the stage is set by the standard new public buildings and public-built loop road surrounding the business center, with appurtenant parking areas. These types are:

More, and more modern, office buildings, as many as optimistic market prognostications seem to make possible.

Modernization of department stores and new ones wherever possible.

Middle- and higher-income apartments.

A cultural center: always an art museum, usually one or two other museums, a concert hall, around a plaza.[8]

Institutional expansions (such as universities, churches, government buildings).

The trouble with the group of standard installations is twofold. First, the private enterpriseur customarily builds office and apartment buildings that are taller and much more densely spaced in relation to each other than what is being replaced and/or is being made obsolete. The amount of new space available to be occupied soon exceeds the anticipated expansion in demand, so that while the early sponsor-entrepreneurs may do well (which often is not the case even now), a point is reached where present and future demands are satisfied, while there are still large available areas of empty land of presently or imminently obsolete buildings in the central business district. Thus we find ourselves with a new induced crop of obsolescence and slum or "the blight of surplus," e.g., many existing office buildings and marginal stores which have become

surplus. These cannot be profitably absorbed or modernized. Second, the new buildings, a very considerable improvement over what has been replaced, are yet not greatly if any better than what is created and is constantly being enhanced in the attractive new outlying regional shopping and entertainment centers, so that there is only a rather low increase in the city's attraction for its outlying areas and indeed for its own citizens. And with our new high-speed road systems and plane services, the time distance from almost anywhere to one of the great metropolises has been so reduced that when one requires truly more glittering merchandise and style—in essence, a wider choice—one readily has that alternative.

The Middle-sized City: Realizing the Potential

Does this mean that the middle-sized city and its regional hinterland are doomed increasingly to desiccation by the great metropolises and megalopolises? This is highly undesirable. And it need not be inevitably so. We must find the key to open the doors to many kinds of magnetic uses which may not be demonstrably and predictably profitable or ever profitable (they *may* turn out to be so), which can add to the inherent advantages, galvanize our smaller region, make it much more competitive with the great metropolis. But to embark on them means to shift from the 100 per cent sacredness of private enterprise to providing the mechanisms and the finances for the life-giving activities that would enrich the city, as well as its region, beyond its present rather meager man-made endowment.

We want a new kind of central city in the middle range, more festive and adventurous in character and range of action, with a galaxy of new land uses and developments, to give it quite new magnetic character, not just make it an improved version of the old. We want infusion of central green public spaces at various scales, for animation and relaxation. (No profit here.) We want such enterprises as a suitable version of a central Tivoli (the famous original one in Copenhagen did not originally pay, pays fabulously now, and is, of course, a most entrancing experience); a miniature child-scaled city such as the fabulous and successful Madurodam in The Hague, a special children's zoo, a children's museum (and stimulating central attended "parking" for children is at least as important as automobile parking). We want comprehensively articulated displays of architectural and building products and processes, with a color-microfilm library; a de-

---

[8] This is not private enterprise in the individual sense. It is private in that a large group of businessmen undertake a campaign to raise money from wealthy citizens and foundations.

sign center for interiors and fabrics and furnishings; an arboretum, a planetarium, special museums.

Such elements call for various mechanisms in addition to straight private enterprise. They call for a varied panel of devices—public, public-private, and industry-wide associations. A specific example: Rotterdam's outstanding and renowned building and design center, the Bouwcentrum, at the start was financed by government with an interest-free loan. It is now self-supporting and operated by a nonprofit private group.

In our urban renewal chapter we noted grave defects in preparing so exclusively for private enterprise and then depending so exclusively on the limitations of its boom-area dynamic, with its inability to reach low rentals in housing and its unwillingness to let government do it except for minimal amounts as relocation housing to permit the private operations to continue and flourish. In the middle-sized city particularly we have this present additional basic reason. In the case of the hundred or more cultural and drama centers under way around the country, an effective public-private mechanism has been evolved. We must evolve and use this and other new mechanisms and straight municipal help for other large and small enterprises for essentially similar expanded purposes. Here again, we must above all think and act in terms of total equations, adapting our static limited formulas to the requirements of the total situation and taking in more than the single-enterprise profit and loss as our measure.

For All Cities: New Priority for Housing-Community

It has been important, in considering our fast-moving urban scene, to develop the characteristics and problems of both the major metropolitan center and the major center of the middle-sized city. As we have seen, there are such significant differences that the issues in both must be pinpointed, to enable the concerned and motivated, or potentially concerned and activated, citizen to grasp the essentials of both cases. But there are basic similarities, and prominent among them is this one: at both city scales, the psychology of the business-social elite, and of the local government that relies on it, is very much the same.

The dominant conception in the current impulse and surge of urban creative emotion is that of a top power structure which sees urban significance in terms of visible power symbols, in terms of the giant greatest. This may be explicitly stated, as in

Cleveland's University Circle's goal of a center "that rivals any in the world," or it may be simply implicit in the motivating dynamics of Lincoln Center, and the proposed 80,000-seat convention halls. In these cases, the fact is that these centers are equated with the welfare of the city. The stone-by-stone rebuilding of the city for the welfare of the people is consciously put aside to some convenient time after these megacenters have satisfied the mega-egos of the power structure. A diadem is created for a city that is sick; the city which possibly will be operated on later.

I have frequently contrasted the top-circle zeal for creating the great centers with the quasi-invisibility of the slums, the shortage of satisfactory housing which is escalating rather than decreasing. Let me give a few dramatic verifications. We all know that Southern cities are doing handsome central urban renewal, while the Negro sections are often still unpaved and sewerless. On a different plane, consider again Cleveland's University Circle.[9] Quoting again from the 1962 report:

> The Circle's highly trained and well-equipped police force, now numbering 16 men, was formed in 1959. Bolstered by a corps of uniformed attendants in parking areas, it has virtually eliminated crime within the Circle and made it safe for thousands of visitors to use and enjoy. This good influence has had a tendency to spread into neighboring areas and has relieved the city's police force of much of the burden of patrols in the Circle.

Let us see another view. The Cleveland *Plain Dealer* of May 28, 1965, has a full page of photos and comment entitled "Fear Stalks Circle Area Night Workers." Here are the quotes:

> The University Circle Development Foundation supports a private police force, which patrols the area in addition to regular Cleveland police. The force has grown from 15 men at its inception in 1959 to 49 today.
>
> Police and Foundation officials feel the lingering apprehension is unfounded. They cite statistics showing crime, especially to persons, has decreased. In 1962–63, while crime increased 18% in Cleveland as a whole, it dropped 18% in University Circle, Craig E. Michalski, chief of the private force, said.
>
> But the crime fringe that borders University

[9] University Circle is certainly as sensible and well carried out a center as dozens more around the country. I have criticized it relatively often here because I happen to know a good deal about it.

Circle on the north and west affects the psyche of workers and travelers to the cultural center. . . . Some University Circle police admit unofficially that they merely may be pushing crime from their district to fringe areas.

Official accounts of over-all urban renewal programs of a number of cities supplement this Cleveland picture. The main space is devoted to program and accomplishment of the new center or centers, historical restorations, the bad previous slum conditions, and the exact number of slum dwellings *cleared.* The number of new dwellings for the displaced families is generally not mentioned, and is indeed not easy to find out by further inquiry. With few exceptions it is small, and provision of new housing usually does not *precede* the demolition of the old area. Usually, the report contents itself with stating that people have been relocated in standard housing. No mention of *increasing* supply of good low-rental housing; apparently no question of any over-all quantitative program of new housing, especially for those of low income.

The life and health of the significant city of whatever size depends on the penetrating recognition that the vitality of its parts and of its people living in them is of paramount importance. In the preceding chapter, we worked out the thesis that for the health and vibrancy of the total city, it is essential to conceive it as an anatomy of localities, to achieve an awareness of the need for organic locality, local identification, local inspiration. In this chapter, we have considered the validity and positive importance of major centers in their own terms, and have noted in some detail that even from their point of view, there is a point of diminishing returns

with size. The major centers themselves are more truly effective, not only lose nothing of their brilliance and quality if their "bulk content" is analyzed and burnished down to their authentic glitter, but they actually gain in terms of the performance of those working in them and in terms of the experience of visitors, or "consumers"—and indeed in terms of architectural clarity and conviction. In Mies van der Rohe's compelling phrase, "Less is More."

We arrive at a constellation composed of locality centers in the city and of the main center or centers in the main city and the smaller cities in the great metropolitan region and in the less outsized metropolitan region as well. We must start thinking in simultaneous terms. Each has tremendous validity. The vitality and brilliance and optimum fulfillment of each depends on active recognition of the equality of validity of the various levels.

Beyond and underlying that, the invisible parts of our cities, the matrix of living, the housing communities of our people, have to command a drastically greater and earlier driving recognition by those who are so single-mindedly and dramatically pushing the great centers. The Demonstration Cities Act of 1966 (now referred to as Model Cities) is a modest start in the right direction. We must not only distribute funds between major centers and subcenters, but include in our equations, as of even greater importance, a higher quality of daily living and a far more adequate quantity of good housing community. It is only out of such a matrix that the great towers and spires can genuinely reach upward. Only when we have it will our cities be fulfilling the obligation of our time.

CHAPTER NINE

FROM CITY TO CITY-REGION: METROPOLITAN PLANNING. FEDERATED METROPOLITAN GOVERNMENTS

The keys to the metropolitan symphony are the bold establishment of genuine New Towns with their potentials of new life, of happier relationship to nature and environment; dramatic reversal of city fringe and of leapfrogging; reconception and redirection of the new freedom and the new bondage of the automobile; redirection of the mounting trends in costs and tensions of traffic; formation of the region into a crystallized entity. Now, we explore questions and crises and opportunities in regional policy.

We shall consider regional policy and its implementation in two different senses: that of local metropolitan regional policy, to be considered in this chapter, and national regional distribution policy, to be considered in the next chapter.

The Urgent Need for Local Metropolitan Regional Policy and Political Structure

By local metropolitan regional policy is meant the analysis and coordination of urgent problems which commonly arise in any city-region and which are constantly becoming more pressing with the rise of population and of in- and out-migration. Such problems are problems of:

Over-all land use and relation of living places and workplaces
Industrial growth and location
Highway location
Drainage and flood control
Air and water pollution
Nature and parks and open spaces
New Town locations and sizes
Population distribution, destratification, and the race issue

In various specific problems, various specific elements will be outstanding. (The aggressive new population surge is common to practically all.) It may be water pollution from industrial wastes miles away upstream, or it may come from overload of septic tanks in the suffering area itself; or it may come from both. The first case requires action far beyond the locality's own jurisdiction. The second requires a sewage-disposal system beyond its financial capacity, and a sewage-disposal system is usually much more economical and effective if it is provided on a much larger than local scale. Again, there often is conflict or neglect in road systems and locations. Floods and flood control provide another recurrent case of the impotence of the locality.

This is not only a question of surveys to establish policy and of planning and advisory bodies, which we are fairly long on in this country. It is urgently a question of setting up methods and mechanisms geared to the complexities of rapid growth and change, of providing governmental forms for effectuation and enforcement and control, and of states of mind that insistently seek these.

It is one thing to recognize need. It is another to conceive and then design solutions; this we have been undertaking in the last chapters. It is still another to propound them convincingly, to debate them, to cause ferment and demand for action. And the final act of determination and creation is to struggle for, and bring into active being, the governmental institutions to anticipate and do what is necessary to do. This is the great subject matter of this chapter.

The Royal Commission which finally recommended the subsequently adopted federal London regional government setup generalized the same universal and growing difficulties from its investigations:

> The [existing] machinery is untidy and full of anomalies. There is overlapping, duplicating, and, in some cases, gaps. . . .
>
> There are great and growing problems to be solved and the present machinery of local government is inadequate to solve them. . . .
>
> We have come across numerous instances in which desirable highway improvements have been postponed or delayed for years, while this tug-of-war continued.[1]

Great cities in metropolitan regions are here. No one can reverse that, whatever his personal Utopias. We *can* make the best of them, in such ways as we have outlined. And we can and must do our best to dampen down their endless indefinite but persistent growth, through a national and local urban regional policy.

Local Metropolitan Regional Policy and Execution

Now as to local regional policy and administrative requirements. Perceptive people everywhere recognize the necessity for comprehensive metropolitan regional surveys, research, and coordinated study *and action*. But they simply have not yet made themselves adequately heard in effective action terms.

There are over two hundred metropolitan areas in the United States. Although half of them already have some form of setup for dealing with metropolitan problems, in most cases it is quite lacking in authority. Some are fairly influential and pervasive; almost none are very strong. There are the private voluntary group, e.g., the Regional Plan Association of New York; the public body authorized by statute, with members from constituent communities but with no legal enforcement power, e.g., in the Chicago area, the Northwestern Illinois Metropolitan Area Planning Commission; the public metropolitan body with specific defined powers for construction and operation, e.g., the Port of New York Authority and the Bi-State Development Agency (Illinois and Missouri) for the St. Louis metropolitan area. Then there is (rarely) the most thoroughgoing setup of all, metropolitan government. Examples are the Greater London Council;[2] the Toronto "Metro" government, now in its thirteenth year; Metropolitan Dade County in Florida, established in 1959 (Miami being the chief city); and the metropolitan government of Nashville and Davidson County, Tennessee, in operation about three years. The two former are federated, or federal, forms, with regional matters handled by the metropolitan body with its own budget and power, and with the bulk of local powers in the control of the individual constituent communities.

This specimen listing indicates how widely the need has been felt and action taken, varying from mostly quite weak to a few decisive ones should bring home sharply the oneness of metropolitan-wide problems and the urgency of the need that has led to the current expansion of metropolitan-wide planning and powers. It is inevitable that planning will come to all metropolitan areas, and in its fullest version. The burning question is this: Will it come now, or will it come after much more metropolitan spoilage has taken place, much more new land has been prodigally and fragmentarily used up, and the results of metropolitan anarchy are much more evident and irreversible both in the central city and in the outer areas?

As far as studies and recommendations are concerned, most of these have gone a considerable distance. In some cases, such as the Baltimore and

---

[1] Report of the Royal Commission on Local Government in Greater London 1164, H. M. Stationery Office, London, 1960. In order quoted, paragraphs 286, 707, and 410.

[2] As previously noted, London metropolitan government has recently increased in area and population controlled and in strength of control, as the result of long study and the recommendations of a Royal Commission. This significant step, showing both the changing needs and the accumulated confidence of a region which had had previous experience with metropolitan government, is well described in a pamphlet by William A. Robson, *The World's Greatest Metropolis: Planning and Government in Greater London*, Institute of Local Government, University of Pittsburgh, Pittsburgh, Pa., 1963.

Washington areas, New Town locations have been roughly indicated in regional master plans. In others, there are enough data at hand to facilitate choice of some sites. In the case of New York State, a proposed framework of regions announced in 1964 by Governor Rockefeller includes illustrative locations and envelopic sizes of a number of New Town or expanded town galaxies, indicative of the state's development policy. Thus we have arrived at, or can readily arrive at, the specific locations of early New Towns.

Chapter 6 delineated, in analytic terms, the internal social, economic, and physical composition of New Towns, and described a feasible initial setup for creating them. Now that the location problem is on the way to specific solutions, there is no doubt that a substantial number of New Towns in our sense can be created soon. But the maximum advantage will accrue in any individual case only if at the earliest moment a metropolitan government can set out a complete plan, can closely link solution of population problems with the other urgent physical, social, and transport-communications decisions, and can gain the maximum value in action from this coordinated decision-making and execution. That is why it is so late in the day and so very urgent to move a thoroughgoing metropolitan government setup into action *now*.

This issue is receiving a great deal of many-paged high-level attention. For example, there is the Advisory Committee on Inter-Governmental Relations, a permanent bipartisan committee set up by Congress, composed of distinguished and practical members from local, state, and Federal government. After analyzing the inadequacies of the approach of metropolitan special authorities or single-purpose districts with specialized piecemeal jurisdiction, it has advocated what it considers a first move: "the metropolitan service corporation." This would have jurisdiction over, and perform area-wide services of, sewage disposal and water supply, transportation, housing, parks, flood control, etc.—all the area-wide needs that the localities simply cannot cope with. Its board of directors would be persons who hold local office in cities and counties of the metropolitan area, and thus persons with direct responsibility to the people. But at this late date such partial setups are inadequate.

Causes of Inaction and Half Action

The *need*, then, is well recognized. Why is action usually so meager, usually so halfway or less than halfway where there is action at all? Even in

Washington, where the internal-city planning is as determined and alert as anywhere in the country perhaps, or in the world, we have immediately beyond its borders, and as disturbingly visible as though inside the city, the anarchic proliferation of skyscrapers across the Potomac at Rosslyn, the beginnings of the same around Arlington; the shambles and traffic mess of Silver Spring; and Friendship Heights, where in the last few years a number of 17-story buildings have been erected at the incredible density of 400 dwelling units per acre!

One may discern three reasons:

Those who clearly recognize the need are intellectually involved, not passionately involved. They are too ready to accept the shadow for the substance: research, reports, and discussion without timetable; voluntary associations and statutory bodies without enforcing power.

The hard-boiled suburban-oriented local people are persistently wedded to the exclusionary second rate, and mean to hold on to it. Or, recognizing their multiplying difficulties and shortcomings, still more do they fear change.

Most elements of the general citizenry, on whose sensitive and passionate involvement all effective political action depends, are substantially unaware and uninvolved as of now.

Let us analyze these groups, and see what to do.

The political scientists and the professional planners are basically not action-oriented. Planners are by tradition above the melee, pointing out the pros and cons, making recommendations, but only in the case of exceptional personalities getting into the actual struggle for accomplishment. They are not seared by the mounting discrepancy between multi-fronted deterioration and available effective measures for new creation, in contrast to paper arrangements, postdated checks, and voluntary gradualist associations expected to grow at some future time into decisive metropolitan authorities. There is the shambles in the metropolitan area beyond Washington, and the deterioration of the great Potomac itself. Yet the Washington metropolitan region is awash with planning bodies, with such important titles as the Metropolitan Washington Council of Governments and the National Capital Regional Planning Council; there are a dozen others. Paper tigers. Their existence in addition to many other planning bodies around the country in varying degrees of official and voluntary status is undoubtedly of some value, and yet it may on balance be actually harmful, because by their mere existence and their numerous voluminous publications, they lull citizens into a belief that they are the real thing.

Washington Plan
Year 2000

But, not enforceable without metropolitan government. Its very publication encourages land speculation, which will probably make it impossible to accomplish.

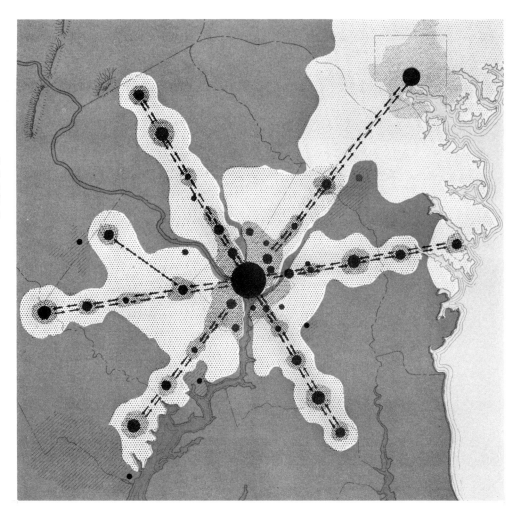

Across the Potomac
from Washington

1. *View of Rosslyn, in foreground, one of the booming suburbs*

Another instance is the viewpoint of the planning profession, its state of euphoria which takes the form for the substance. The American Institute of Planners, the representative body of the profession, made this statement at a congressional hearing: "Now nearly every metropolitan area has some sort of comprehensive planning framework and some mechanism for cooperation among local governments to solve common problems. The emphasis now must shift to the area outside the Standard Metropolitan Statistical Area—the land to be urbanized in the next several decades."[3]

Of course, what is sought beyond the metropolitan area is desirable. But the point is that the institute is evidently pleased that nearly every metropolitan area has *some sort* of planning framework. The mere existence is taken as satisfactory, symbolically, as it were. But the crux is the extent and quality of authority, of legal and pragmatic power. These are the real-life criteria. The dominant motivations and tactics of the planning profession are in urgent need of a leaven of political understanding. And political vitality: for the planner must furnish not only analysis, but the power of his vision, the spark, the drive. The planner's role is that of Paul Revere. He must ride to goad politicians and people into action.

The people, in this context, fall into two categories, central urban and suburban-exurban. The latter are rapidly finding that their idyllic conditions no longer exist: that their septic tanks are overloaded and water pollution is becoming a menace, that costs to maintain and update their originally good school systems are prohibitive, that they are being overrun and run through with disruptive roads. They are facing a myriad of problems and momentarily attempting to meet them by a myriad of single devices—special districts, new departments —each a finger in a dike with many leaks. They are not yet grasping that at this complex stage of our development, these apparently single problems are not single and these single devices are quite outdated—that there is now a functional and territorial interrelatedness of problems, and solutions, including finances and other resources, for which the single ad hoc bodies are not adequate, get in each other's way.[4]

Nor have the general citizenry of the central city, and their mayors, grappled with the totality of their situation. They are frantically aware of the desperate nature of their problems of crime, schools, slums, and race but they fail to recognize the meagerness of their weapons. Slum clearance, urban renewal as it mostly exists, rehabilitation; multistory housing, inappropriate for families; subsidized remedies for impossible in-city traffic—these are expensively misleading, and their effectiveness is actually receding relative to the growth of the problems. These have been all internal and in-city remedies, moreover, while the problems involve the city-region. Still, attempts at remedies or even at re-creation could get somewhere if the other areas of the city-region could be integrally called on, consciously involved, as in the crowding reality of this age of the automobile and exploding population, they so closely and inextricably are.

Meeting the New Needs: Articles of Confederation or Constitution?

This is the poised moment. Serious delay in joint decisive action could be fatal. In our twentieth-century environment, only a very few regions have reached a point comparable even to the Articles of Confederation stage of our early nation's life. The Articles of Confederation were too partial, too feeble to cope with onrushing reality, and the realization came that drastic change, though painful, was imperative, and so the Constitution was created. Now, as then, we need the breadth and firmness of a constitution. And an interesting similarity: the kind of metropolitan constitution we need is, equally, a federal one. Not an attempt to erase local initiative and self-reliance, but a two-level setup, a setup of full local representation at a strong higher level, to produce the optimum totality. Thus a strengthening of local government, a remedy for bewildered anarchy.[5]

[3] From American Institute of Planners *Newsletter*, June, 1965, p. 3, covering testimony on May 27 before Joint Committee on Intergovernmental Relations.

[4] For an informed tragicomic tale of suburban futility, of the need for action versus the many lags and gaps and governmental entities it encounters, read Charles M. Stonier, "Planning in the Maturing Suburb," *Traffic Quartely*, Eno Foundation for Highway Traffic Control, Saugatuck, Conn., April, 1965. With a few substitutions as you go along, it is your own case of travail and frustrations: the so many problems that originate beyond your domain, the so many problems that *seem* internal but that you must leave your domain to tackle.

[5] The Committee for Economic Development, a well-known sober national business group, makes a cogent statement of the case: "Failure to establish metropolitan governments with wide powers *will lead to a greater loss of self-determination in local affairs* through the continuous transfer of responsibility to the State and Federal governments [italics mine]." From *Guiding Metropolitan Growth*, Committee for Economic Development, August, 1960, p. 9.

Let us now examine precedents, successful precursors on this road. And then let us see what orchestration of measures and institutions *we* apply to make a workable and happy path *for us.* Our main cases are the metropolitan government of Toronto and the London region considered again from this fresh point of view. We also consider our own Miami and Nashville.

Inspired Pioneering: Toronto's *Metro*

Toronto's is a most convincing case. The metropolitan government started on April 15, 1953, in an atmosphere of much doubting, under pressure from the government of Ontario. Twelve years later a commission named to study desirable changes received not a single submission advocating any serious changes or advocating return to the replaced system of independent municipalities.

Metro, as the metropolitan government is called, was formed by putting together a total of thirteen independent municipal areas—Toronto and twelve others. It has a population of 1¾ million, and the population is growing at the rate of 50,000 a year. Plans provide for an additional 750,000 within the present area. The government of this new Metropolitan Toronto is a council of twenty-four members. Half are elected officers of Toronto's city government. The other half are the mayors of the other twelve municipalities. Experience had shown that through this setup there is no domination by the central city. Metro has been responsible for, among much else, striking physical accomplishments, such as trunk water distribution, improved sewerage and drainage systems, outstanding river-valley parks, and a system of expressways and parkways. These are not discrete accomplishments of single authorities or special districts, but an interconnected web of accomplishments. And, what has appealed particularly to the suburbs which became members, the consolidated borrowing power of Metro has lowered financing costs for each.

As this indicates, Metro creates total solutions. In an increasingly industrial and automobile age, water pollution has become an area-wide problem beyond the control of single municipalities, and air pollution is literally a galloping menace with gasoline fumes from the hundreds of thousands of fast-traveling cars respecting no boundaries. Metro handles the problems of water pollution and air pollution. It also handles aspects of public education and welfare, and over-all land use. And it has recently recognized housing as a city-regional problem and initiated a program of public housing on open land in the suburbs which are part of the Metro.

In the beginning, the powers and their exercise were taken on in a gingerly way. But in the years of Metro's existence and experience, need and consensus have led to further forms of coordinated power. Now, the Metropolitan Toronto Urban Renewal Study is a two-year project of the Metro Toronto Planning Board and Metro itself. Its aim is an integrated urban renewal plan and program for the total area. Reflect on our fragmented urban renewal and on how much more could be accomplished by such an integrated approach.

This is heady and wonderful stuff. Of course they are not all living happily ever after. In the two-tier system of government there are a number of areas of doubt and serious differences of opinion and of interest. These are inevitable irreducible accompaniments of human and institutional complexities. But the system makes inspired sense.

More about Greater London: Miami and Nashville

In Chapter 7 we considered the case of Greater London from the inside out as it were, mainly from the viewpoint of the subcities or boroughs within. Now consider it from the obverse view: as a second action example of federated regional government. The new Greater London Council region has a population of some 8 million, as compared with its predecessor London County Council of 3 million. It covers 600 square miles. It had the usual anarchic and overlapping assortment: 100 separate local governments, special districts, boards, authorities, commissions.

The Royal Commission set up by the British government recognized the same points that bother us. "The Commission were impressed with the need to keep local governments in the area local and accessible. . . . A single gigantic authority covering all aspects of Greater London government would be too remote." [6] But in contrast to us, they weighed the forces of reality and went ahead and did a job of federation that met this need. The Greater London Council is directly elected, on the basis of whole boroughs. Thus there is no overweighting. The GLC is elected differently from the Toronto Metro, but accomplishes the same objectives and has jurisdiction over much the same necessary spheres of action. Central and crucial are two ele-

[6] *Greater London Government,* Conservative Political Centre, Local Government Series, no. 11, London, 1964, p. 10.

legend

 Centers

 Transportation Emphasized — Expressways

 Rapid Transit

 Work Places

 Residence — High Density

 Medium Density

 Low Density

 Public Open Space

Farming

Intelligent Presentation of Metropolitan Alternatives

For public discussion and choice. By Northeast Illinois Metropolitan Area Planning Commission, which has no power to turn it into reality.

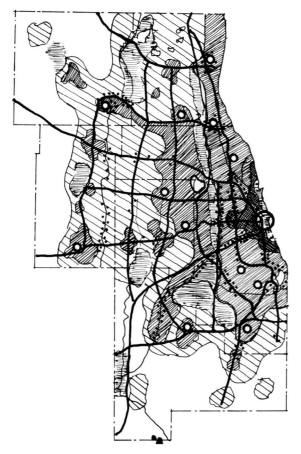

trends

The Trends alternative reflects some parts of all the planned alternatives.

The lower residential densities of the "Dispersed" plan but with more apartments as in "Multi-Towns."

The stream valley orientation of open space continues established forest preserve policy.

Some additional rapid transit and commuter service are added similar to "Satellite Cities" primary emphasis on expressway travel.

Jobs are dispersed somewhat but not so widely as in the "Dispersed" plan.

Individual communities show some of the "Multi-towns" specialization in providing for shopping, culture or entertainment.

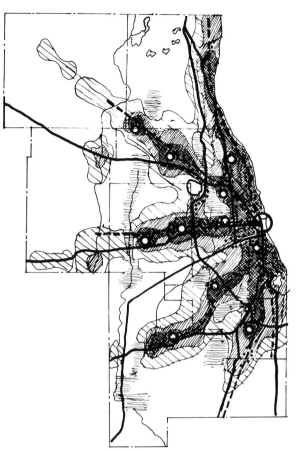

finger plan

A major alternative to automobile emphasis and the increasing rate of land consumption.

Rapid transit lines radiate from the Loop and form an interconnected grid east of the Tri-State expressway.

Many people (70%) choose to live in apartments and town houses convenient to the rapid transportation.

Each residential area is close to major parks and forest preserves and farms.

Jobs are quickly and cheaply accessible, though possibly distant, to anyone via high speed trains.

Higher residential densities bring more shopping and cultural facilities close to home.

satellite cities
greenbelt plan

Five or six major cities evolve in the region, with the City of Chicago remaining as a hub for culture, communication and transportation.

The cities are set apart from one another by a low density residential "Greenbelt" with some farming and major areas of permanent open space, much of which is available for public recreation use.

Natural Resources are conserved by concentrating population and building large reservoirs.

Movement between cities is fast and easy due to rapid trains and helicopters as well as expressways.

Several large industrial parks are found in each city.

Retail, culture, education and entertainment centers are in each city.

multitowns plan

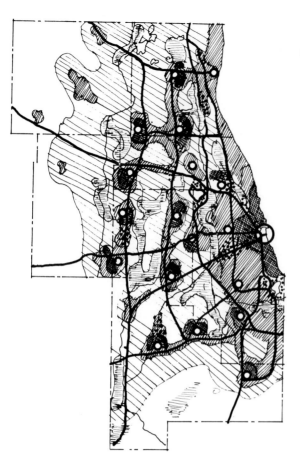

Wide variety of communities, differing in size and character.

Narrow, but continuous bands of open space divide the otherwise continuous expansion of developed land. (Swiss Cheese)

Overall population is similar to today's.

Some communities are only for residence, featuring one housing type or another.

Some communities contain major work places.

Others have a regional shopping center, or possibly a cultural center or a major university.

dispersed regional city plan

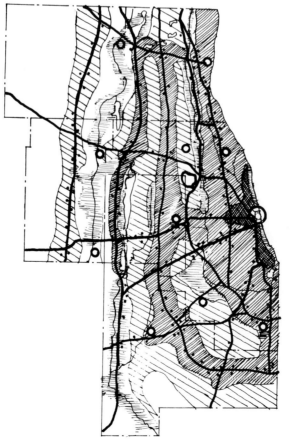

A region organized in harmony with its natural environment in particular the North-South river valleys.

Principally (70%) occupied by single family homes on medium and large lots.

Served by expressways.

Combined centers for shopping culture, and entertainment serve a dozen major sub-regions.

Widely dispersed small industrial parks and office centers.

ments of the GLC's powers: The master development plan (the boroughs do town planning within their own area, in accord with the GLC's general pattern of communications, industrial location, and land use), and GLC control of certain aspects of housing. Note that this federal city-regional system was the unanimous recommendation of the Royal Commission.

Turning to the United States, Miami and surrounding Dade County formed themselves into a metropolitan government in 1959; Nashville and Davidson County did this in 1963.

Aside from the fact that these are examples in our own country, they are noted here because they were conceived and consummated without pressures or inducements from the outside or above.

Nashville–Davidson County had a total population of only 415,000. That is, the compelling advantages were perceived even in a situation much smaller than one's customary image of a metropolis and its region.

In Nashville, to allay the fears of the suburbs as to heavier taxation, two levels of taxation were set up: a normal level and a lower level in areas not getting full urban services, to be raised by steps only when the level of services was raised.

In the case of Nashville, there was almost as long birth travail as in London. The plan for metropolitan government was issued in October, 1956. The charter for the government failed to win adoption in a referendum in June, 1958. It was revised and finally, in June, 1962, was voted on again and adopted. Metropolitan government was finally initiated on April 1, 1963. Thus more than six years passed between the first real moves and actual operation; seven years in the case of Greater London. This seems about par for the course, and accounts for the urgency of my exhortations *to lose no time in initiating the job.*

In Miami, there have been popular referendums since the original adoption, each time sustaining the original decision.

The form adopted in these two cases was not two-tier–federal, but unitary. There are thus various forms possible. However, having regard to the essential realities of inherent and worthwhile local uniqueness, and to the American tradition and spirit, the federated, or two-tier, setup has the greatest promise for us.

Local Reluctance: Carrot and Stick

There are, then, few but quite convincing cases of real metropolitan government. They point up the importance and attainability of the fully thought-through "Constitution type" of metropolitan setup, in place of the intermediate loose and semianarchic "Articles of Confederation stage." As noted before, we have generally not reached even the Articles of Confederation stage. Indeed, we are still at or before the stage of "ad-hockery." [7] Let us lose no more time in getting from our present morass into a situation where we are in command of instrumentation capable of coping with the complexities of the twentieth-century's city-region.

We need a lot more than brave words. We need a lot more than the existence of precedents elsewhere. We know the resistances. There are the fears of the suburbs, fears they've always had, but now newly crystallized around color and around resistance to the necessity for low-income housing. There are the inertias of the city, daily seeing deterioration and depletion of its population and resources, which are heavily due to regional factors, but hating to look beyond its borders for remedies. Both elements respond minimally to each ill when it becomes intolerable or after it has become intolerable, by limping single efforts and agencies: anything to avoid full confrontation. An interesting and worrisome illustration of the metropolitan action dilemma and current unpreparedness for action comes from a meeting in the St. Louis area, called by the Bi-State Development Agency and attended by members of fourteen local government and planning bodies. As reported in the St. Louis *Post-Dispatch* of June 19, 1964, an agreement was reached to form a highly tentative regional coordinating committee.

> The agreement . . . represents a kind of shotgun marriage, the coercive element being a threat of a withdrawal of Federal funds for urban highway projects next year. The Federal Highway Act of 1962 specifies that the Bureau of Roads will not approve any more projects in urban areas of more than 50,000 population after July 1, 1965, unless they are based on a continuing comprehensive metropolitan planning process. . . .
>
> Richard Ives, deputy assistant commissioner for urban planning of the Urban Renewal Administration, also had a warning for the group. . . . [He said] that hereafter, funds will be available for smaller agencies only where their planning functions are coordinated with others in the metropolitan area.
>
> When some delegates questioned the Federal

---

[7] Prof. William A. Robson's felicitous expression for the proliferation of single-purpose authorities, special districts, commissions, committees, study groups, etc.

officials on how minimal the regional planning could be and still qualify for funds, Laurence K. Roose, St. Louis county supervisor, said he was concerned with the direction of the discussion.

"It seems to me the question before us is whether we establish a coordinating committee to meet all the needs of our community. I don't think it is a businesslike approach to regional planning to just find out the minimum things we must do to get this Federal road money. We ought to find out and define the areas in which regional planning coordination is in order."

A major consideration in introducing the cases of Toronto and London was that the local states of mind that preceded their solutions were somewhat similar to ours now: unawareness, then indifference, then inertia and vested interest, then single responses to the sharpest troubles as they could no longer be ignored, with enough troubled and far-sighted people to produce a continuing persistent thread of agitation for the broad federated metropolitan answer.

Higher levels of government saw the city-regional issues more clearly and urgently than all but a few, and stepped in with their powerful arsenal of weapons—prodding, withholding, inducement, greatly superior financial resources. The provincial government of Ontario, in the one case, and the central British government, in the other, were able to get results, not fast, but years faster than any local regional consensus and local electoral process would have done. Gradualism had done its part and had then become quite inadequate. Finally, decisiveness had to supervene.

The same kind of process has to take place here. And there is plenty of analogous experience. One encouraging and effective precedent is the Federal Highway Act of 1962 mentioned in the above quotation from St. Louis. In it, Congress made it mandatory after July 1, 1965, for metropolitan areas to present a master plan of roads and to have a comprehensive planning process before the Federal government would make its 90 per cent subsidy available for the strategic interstate roads. The prospect of delay or suspension has had a galvanizing effect in production of the necessary planning machinery and actuality. This is negative inducement, or stick. An example of positive inducement, or carrot, comes from another part of the road program. States which have aggressively been pushing their work have been able to consume appropriations left unclaimed by laggard states. Other examples of similar action:

Federal aid to school districts is withheld if there is not submitted a plan and timetable for integra-

tion. And it's not just the fact of *a* plan and *a* timetable: these are being rejected if their substance is unsatisfactory. The Federal Equal Employment Opportunities Commission withholds consent for the award of enormous Federal contracts if its investigation indicates unsatisfactory practices or until proper practices are initiated.

Other Federal programs which could more fully apply this principle and practice are the Community Facilities Administration and the Urban Renewal Administration, whose help is now much sought in the suburban areas.[8] They could require the metropolitan synthesis as a condition of help or could make the degree of help contingent on it. This kind of attitude and pressure, joined to a really energetic determination on the part of those citizens of the city-region who understand the need, could snap the tether of inertia and gradualism, bring about effective decision and action.

The Demonstration Cities and Metropolitan Development Act of 1966: Grants for Planned Metropolitan Development

Since the above section was written, The Demonstration Cities and Metropolitan Development Act of 1966 was introduced in Congress and has become law. It marks an important step toward the aims stated in this chapter, and specifically toward applying carrot inducements. Briefly, some significant elements:

Sub-section (b) of Section 101 would declare that the purpose of this title is to provide additional encouragement and assistance to States and localities, through supplementary grants for certain Federally-assisted development projects, for making effective comprehensive metropolitan planning and programming. . . .

In addition [under Section 102], no metropolitan area would be eligible for the grants unless it is demonstrated to the satisfaction of the Secretary that adequate metropolitan-wide institutional or other arrangements, such as a metropolitan council of governments, exist for coordinating local public development policies and activities on the basis of the metropolitan-wide comprehensive planning and programming; and that public facility projects and other land development or uses [public or private] which have a major impact on the development of the area are, in fact, being carried out

[8] Under new names and relationships, these are now under the newly organized Department of Housing and Urban Development, under the Assistant Secretary for Renewal and Housing Assistance.

in accord with the metropolitan-wide comprehensive planning and programming. . . .

Subsection (a) of Section 103 would limit a grant under this title to *20 percent of the cost of the project for which the grant is made.*[9]

This bill is a real beginning, and should be strongly supported. But it is essential that much more than is provided in it be accomplished, and promptly, part at the Federal level, part at the state level:

■ At the Federal level. To qualify for grant, one of the requirements is "metropolitan-wide institutional or other arrangements, such as a metropolitan council of governments." We have seen that this kind of interim arrangement is not enough. We should push for the provision of an additional grant *beyond* the extra 20 per cent of the present bill for those areas which have or set up a genuine federated metropolitan government.

■ At the state level. Everyone knows that the strongest block to real metropolitan government is the racial and economic issue—that the suburbs want to keep out Negroes and Puerto Ricans (as well as low-income people and large families in general). At the present juncture, a bill that would require a genuine and strong open policy would not pass Congress. But in a number of states, positive sentiment is latent or active. In these states, it is our urgent duty to produce legislation that will add *its* grants to areas where the metropolitan government to be set up specifically has the power to deal with this issue and come up with positive action.[10]

A New Synthesis

Within the city, we need a two-tier federalism. In the subcity or district, we need local awareness,

[9] The quotations are from "Section-by-Section Summary," Department of Housing and Urban Development, Feb. 21, 1966, pp. 1, 2, and 3 of the predecessor bill.

[10] In Connecticut, the State General Assembly has appointed a bipartisan Commission to Study the Necessity and Feasibility of Metropolitan Government. Its report is due in January, 1967. This is encouraging. Negotiations are under way to form a regional government in the San Francisco Bay Area.

local effective spheres of authority, and local architectural embodiment, as the humane complement of a remote city hall. These fill the local vacuum of frustration with vitality. In the metropolitan area, or city-region, we likewise need a two-tier federalism, coming from the opposite direction. At this level, the originally healthy local loyalty and independence are simply no longer adequate to deal with the problems. We are barnacled by an excessive and obsessive localism.

I return to the parallel of the birth of the Constitution. This evocation is not just a self-serving tour de force. What had been healthy independence finally had to give way to a more mature and comprehensive outlook, and this had to be translated into a strong federated governmental form. To create a strong federation was a painful decision to make, then as now. But today even our most maddening neoconservatives are not suggesting any retrogression into the early inadequacy of the pre-Constitution government. Many of our metropolitan areas now have a population considerably greater than all the original Colonies, and are beset by problems of the most formidable scale and complexity. For these areas and for those that are still evolving toward this situation, we desperately require strong metropolitan structure.

We have considered the sometimes painful birth but also the success of a number of metropolitan governments. I am convinced that, once the deed is done, for all of us who live in or near cities, the fears and insecurities that beset us now will be transformed into a high spiritual satisfaction, a sense of wholeness and of effectiveness, of being much more equal to the many-dimensioned situations that face us. We will then be able to implement and supplement the healthy and dynamic elements in localism, by extending its strengths.

Once we have roused ourselves to take action *now* on the metropolitan-federated plane, we will experience a freeing and a flowering, a gushing forth of dammed-up springs, a surge of powerful impulse and accomplishment, a great and fruitful new adventure on many planes.

CHAPTER TEN

TWENTIETH-CENTURY PIONEERING: RESTRUCTURED REGIONS AND NEW REGIONS. RATIONAL CITY SCALES. THE REGIONAL CITY

The great adventure which we have just traced from the small neighborhood to the city-region can re-create our lives and reshape our environment in the regions where, by and large, we are. But the order of magnitude of the accepted population-growth projections, and the horrendous specific situations that already arise on all sides and illustrate the dire nature of things to come, piled on top of our existing confusion and congestion, points inescapably to the conclusion that in most of our developed regions, we very quickly have to deflect growth into "new regions" and into less intensely and tensely developed portions of our old regions.

National Urban Regional Policy

There are important and urgent alternatives to even the most intelligent development of the major metropolitan areas. If there is one great characteristic of these United States, its genius, its ethos, it is *pluralism*. Let us capitalize on our competitive spirit, raise it to a new and compelling dimension. Let us in this vast country, with its vast spaces and initiative, create important alternatives to the outsized metropolitan regions. They will be better places for living. To say the least of it, many, many people's values would be better fulfilled. And in our age of overflowing technology, we owe it to ourselves to create these alternatives and give them a real chance. I believe that they will prove themselves out, economically, socially, and spiritually.

There are several great alternatives to the major metropolitan regions. One sees three such:

Development of middle-sized metropolitan regions

Development of galaxies of smaller cities

Development of almost new areas

By national urban regional policy we mean first an urgent national debate, then a consensus, and then a national implementation of new or guided distribution of population, industry and employment, recreation, and highway network. Do we continue to accept the overwhelming increase in the size of existing regions, and try only or mainly by New Towns and restructured cities in those regions to make them work more rationally? Should we not also very positively seek to take the very major part of the increase and dispose it in alternative ways? We must not go along with the fashion and add to the ever-increasing megalopolis tendency of Boston–New York–Philadelphia–Baltimore–Washington, of the Los Angeles–San Diego stretch, and others. Let us embrace a valiant twentieth-century equivalent of pioneering: urban regional pioneering.

Before looking closely at the splendid potentials and the way into them, let us face some of the striking evidence of the necessity. Then let us consider some current efforts and precedents from other Western countries which are—contrary to our cherished self-images—outpioneering us.

Samples of What Is Facing Us

■ Population. A few random figures. By the year 2010 it will more than double in the United States. In New York State, one of the lesser increase areas, the projection is from 16 million in 1965 to 30 million in 2020: practically twice as many people. In the San Francisco Bay Area, the Conservation Study Commission in 1965 reported to the California State Legislature an estimated growth from present population of 4 million to 14 million in the year 2020: 3½ times as many people. Perhaps these tremendous figures will not be fully realized, will be mitigated by a new increase of birth control. But this is notoriously slow to catch on, and even if growth were cut by 25 per cent, the *nature* of the problem and the difficulties would be much the same. And of this tremendous growth, 80 per cent will be in the already outsized overcongested metropolitan areas. *This* we *can* do much about, if we get started. That is what this chapter is about.

■ Traffic. Figures of traffic increase are still more staggering. The increase in total numbers of cars we probably cannot seriously affect because it is a function of both increased leisure and increased affluence. But the all-critical matter of peak traffic volumes we can affect. We have seen the *intrametropolitan* dampening down which will result mainly from New Towns and from other measures for better relationships between work, residence, recreation, and open space. By *interregional* redistribution, consciously channeling growth to new regions, we can reduce such frightening figures as the predicted *150 to 200 per cent traffic increase by 1980* in the Northeast corridor, from Washington to Baltimore to Philadelphia to New York to Boston. And, of course, there is nothing terminal about 1980 or any other chosen year. Such increases will go on, to become still more impossibly stifling in the year 1990 and in 2000 and beyond.

Still using the Northeast corridor as an example, passenger air travel between Washington, New York, and Boston shows a traffic increase four times the national average which is in itself huge. The Port of New York Authority, in a search over

several years to find a site for a required additional airport, has with finality been rebuffed by the one locality where it had hoped to do an economically viable job, and has since been reporting prohibitively high costs for a number of other sites considered. Meantime, several plane collisions in the region have been attributed to the overcrowded skyways. In Philadelphia, it is predicted that by 1985 air traffic will increase to 3½ times its 1965 volume: 13 million air passengers as compared with 3.5 million. Consultants have recommended a new airport to cost $75 million, with parking to be increased from the present 2,280 cars to a figure of 12,000. It has already been noted that the Los Angeles Airport, which when completed in 1959 was figured to need 9,000 parking spaces, is now having to increase this to 27,000. Air-traffic increase adds a major component to highway traffic. A personal experience: The flight from New York to Washington used to take an hour. Lately, it rarely takes less than an hour and a half, because of stacking and circling at the two airports. On a recent trip the pilot apologized and explained the delay: "The best way I can explain it: it's like bumper-to-bumper traffic on a highway." I've had the same experience on the Los Angeles–San Francisco flight. Such experiences are previews of the final impasse being reached in various ways in the congested older regions.

■ Open space for recreation. It is a cliché documented by innumerable official and unofficial reports and the personal experience of every one of us, that open space for recreation in our overdeveloped regions becomes scarcer each year relative to our needs, becomes more difficult and irritating and exhausting to reach, becomes more crowded and less satisfactory when we get there.

Some Examples of Action Abroad

On the twentieth-century trail to regional pioneering we have current guideposts in the British study and announcement of a new southeast region and in Holland's policy of developing its underdeveloped east regions to minimize the flow of population into its present great cities and their environs. France is purposefully redressing the imbalance created by the high concentration of the Paris metropolitan area, by way of provincial centers.

The western part of Holland contains all its large cities—Amsterdam, Rotterdam, The Hague, Utrecht, Haarlem—in the ring called the Randstad. Though there was still a fairly open and rural central area and though the cities were still sep-

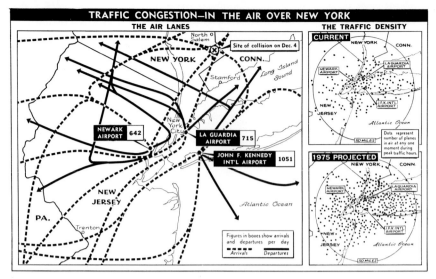

1. *On collision course* (*From* New York Times, *December 12, 1965*)

**Push and Pull
from the Congested Regions**

2. *"Recreation"
in the overcrowded regions*

3. *There's still plenty of room for
twentieth-century pioneering*

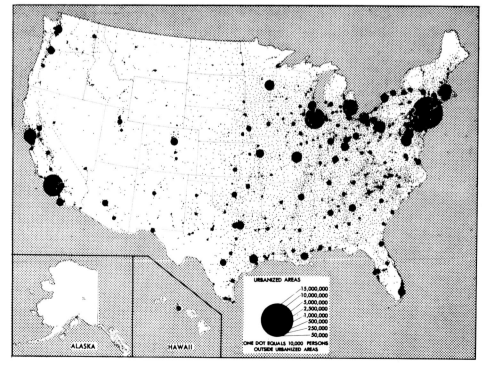

arated from each other around this ring by green space, population was rapidly increasing, and the cities were threatening to ooze together into one solid megalopolis. Some six years ago, the Dutch energetically initiated countermeasures and channeling measures of development. They have been pushing the less developed eastern regions by accelerated public resource development and subsidies to industries, to divert in considerable measure what they consider the excessive Randstad growth.[1]

In England, we know, of course, of the notable New Towns effort, around London, Glasgow, and now Birmingham and Liverpool. The British have concluded too that an ever more decisive national urban regional planning effort is necessary. In 1964 the government announced the first of these, an effort that officials describe as "the biggest planning project in the free world." They propose a regional plan for the entire southeast, to meet a chunk of population explosion of the order of 3.5 million people. It involves three major new cities, New Towns, expansion of towns, *and* doubling the size of the greenbelt surrounding London "to prevent the capital from spreading endlessly into the countryside."[2] Immediate policy toward this end includes a campaign of persuasion (utilizing cartoons, films, broadcasts, advertisements) and legal limitation, and by the government decision to locate no more of its own offices there; to relocate some existing ones away from London.

In France, the plan for the year 2000, promulgated in detail in 1963, includes both the restructuring of the Paris region by New Towns and the accentuated development of eight regional centers such as Marseille, Lyon, Lille, and Strasbourg. These steps are intended to reverse or severely modify the high trend of in-migration into Paris, which has been growing at a much faster rate than the rest of France. It is planned to more than double the population of the regional centers and qualitatively enhance them as counter-magnets. The plan is intended to progressively dampen the Paris in-migration from its current 70,000 to 80,000

per year to an average of 25,000 over the period. It is planned that this reduced growth will be taken up by eight new or enlarged cities in the Paris orbit.

Thus in Western Europe we have a series of adventurous and determined breakthroughs—some brake on the gargantuan present metropolitan population increases and energetic creation of alternatives.

Now as to our own United States. What are some of the new emerging factors in twentieth-century life that insistently demand the more intensive settlement of less developed regions?

New Elements for a New American Policy

Recreation is one key factor. Automation, drastic decrease in the work week, increase in leisure time and mobility range, scarcity of available open space, and the almost unbelievable projections of open-space need—all these compel an examination of recreation as a newly emerging major factor in regional location. Consider a single, not extreme instance. A study by its consultant has led to a recommendation that St. Louis County should within decades have 31,000 additional acres for recreation within an hour's drive of the major urban area. The land-acquisition cost alone will reach something like $125 million. Such amounts are and will increasingly become major items of cost for developed metropolitan areas. In a number of less developed regions, the cost would be a fraction. This indeed is a new dimension in our cost equations.

In our big metropolitan regions, the access journey to recreation constantly increases. Lewis Mumford has made a forceful and succinct statement of this dilemma and its ramifications:

> When it [the city] wipes out the valuable reserves of countryside close at hand, instead of zealously preserving them, its inhabitants are still dependent for recreation and change of scene on some more distant area. Unfortunately, the more distant the area, the less open to daily common use, the more tedious to reach by motor car, the more costly to get to by plane, and the more empty it will ultimately be of recreation value, since crowds of people from other areas will likewise be drawn to it—thus turning the most striking natural landscape *into a kind of recreation slum,* like Yosemite in midsummer.[3]

Again, consider the costs of building. It has been previously noted that housing costs are constantly

[1] This policy and its effectuation are described in a number of publications by the Dutch government. I have made my résumé chiefly from G. A. Wissink, *Metropolitan Planning Problems in the Netherlands,* a mimeograph published by the Planning Department (Rijksdienst voor Nationale Plan), The Hague, September, 1961.

[2] From an account in the New York *Times,* Mar. 20, 1964. This was based on a British government white paper on southeast England. The government has also published *South-East Study,* a report affirming its basic commitment "to moderate the dominance of London" by developing "centers of growth alternative to London."

[3] From "A New Regional Plan to Arrest Megalopolis," *Architectural Record,* March, 1965, p. 149.

rising at an accelerating tempo, that in metropolitan areas the price of developed land has gone from 10 per cent to 20 per cent of the total cost of the home and is still rising. In the relatively new region the speculative and related factors have in most cases not yet been seriously operating. By public purchase and permanent control of massive chunks of land in the new areas, the people can retain for always the benefit of these low costs, particularly of raw land for new towns. And this competition by new regions will operate to dampen, for the future, the egregious rises in cost of land in the old regions.

The opportunity to accentuate development of middle-sized metropolitan areas and new urban regions is made realistic by the communications developments of the last decades, which make certain types of industry all but independent of proximity to market or to raw-material sources. The car, the truck, the plane, road networks, and airways greatly narrow the distance factor; telephone and teletype, wave communication generally, operate further to obliterate it. However, as of now, the vast new interstate superhighway system does its very effective utmost to further accentuate concentration and congestion of cities and regions, to make minimal the effort to activate less developed regions. How?

Application of the cost-benefit ratio to a very short time range means naturally that we increase highway capacity and, temporarily, the attainable over-the-road speed between and around the already congested centers, where demand is insatiable. In the process, of course, we increase the numbers, later the congestion again, and thus we also bind future highway expenditures to more of the same, ad infinitum. We must break loose from this compulsive tie. The public cost-benefit ratio must have a different time orientation from that of private enterprise. Indeed, these matters, being public, should have a different set of governing equations.

Recreation and Re-creation

Development of three major types of new regions is readily possible if we have the imagination and the determination, and they would in a happy way decelerate megalopolitan ooze and eventually put a stop to it. A major accomplishment. But in a sense this is a negative statement; for on the positive side, our alternatives would produce a realization of many of the suppressed potentials of our culture, including importantly an easier tempo of living and a warmer closeness of man to nature. Our twentieth century's multifarious technology and dawning spirit permit these potentials—permit us to "start nearer to the beginning," as it were. (Of course it would be naïve to think we can start altogether from the beginning.) Hence our immediate emphasis on New Towns to meet the undoubtedly inevitable further growth of megalopolis, and on metropolitan planning-development and government. By the way of introduction to the recommended alternative regions, I want to pause to consider more penetratingly the word "recreation" and what it implies. Recreation is becoming, especially with the new leisure, an increasingly major factor in our lives, in our local and national government budgets, in our private budgets, and in our planning ahead, whatever our outlook or economic background. And there are all kinds of positives in recreation. It is pleasurable and healthy and brings out or develops important skills and qualities of sportsmanship and relationship. Some of its various synonyms are relaxation, sport, change, refreshment of body or mind after toil.

Still, the word itself and the concept behind it have in an important sense degenerated. "Recreation" is a homogenized contraction of "re-creation." One can achieve recreation in major metropolitan areas, though at increasing costs and with increasing effort to make the journey to recreation, and limp back from it. But re-creation? A basic element in re-creation is our relation to land and the growth it sustains in animal life and plant life and food. Inhabitants of the great metropolitan areas forfeit these organic, re-creative, meaningful relationships. To them these are distant processes without essential or firsthand emotional meaning, except most meagerly by way of the zoo or occasionally the private garden.

It is necessary that the organic quality of the growth process be retained or regained as part of directly transmitted feeling and experience, by a much more substantial number of people, even by city people. While in outlying New Towns in major metropolitan areas, the people are physically closer to nature in this re-creative sense, especially by virtue of the surrounding greenbelts, it is in what I have called new regions that cities of moderate size, adjacent active farm and dairy production, and in most cases virgin nature can be positively related and sufficiently close to each other to promote fully this natural contact and emotional penetration.

The Three Alternatives

Here are the three types of alternatives to un-

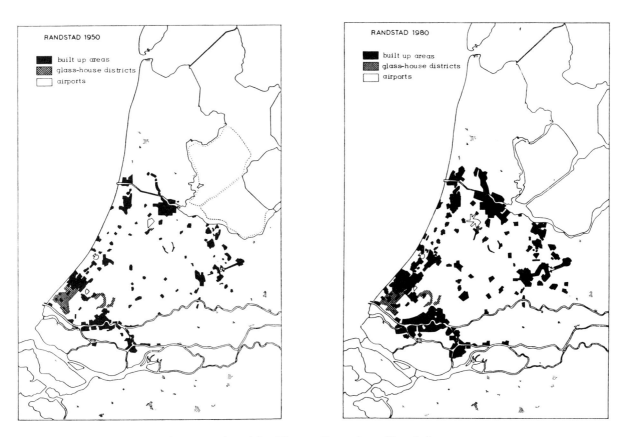

1 and 2. *Randstad (Amsterdam, Haarlem, The Hague, Rotterdam, Utrecht)*
in danger of becoming Megalopolis

3. *Alternative: Government determination to*
redirect population trend

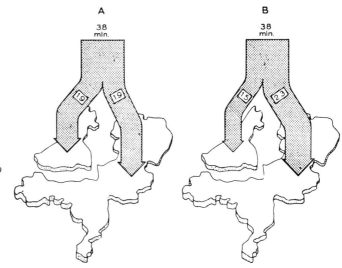

135

France's Policy: Damping Population Growth of
Paris Region: Channeling into Regional Centers

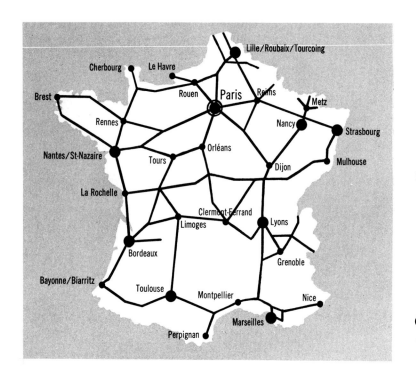

The Regional Metropolises

Proposed Superhighway System

● Regional centers

● Other cities

1. Diverting new growth from Paris. Emphasis on developing the Regional Metropolises (and Sub-Regional Centers) "into real economic and social leaders": high-level facilities for culture, research, higher education, medicine, government, communications.

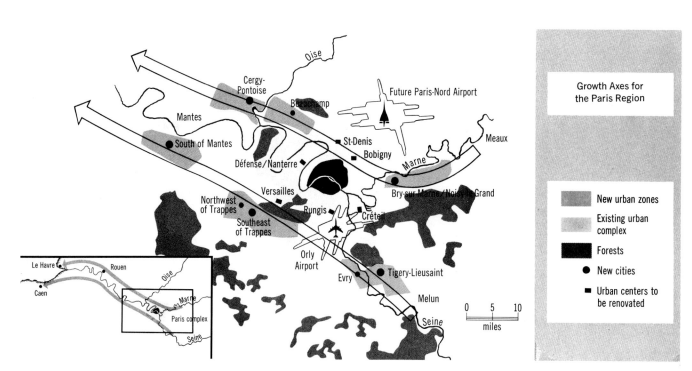

Growth Axes for
the Paris Region

New urban zones

Existing urban
complex

Forests

● New cities

■ Urban centers to
be renovated

2. Paris in the Year 2000. Development of new cities in the region to absorb residual increases

limited accretion and spread of the major metropolitan areas. Progressively they offer sharper alternatives and opportunities. Progressively they involve less of the fixed and barnacled aspects of past development.

1. *The Middle-sized Metropolitan Region: Zurich as a Beau Ideal.* A number of middle-sized metropolitan areas can offer a *kind* of living that is comparable in style and content with the major ones, but with these differences. The tempo is less frenetic; there is less sense of anonymity, more direct human participation and contact; open space and nature are intimately closer. These locales can be counter-magnets to the gargantuan metropolises if they acquire more of, and more distinction in, the cultural and entertainment opportunities now fully available in the great metropolises. And this can happen, and in many cases is attained.[4]

Increase in size will enable middle-sized metropolitan areas to encourage and to support this higher level and variety. More fully, with intentionally accentuated (but not unlimited) growth of the middle-sized metropolitan center itself and of New Towns or guided-growth towns in its orbit, we can have a more humane competitive version of the major metropolitan area: the same kind of living with the excesses mainly shorn away or, rather, never allowed to develop; and positive conditions and opportunities which it is now too late for the major metropolises to attain.

Great further growth adds nothing significant to present major metropolitan areas, but simply accentuates already very serious problems; middle-sized center cities and their metropolitan areas and new towns will gain in quality and character by substantial but, again, not unlimited planned growth. There are numerous examples or candidates around the country. Syracuse, in the center of New York State, is one. It is a core city of some 216,000 in a metropolitan area of some 500,000. Such an area can stand, and can benefit from planned (and limited) growth of intentionally very substantial induced

proportions. It is at an important node of the new communications: a new crossroads of the east-west New York State Thruway and the north-south Penn-Can Highway. It has a great and adventurous university, one essential core of an alternative region. It has a lively significant local quarterly called *Event*. The New York State plan already referred to calls for other such potential medium metropolitan centers.

Around the country, Nashville, Hartford, Spokane, and Des Moines, among many possible cities, are of size, character, and "independent" location, not too close in the suction orbit of a great metropolis, to serve as illustrations of the case for intentional increase.

There is, of course, a typically American danger in recommended expansion: that it then simply goes wild, producing all the undesirable and ugly excesses of, say, the new Phoenix boom area in the Southwest, repeating the old speculative drives and mistakes in accentuated, expanded, automobilized form. We must avoid conceiving of growth as an infinite upward spiral. It is worthwhile, therefore, to consider what size a city needs to reach to have the cultural and market-place characteristics and stimuli and varieties of choice of the massive metropolis and still retain its relatively humane internal quality and relation to the countryside. How large the middle-sized metropolis?

Zurich as a Beau Ideal

I would say that a city of around 500,000 can achieve the kind of life and animation we are seeking, the atmosphere and accoutrements of the population-great metropolis. In place of theoretical argument here, I will describe the city of Zurich, my favorite exemplar. Population, 460,000. First-class department stores, a galaxy of specialty shops, smart fashion shops, gourmet centers, big business and office buildings, banks, important newspapers and weeklies. To give the flavor, let me summarize, from my last visit there, the entertainment section in *Zürcher Woche*, "Diese Woche in Zurich" ("This Week in Zurich"):

Four theaters, mainly repertory: plays by Giraudoux, Nestroy, Zuckmayer, and Beckett.

Opera House: *Don Giovanni, Falstaff,* and operettas.

Kongresshaus: ballet, including performances by the National Korean Company; Bishop Kelsey's Spiritual and Gospel Festival from the United States.

Twelve commercial art galleries: shows include

---

[4] Consider a few random examples from our remarkable widespread cultural explosion:

Opera newly set up in Kansas City, Missouri (population 475,000); the Performing Arts Foundation formed last year says, "Kansas City needs to feel the pride of creation." The North Carolina School of the Arts in Winston-Salem (111,135), whose voice department is headed by Rose Bampton of the Met. The outstanding Tyrone Guthrie theater in Minneapolis (482,000). In *Life* of Apr. 2, 1965, we read: "O'Casey in Seattle, Chekhov in Milwaukee, Euripides in Houston. Name any world-famous playwright and you'll find his works in repertory across the country." There are thirty such distinguished repertory theaters.

1. *Bahnhofstrasse*

2. *Import Fair in the Hallen Stadium*

Alternative to The Great City:
Middle-Sized Zurich

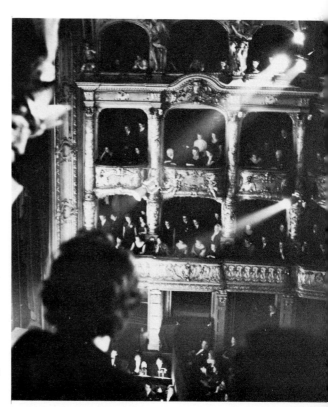

3. *Opera*

4. City

5. Altstadt

6. Countryside: an easy walk

139

Pollock, de Kooning, Pop Art, Surrealists, and Italian Still Life from Caravaggio to de Chirico and Morandi.

The Kronenhalle Restaurant at the threshold of the University Quarter has on its walls paintings by Braque, Picasso, Matisse, Klee, and Chagall.

Note, please, that this rich variety of events and opportunities (and many others, including some delightful cabarets and night clubs, and a variety of museums, of course) were available during a week in early spring, in the nontourist season.

This is a city that sparkles, that is always animating and various, without that frenetic character, huge size, and fantastic traffic that we have come to feel are the price we must pay for sparkle, animation, and variety. Within less than twenty minutes, the countryside!

I am far from maintaining here that to provide the best life, a city needs to be 460,000 or 500,000. All I am saying is that a city of around 500,000 population can supply the excitements and splendors and varied choices and cultural experiences and opportunities that our macrometropolis does— can be a challenge to our macrometropolis *on its own terms,* and often a superior alternative to it.

2. *Galaxies of Smaller Cities.* A second type of urban region where growth should be encouraged, as alternative and competitor to the great metropolitan areas, consists of galaxies of small cities of special promise and perhaps of already special achievement in manufacturing, education, research, abundant cheap power (available or potential) and scenic values. An example is the Piedmont Crescent in North Carolina, with a present total population of 1.5 million in an area of some 6,000 square miles, and with about 60 per cent of this population in a dozen cities, the largest of which is Charlotte, with 200,000. These are still-distinct, well-separated communities which could be very substantially increased, probably *should be doubled intentionally* by 1980. By sensitive planning and determined land-use control involving public ownership, we could keep free and productive land between them, avoid the fringe-and-ooze-together of the already fringed-and-oozed viscous great metropolitan area. Within this Piedmont Crescent, there are important specialized assets: Duke University in Durham, the University of North Carolina in Chapel Hill, and North Carolina State in Raleigh (the Research Triangle); a natural subarea is the Five Cities area, in which Winston-Salem, Greensboro, and High Point are the best-known cities.

There is a tremendous opportunity in such areas

if it is grasped in good time (now) and we do not repeat our other monumental carelessnesses and drifts into unmanageability. This second alternative to megalopolis could have a distinctive new kind of pattern: no single predominant metropolitan center or focus, but a distribution of foci and regional functions into a total configuration that Clarence Stein calls the "regional city." A regional city would be not a major city in the ordinary sense. It would be a constellation of distinctive moderate-sized communities, separated by open areas but bound closely by "townless highways" that would not pierce them. Each constituent town would have its own size, character, and cultural elements, including all the day-to-day activities and attractions of any American community. But there would be no parochialism, because the towns would be performing complementary regional functions, and there would be constant intervisiting related to these higher functions. Such a galaxy forming a regional city could of course equally well or better be composed of New Towns.[5]

Another example, different but of this galaxy character, is the well-located, well-variegated triangle of Albany (the capital of New York State) and Schenectady and Troy (industrial and educational). By the way, this area is similar, in miniature, to the Randstad in Holland; or at any rate, this was true until a few years ago: the oozing together and overlapping development may now have gone too far. Such situations are indeed galloping away from us in the ubiquitous spread of speculative *laissez faire.*

Let us note still another example of both the galaxy type, and of a quite small-scale metropolis-region type—as prototype or forerunner of the potential of such areas, in this epoch of genuine cultural decentralization not of the hand-me-down variety but of genuine distinction. It is known as the Tri-Cities area in the Southern Tier (south center) of New York State. The three cities are Binghamton (population 75,000), Endicott (18,000), and Johnson City (21,000). All three have interesting cultural activities. The latter two have substantial industrial base (among other enterprises a major IBM plant, ANSCO, General Electric, and large

[5] Studies in the United States and in England point strongly to the conclusion that when a city's population gets much beyond 150,000, there is a rise in capital and operating costs and thus in taxes. In these days of rising taxes for improvements in education, welfare, etc., we have here an additional factor in favor of the regional-city concept. K. S. Lomax in *Journal Royal Statistical Society,* 1943, pp. 51–59; Werner Z. Hirsch in *Review of Economics & Statistics,* August, 1959, pp. 232–241.

shoe-manufacturing plants of Endicott-Johnson). Binghamton is the leader, the capital of Broome County and the focus of a charming small region. It is situated on the Chenango River, which curves through it, and on the Susquehanna, which borders it.

Binghamton has a remarkable and quite various cultural life that flourishes with distinction on three planes: audience, adult learner, and active artistic participant. The city's alert educational institutions include a state university, the Civic Theater and its heavily participated-in workshop; the Tri-Cities Opera workshop.[6] In addition, Binghamton is the locus of Roberson Memorial Center. This is a dynamic cultural influence and beacon beautifully set on the banks of the Chenango, in the heart of the city. It functions as an arts council; it is the home of ten groups and provides facilities for *forty-five* others. The basic ten are the:

Fine Arts Society
Folk Dancers
Garden Center
Historical Society
Musical Arts Society
Photographic Society
Potters' Guild
Science Association
World Affairs Council
Astronomy Society

All this cultural-entertainment ebullience is not just a summer-festival sort of thing, but lasts throughout the year. And it is locally inspired, locally sustained and sustaining.

What does this case illustrate? In Zurich, as a middle-sized metropolis, we have in actuality the full equivalent, on a more humane scale, of what our present vast metropolises offer. In the Piedmont Crescent of North Carolina, as a galaxy of small cities, we have the potential of such equivalence. In the Binghamton Tri-Cities area, there is not such an equivalence or challenge to it. But we find that in terms of twentieth-century affluence, cultural command, and technology, such a smaller galaxy is no longer a backwater, and has several elements uniquely its own. There is a much greater permeation and intensity of creative cultural *participation* and *contribution* by far larger numbers of individuals (as compared with higher and more frequent

major-metropolis peaks of spectator culture). There are a face-to-face personal intimacy, a significance of the individual, and a close awareness of the polis that no major or even middle-sized city offers. And there is an urban-rural interpenetration, not just proximity, that is deeply satisfying. These are the twentieth-century small-region values that the Binghamton area represents.

3. *Development of New (Almost New) Areas.* There is a third type of alternative to the growth of megalopolis: intentional accentuated development of regions where development patterns and land use are still sufficiently unformed that all our best mid-twentieth-century technology, social understanding and thinking, and dawning efforts in regional architectural synthesis and design can be fully brought to bear. Among these, out of a number of potential areas, are the Columbia Valley region in the Northwest, the Tennessee Valley Authority region, and Appalachia. We shall consider the latter two.

The TVA region is an almost unfair example, with its already well-developed regional-planned power resources, important industries and agriculture, natural and man-made recreation areas, its high level of social and government extension services, its few small cities and its towns of various sizes. But here is an area which, even in its present state of relative well-being, could gain much by very considerable planned increases in population and enterprise, New Towns, regional-city groupings, and diverse and more excellent cultural resources. And it is still a relatively virgin area in terms of its relatively low degree of urban developemnt and the still very close physical and social relationship between urban settlements and productive rural land. A sensitive and knowledgeable person to whom I mentioned the TVA region in this context went even further. He felt that there is a modern-day experiment and yardstick function for TVA in terms of humane living, a challenging successor to its power yardstick function of thirty years ago, and an important complement of it.

Our second example is Appalachia. At the mention of Appalachia one's first reaction is to equate it with poverty, backwardness, exhaustion or competitive killing of its major resource of coal, national headache, halting government efforts at improvement by way of a road-building program and maybe tourism. But surprisingly, to me at least, large portions of Appalachia are found to have already partially developed the potentialities for a fresh and exciting future such as we have been visualizing in considering other areas. It is not only a "new" re-

---

[6] Broome County has in the workshop one of the finest nonprofessional operatic groups in the country. According to a report in the New York *Times* of Sept. 13, 1965, it is being transformed into a full-time professional opera company. The Ballet Society is to be a full-scale regional ballet company.

Nervi in Norfolk, Virginia (population 304,869)

The middle-sized city effectively reaches for distinction.

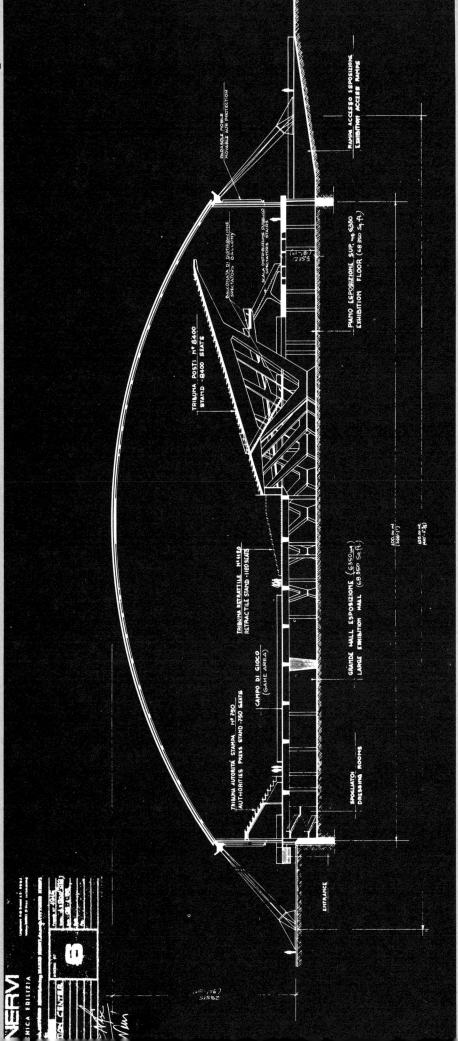

NERVI

NICA EDILIZIA

6

PARASOLE MOBILE
MOVABLE SUN PROTECTION

RAMPA ACCESSO ESPOSIZIONE
EXHIBITION ACCESS RAMPS

TRIBUNA POSTI N° 8400
STAND · 8400 SEATS

BALCONATA DI DISTRIBUZIONE
SPECTATOR GALLERY

SALA DISTRIBUZIONE PUBBLICO
SPECTATOR'S FOYER

6,515
(21'-8")

PIANO ESPOSIZIONE SUP. ≃ 6350
EXHIBITION FLOOR (68 350 Sq.ft.)

TRIBUNA RETRATTILE N° 1120
RETRACTILE STAND · 1120 SEATS

CAMPO DI GIOCO
(GAME AREA)

GRANDE HALL ESPOSIZIONE (6350 m²)
LARGE EXHIBITION HALL (68 350 Sq.ft.)

TRIBUNA AUTORITÀ STAMPA N° 780
AUTHORITIES PRESS STAND · 780 SEATS

SPOGLIATOI
DRESSING ROOMS

ENTRANCE

100,00 ml
(328'-1")

125,00 ml
(410'-2")

28515

1 and 2. *For a focal location: Nervi is designing a 12,000-seat auditorium and exhibit hall, and a 2,500-seat theater.*

Alternative: Galaxies of Smaller Cities
Piedmont Crescent, North Carolina

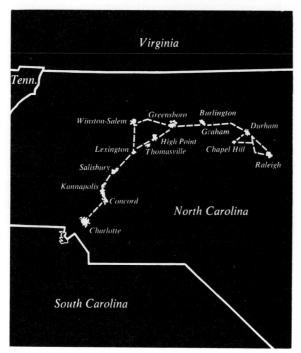

1. *Location*

2. *Configuration*

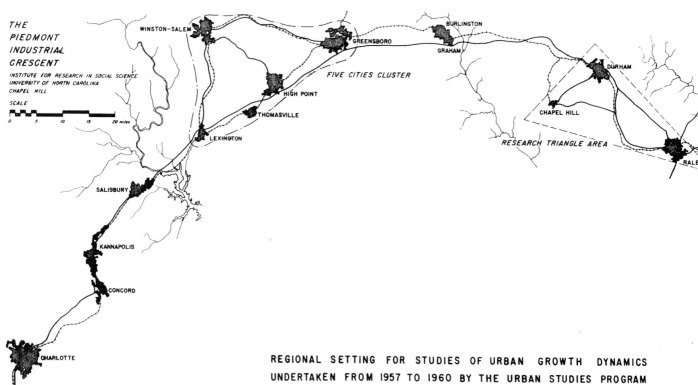

REGIONAL SETTING FOR STUDIES OF URBAN GROWTH DYNAMICS
UNDERTAKEN FROM 1957 TO 1960 BY THE URBAN STUDIES PROGRAM

gion, but it strikingly illustrates our leit motiv that trend is not destiny, but can be changed.

Appalachia had been in the course of intentional and effective change some years when government got around to it. I first learned this stirring fact when I saw a full-page ad in the New York *Times* of September 3, 1965: the American Electric Power System was spending $370 million to produce an additional 2 million kilowatts of power in Appalachia. Obviously the AEP's planning and commitments must have preceded the government's efforts, for such big enterprises take years to plan, to program, to schedule before construction begins. I found that they had, by about ten years. An AEP official infomed me that this expansion was based on anticipated "natural" demand growth and, heavily, on what he called "promoted growth." This was a combination of technical research to produce cheaper power and hence attract industry, helping communities to become more attractive to the kind of skilled and technical personnel that industry would bring, and what is commonly thought of as normal promotion by business.

The story briefly: Anticipating general further growth of the aluminum industry in particular and an imminent rise in cost of hydroelectric power, on which this industry had always relied for its vast requirements, the AEP visualized that coal might again come into its own. So it intensively studied and researched two related possibilities: that of making coal cheaply available by mine mechanization, and that of developing more efficient coal-produced power. The AEP succeeded in both projects. Kaiser Aluminum has opened a large new smelter in the Ohio Valley; Olin Mathieson also. A dramatic aspect of resuscitation of coal by mechanization is this: One of the greatest blows to the old coal industry and the employment it provided was loss of the home-heating market to oil and gas heat. Now, with the new cheap electricity available through the use of coal, electric heating of homes is making rapid strides. Already two million homes in the United States are heated this way. Thus coal, kicked out as a direct source of heat, comes back by way of electric heating as well as newly competitive source of power.

In Appalachia, then, by human determination and resourcefulness, we see under way the beginnings of a dramatic reversal of trend. And we have a great opportunity for regional development in a highly scenic area of natural attractions, in relatively virginal conditions (this whole major area contains only three cities of over 100,000 population). A happy statistic: in the state of West Virginia there is ½ acre of open space for every man, woman, and child, i.e., the incredible figure of 500 acres per thousand persons is available. We ought to make of Appalachia a wonderful exemplar of all that we now know of dynamic and effective development, of nonspeculative land accumulation and optimum use, of nature creatively preserved and developed close at hand, of the various essentials of creative living well related and handsomely articulated in design. Thus we can fulfill the promise in the economic start that has been here briefly sketched out, by producing a rounded and unique region physically, socially, economically, ecologically.

But will we? We can, but we must be highly vigilant. In the first place, the present program for Appalachia is not a massive attack, a steering of government contracts, and thus industry. Of the $1.1 billion appropriated, 76 per cent is for roads in eleven states, stretched over a six-year period; some money for airports, water resources and sewage treatment, etc. Important but meager. Certainly not a great push. Also, we must insist on applying the best of what we know in this century, and sternly rule out the laissez-faire opportunism which is only too likely to take hold in the wake of, or accompanying, the government's program. Consider two instances which warrant this alarm.

Strip mining, which one used to associate with desperate ex-miners out of work, scratching a bare living out of the hillside with hand tools, is no longer that sort of undertaking at all. It is in reality a huge industry in which major and very respectable corporations with giant equipment have destroyed and continue to destroy millions of acres, making them useless for the future. This goes on, destroying land at a far greater rate than our conservation efforts for redwoods, for sand dunes, and for wildernesses can save in generations. [7]

On another plane, we find forms of spoliation that are more familiar to us. In the Long Island *Newsday* of April 11, 1966, reporter Bernie Bookbinder writes of his visit to Appalachia. He says that in many places no progress is visible.

> Then, suddenly, one encounters spectacular progress. Outside Abingdon, Va., a once-pastoral crossroads has been transformed into a modernistic complex of motels, restaurants and gas stations by the construction of four-lane Interstate Route 81. The change is so striking that the Appalachian

[7] Only one state, Kentucky, with Governor Breathitt's determined pushing, has recently taken measures to begin to bring these disastrous activities under control.

Alternative: The Small Galaxy,
the Small Metropolis

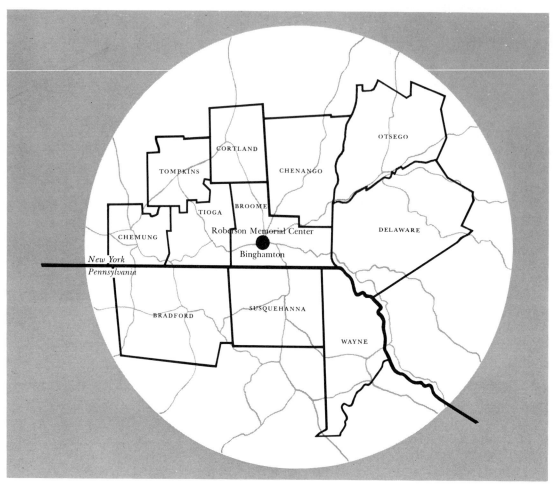

1. *Binghamton, the Center*

2. *Town and Country*

146

Roberson Memorial Center

Board of Directors

Director and Staff

Museum Functions
Exhibitions
Planetarium
House of Science

Educational Functions
Classes
School Class Tours
TV Programs
Workshops

General Cultural Functions
Concerts and Recitals
Lectures
Plays
Films
Seminars
"Open House"
Talent Contests
Vocational Guidance

Regional Museum Service Center
(Proposed)

**Eleven
Constituent
Organizations**

Astronomical Society
Binghamton Museum
of Fine Arts
Civic Theatre
Fine Arts Society
Roberson Folk Dancers
Garden Center
Broome County Historical Society
Musical Arts Society
Photographic Center
Potters' Guild
World Affairs Council

…working with
the Center's Director
through a
Program Council

**Forty-Two
Affiliated Societies**

American Guild of Organists
Antique Society
Ansco Camera Club
Beta Sigma Phi
Broome Tech. Science Club
Chamber Music Society
Choral Society of Triple Cities
Civic Music Association of Southern Tier
The Clef Club
Community Ambassador Project
Community Symphony Society
Endwell Camera Club
Harmony Club
Naturalists Club
SPSE (Society of Photographic
Scientists & Engineers)
Southern Tier Aquarium Society
Tri-Cities Opera
Vocano Musical Society
and 23 Garden Clubs
in 14 communities

3. Cultural Heart

The People of Binghamton, Endicott,
Johnson City and 11 Counties in the
Upper Valley of the Susquehanna
in New York and Pennsylvania

Regional Commission's plan to build 2,350 miles of development highways over a six-year period prompts visions of a new Appalachia.

A new Appalachia indeed! One can just visualize this crossroads complex, because one has seen this kind of shambles a thousand times. Are we doomed always to repeat our errors and excesses? Cannot the government, which is so sensitive about beauty and roadside billboards, attach real conditions to its grants for roads and public works, so that this fresh region will not be disfigured in a fundamental way?

In the new regions, then, we don't leave the eternally crucial issues behind. We are simply given a splendid chance to move in uncrowded, potentially great areas where speculative land prices have still not taken hold and where we are physically able to start almost freshly. It is up to us to do a significant and creative job.

How Do We Do It?

Of course, in this country there is rightly no enforceable way to channel people into one area or region as compared to another, even if it is agreed that the results will be most desirable. But there are all sorts of very legitimate occasions for powerfully influencing movements: such as a creative location policy for the superhighway system, for government manufacturing contracts and hence plants, for national and state government regional offices, for research and educational contracts, for various types of subsidy and special programs.

In fact, location of government enterprises is right now and almost daily having a powerful effect on regional development and prosperity and growth, as in the case of the Space Center at Houston and the Rocket Center in Florida, or, negatively, as in the relative neglect of areas in the Middle West. But location is haphazard, a matter of pressures and short-time decisions, not the purposeful expression of a debated and adopted national policy which it should be and must be. Another factor of great potency is the location of new educational and research institutions, now in a state of sharp growth, and expansion of less powerful existing ones. A first-class example of using this factor is the creative meshing of the New York State plan and the great new expansion of institutions of higher education by the University of the State of New York.[8]

[8] This New York State plan, which has been referred to at a number of points, has been published under the title *Change, Challenge, Response*. It is an excellent contribution to regional development, after one has skipped its Madison Avenue introductions.

Another illustration of the idea that one need not simply rely on and extrapolate upward the concentrations of a Boston–Cambridge, of a Berkeley–Stanford–Palo Alto, is being given dramatic exemplification by the burgeoning Graduate Research Center for the Southwest and the Southwest Center of Advanced Studies, a remarkable institution now set up at Dallas, which is changing the intellectual climate of the South. While in some respects it starts from scratch, it is utilizing and enhancing a number of existing educational institutions. This kind of creative crystallization is an emerging indicator of the possibilities of newly adjusting regional balances, and of what can be accomplished, with vision and determination, to counter trend.

Adventure and settlement of new areas is still a vital impulse of Americans. Witness the present surges into Florida, California, and Arizona. Witness that as a race of modern nomads, we change residence and move on, once in five years on the national average. So *purposeful* redisposition of (mainly future) population, instead of further overcrowding the old areas and newly overcrowding the favored new areas, harmonizes with our traditional and still vital impulse.

But in these matters a common sense of urgency is sadly absent. There is a widespread lack of consciousness, or there is a lack of willingness to face up to the need for, and benefit from creative *intentional* change. The problem is to enhance the ingrained impulse for change and make its realization more fully humane, by the over-all intentional configuration and regional disposition of administrative and regional government and other locations that this late stage of pioneering requires. Let us devote enough resources and inducements and determination to these varied regional programs to make them compellingly attractive, both to relieve further macrometropolitan accretion and to give new attainable choices to our twentieth century. In other words, we have a dual opportunity. We can employ our insights and techniques to creating syntheses and designs for unprecedented levels of environment. And by the very process of absorbing growth into the new alternative areas, we can make solutions of the old regions' problems more attainable. Thus, at this climactic point in our march forward, we do the same dual job as at every preceding stage: by achievement of the creative new, we can make possible the creative rebuilding of the old.

All this adds up to a modern-day "winning of the West," a new fulfillment of our nation's ethos and destiny.

We have been through an Odyssey of words and concepts. We have tried to visualize a coherent set of objectives and steer a course toward and into them, at the various interlinked scales of modern living.

We have sought to distinguish between genuinely inevitable trend, which covers much less of an arc on the whole horizon of the future than we habitually assume, and our field of choice and, finally, our chosen directions.

We have worked out the elements of attainable and better, purposefully changed, physical-ecological-social environments, from the city neighborhood through the metropolitan complex, and beyond into fresher, pioneering regional alternatives. We have covered substance, arrangement, reasons, aspirations.

What, Finally, Are We Seeking?

The thesis of this whole presentation is twofold:

First, we have it within our grasp to create substantively better environment. However, this will not come in any automatic way from our technological equipment; it will come only if we master in moral terms the essentially amoral new implements, choose among them with connected insight and determination. We must be not victims of an uncontrolled cacophony, but composers of a great symphony.

Second, no matter how excellent the planning that flows from such thinking through, it will not alone achieve ultimate consummation in human terms. To achieve this, the planning must be continuously and unceasingly infused with architectural synthesis at every scale, and sublimation with nature and social and individual life. It is only this interpenetration which speaks with fully emotional power to the human spirit. The architecture is not superior to the plan or to the social operation. But unless these are inextricably intermeshed, none of them reaches its full flowering, none creates emotional wholeness.

Living Architecture: Cradled in Contact with Natural and Social Science

Achievement of this ultimate climax of validity and excellence in architectural expression requires that two conditions inextricably accompany and grow up with the plan formulation.

One condition is that all development, including all urban development, be cradled in nature, be always aware of natural process, have both respect

CHAPTER ELEVEN

SYNTHESIS AND SUBLIMATION: ORGANIC ARCHITECTURE

for natural science and an ethical respect and feeling for terrain and for organic contact. This condition is temporarily obscured by our powerful technology, on two planes. On the gross plane, nature is brutally violated, and the penalties are murderous and massive, as in air pollution, water pollution, disastrous flooding of flood-plain areas that never should have been lived on, erosion due to crass and massive bulldozing. On the subtle plane, by our prideful, wanton command of technology we push nature and natural process, awareness of growth cycle, further and further from the texture of our lives. This kind of sacrilege is less strident, but is no doubt ultimately more brutalizing and lethal for mankind. We must roll back these negatives and fully discover and develop the grand positives. The great point is that we as human beings are no less steeped in nature even though our agriculture is one hundred times more productive, and more distant, our air-transport speed supersonic, our space conquest ever more heroic.

The other condition is this: Staying within this ambit of nature, utilizing nature both as foundation and as an enhancing design element, we fuse with it the individual and social needs and reactions of man, an area in which the social sciences have helped to create and then sharpen our insights. We then produce architecture which is not merely (and only in its highest manifestations) a series of handsome large-scale tours de force, but an inevitable and magnificent expression of our time, significant and possibly breath-taking at all scales and a continuum of sharply articulated scales.

Two Cases, Macroscopic and Microcosmic

Consider now two illustrative cases, the one large and famous, a major and esteemed contribution, the other of an almost anonymous nature in any sense of large prestige. By an initial dramatic contrast, I mean to highlight the equal significance and equal claims of all scales, as well as their sharp differentiation. In this chapter, these and several later examples act as representatives of the whole range. To do appreciably more would take a textbook devoted to this thesis only. (In particular, the design consummation of New Towns, which play so large a part in our thinking and strategy, cannot be carried further here.)

New York's Central Park. The first case is Central Park in New York City, a major city recreational asset, a precious and loved civic ornament in the highest sense.

The establishment, a hundred years or so ago,

of so large an in-city public park, the first one of its kind in this country, was a major act of civic and social statesmanship. Whoever had been entrusted with its design would, of course, have carried out the program and created an important recreational and park resource. But let us see what extraordinary dimensions its designer Olmsted brought to it, not parts of the stated program, that have made it incomparably more useful and emotionally releasing, a genuinely re-creative experience rather than just an area for recreation.[1]

A few specific points will bring these phrases alive. There was a competition to choose who would design the park. The competition program contained the requirement that there be four through-traffic arteries from east to west, through the park. Of all the thirty-two submissions, Olmsted's was the only one which grade-separated this through traffic from pedestrian and vehicular park circulation. And this some thirty-five years before the first automobile! An anticipation inspired by architectural planning, and so skillfully and masterfully designed into the natural topography that from within the park one is not visually or aurally aware of the cross-traffic. Vast enhancement on two planes by the architecture and landscape architecture.

First, then, there was intuitive foresighted enhancement of the program. Second, there was permeation of architectural synthesis.

Now, for other brilliant elements, turn to Olmsted himself:

> The park is to be surrounded by an artificial wall twice as high as the Great Wall of China, composed of urban buildings. Wherever this should appear across the meadow view the imagination would be checked abruptly at short range. Natural objects were thus required to be interposed which, while excluding the buildings as much as possible from view, would leave an uncertainty as to the occupation of the space beyond. . . . The constant suggestion to the imagination of an unlimited range of rural conditions . . . to the visitor, carried by occasional defiles from one field of landscape to another in which a wholly different series of details [experiences] is presented, the extent of the park is practically much greater than it would otherwise be. . . .
>
> The time will come when New York will be built up, when all the grading and filling will be done and when the picturesquely varied rocky formations of the land will have been converted into formations for rows of monotonous straight streets and piles of great buildings. . . . Then the

---

[1] As it nearly was, and would have been had the initial design of the park engineer been used.

Central Park,
New York City

Civic impulse, purpose and program fructified, enhanced, multiplied by architectural intuition, understanding and prevision of their still undisclosed future.

1. *In the heart of the city?*

2. *Indeed in the heart of the city.*

Courtyard: Minimal House in India

The involved architect produces a cell of inspired environment.
(See page 154 for discussion.)

priceless value of the present picturesque outlines of the ground will be more distinctly perceived . . . the constant suggestion of an unlimited range of rural conditions. . . .[2]

And so he kept—and indeed in many places and in many ways enhanced—the rockiness of nature, the quietudes and the contrasts of nature, in the heart of the crowded city.

How vastly important and how vastly successful Olmsted's contributions have proved to be. Thus, to start with, there was the grand civic impulse and concept and action as the jumping-off place; and how incomparably fructified by the environment shaper. This is the kind of interpenetration of understandings and excellences and skills and motivations of various character and levels that we must demand of ourselves in order to create a happier twentieth-century environment.

A Small Community Center, Anywhere. Now turn to a quite different situation and scale, for our urban regional symphony comprises both, in a sort of moral and social theme. Consider the community facilities appurtenant to a low-cost housing development. Individually, physically small: a great contrast in scale to our great Central Park. Yet in one major sense, there is a seeming contrast only. There could be no better illustration of a "minor" design job not at all minor in the intensity of its social importance in each case. Indeed, this intensity is quite major, and so is the cumulative effect on our national life of the thousands of such situations around the country. There could be no better illustration of the need for decentralization of excellence: these "small," rather prestigeless situations cry out for the best imagination, skill, and devotion that we command.

The space program for the community center in a low-cost housing development generally calls for so many square feet, divided into classrooms and committee rooms, craft room, kitchen, maybe a larger room for auditorium. There are variations, more and less elaborate. This layout is the jumping-off place, the bare bones. What is the function of the center? Briefly, it serves as a social and social-educational focus for the life and self-expression of the community. Where is this function met? Sometimes the square feet are found in one or several basements, with no daylight, or gray light from areaway windows. Sometimes the center is raised to the first-floor level, where the

column spacing, determined by typical floor columns above, produces different awkward conditions. An outsider doesn't too readily locate these centers because there is usually no identification, to say nothing of the kind of stirring identification that would be commensurate with their stirring function and potential. In much rarer cases, there is a separate wing, and in a very few, a separate building.

But whatever it is, my close observation over a long period is that to most architects [3] the community center is an appendage, a small mechanically laid-out element hung on to a large project, not a challenging social-architectural obligation and opportunity. And this is exactly what it should be, must become, even granting the minimal budget. The architect must want to create an aura, a sense of pride and allegiance, a visible invitation to those within the development and beyond. He must want to sit down with local social workers and thinkers, with neighborhood people, and absorb as raw material their thinking and experience and outlook, sublimate their mute or latent aspirations, produce DESIGN, HUMAN EVOCATION. He must *live through* the process of design at first hand, not merely accept predigested "requirements."

To put a point on this: I was once called in as a consultant by a neighborhood organization to comment on the community center in a large low-rental development. Leaving aside interior layout and function and relationship to other site and surrounding elements, important as they are, note only two facts which symbolize the situation and the crucial attitudes:

The two-story community center was attached to one of the tall residential buildings, not because there was any functional or three-dimensional rationale in this, but just because this was a convenient thing to do. The site plan of tall buildings had been arrived at without particular regard to the small community element. To have allowed this to stand would have made it evident that visually and spiritually this was just an afterthought, whereas we considered it the heart of this development and of the neighborhood. It had to have separate location and *separate identity* to express that. After a considerable hassle and numerous alternative sketches as challenges, this end was finally agreed to. But the building was still to be of the same dull red brick as the total job, again a denial of its identity and symbolic importance. Again a hassle to establish the viewpoint that this was well worth bothering about,

[2] Frederick Law Olmsted, *Forty Years of Landscape Architecture,* G. P. Putnam's Sons, New York, 1928, p. 239.

[3] Or, rather, to most architectural offices, because in general the architect himself doesn't fool around with this small matter.

well worth arousing the public authority's attention about; and then the job of bearding him. Finally we attained not the stirring design crystallization of a deeply important function, but at least not a denial and a denigration of this.

Bear in mind that this halfway case is better than all but a few. And bear in mind, too, that in the case of the open-space-community equivalent we are scarcely this far, except in a negligibly small number of cases. In the vast nonproject areas in our cities, and generally even in the urban renewal and rehabilitation areas, we do not set up those social plazas and community activity foci so modest in cost, so pregnant in effect, which were particularly emphasized in the urban renewal chapter under "Creative Dispersion of Renewal."

Still Lower in Scale, and Upward

Now let us trace an adventurous path from the basic nucleus of living and design through to great regional compositions and quests. We will pursue architectural sensitivities and sublimations at a number of stages or scales that are a symbiosis with the substantive development elements and with the social sensitivity and natural environment. This will not, of course, be a fully satisfying continuous path, because we do not yet have a full range of significant points to stop at along the way.

To begin with, let us see how the small low-cost family unit has in sensitive hands (though too rarely) commanded imaginative thought and study, leading to an architectural resolution of perhaps even more thoroughness and imagination than the XYZ Bank and Trust Company's new 60-story monument.

The first case is Matthew Nowicki's perspective sketch for low-cost living quarters in a proposed new city in India, illustrated on page 152. There, the climate is burning in summer, and the wind is strong and searing. The people are still villagers really, in psychology and in social habits. Since independence, hundreds of thousands of dwellings have been built in cities for such people, refugees from partition and immigrants from rural areas. The answer has invariably been the quick, mass job: long ribbons of white stucco flats. That is, shelter. Nowicki reconsidered and reformulated. He designed a row house, tiny because the people are poor. But it has at its heart the inner courtyard giving refuge from the murderous heat, glare, and harsh winds: a close response to natural conditions. Socially, the courtyard re-creates the family and household center and restimulates the familiar psy-

chological security of inward-lookingness. Note too the grace of the upper passage and the familiar wall graffiti, which the people themselves do. An epitome of all the factors we emphasize. Truly, the essence of its region and the heart of its nation.

Another example at this nuclear scale. William Kessler was given the job of designing a public housing development for large families. The program handed out for the four-bedroom unit, a program handed out a thousand times, was so many square feet total area for the dwelling, so many square feet for each bedroom (to contain listed furniture requirements), so many square feet for living room–dining area–kitchen. Now everyone who has given thought to how large families live knows that everyone is always on top of everyone else: no separate place for lessons, no place for kids to entertain friends, kids under foot in the kitchen, nothing corresponding to the middle-class family room. Kessler had observed these matters, and he pondered. He came up with a simple, brilliant answer. By reducing the bedrooms, with the exception of the master bedroom, to the minimum size that could hold the furniture, he managed to save enough space to create an extra room for the kids— for study, for games, for entertainment of their friends. Functionally this was very much better than, or at least a fine alternative to, the traditional arrangement. And the extra dimension gave a psychological lift by making possible a more self-regarding way of life.

Our third case in this series is an effort to close a suddenly recognized multiple individual and social gap in social possibilities outside the home. In this case, an architectural solution has been arrived at which is really an inevitable translation of a new social formulation into physical structure.

In an existing large-scale low-rent housing community which was experiencing critical breakdowns of real community, architect and social students jointly noted the following conditions. The very large families had the usual quite inadequate social space in the home, as in the Kessler example; there was an intense need for some reasonable supplementation for boy to meet girl or indeed for any family member to satisfy reasonable social needs. Among the assets of the development was a central community building with space available for groups, committees, organized activity of many kinds. But the key word was "organized," as contrasted with spontaneous. The available social area was located on the second floor, above management and rent-paying operations. Because of this, and because of its sizable physical distance from the homes of many

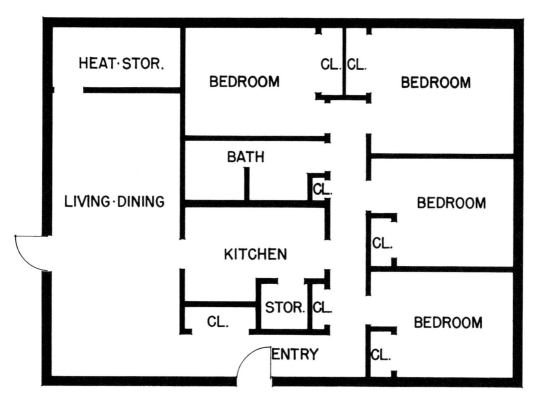

The involved architect transforms the normal stereotyped space (above)

into family-social potential. (See page 154 for discussion.)

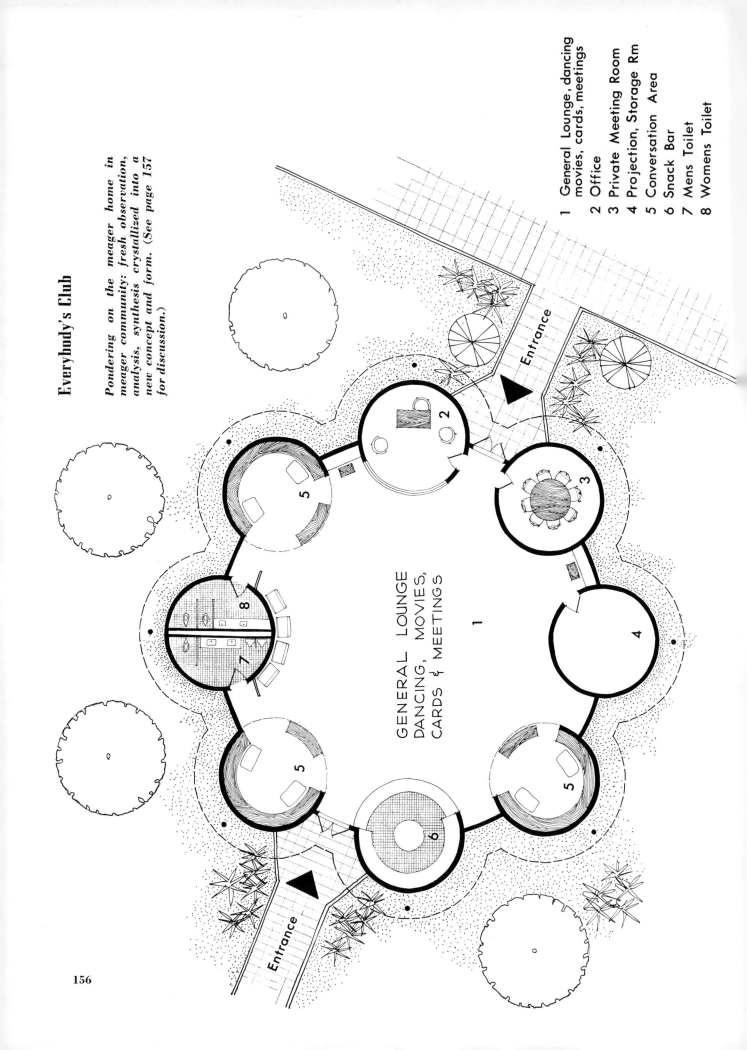

Everybody's Club

Pondering on the meager home in meager community: fresh observation, analysis, synthesis crystallized into a new concept and form. (See page 157 for discussion.)

1 General Lounge, dancing
 movies, cards, meetings
2 Office
3 Private Meeting Room
4 Projection, Storage Rm
5 Conversation Area
6 Snack Bar
7 Mens Toilet
8 Womens Toilet

GENERAL LOUNGE
DANCING, MOVIES,
CARDS & MEETINGS

Entrance

Entrance

of the residents in the large community, the place was certainly not a drop-in place or a casual one. There really was no warm or magnetic place that could meet ordinary social needs, unstructured needs that had never been consciously uncovered and formulated.

Suddenly out of these facts and gaps a new concept was born, on the social plane and almost simultaneously in the architectural form that had to embody it. We called it "Everybody's Club." Its purpose was to be to accommodate anybody who wanted to drop in, just to have a Coke, to meet a few friends, to have the date that couldn't be accommodated in the flat, to play checkers or cards, or to listen to music. There would be an occasional dance or entertainment. What was needed, at low cost, was a place with spaces of various sizes, from fairly intimate niches with a sense of privacy and freedom up to a considerable central space with an atmosphere of natural, unobtrusive control—and with flexibility and merging of space, to structure the unstructured, as it were.

The architectural plan (page 156) worked out of these requirements is a multifoliated form that embodies the multiple social needs. It is a form that uniquely expresses what is taking place socially, and gives psychological identification to the community of which the meeting place is the core. A new form to meet a newly recognized need, not just a denatured minimal hand-me-down that is good enough.

These three cases have this in common: by fresh observation a fresh humane synthesis has been reached; really new, rather than mass-standardized programs and solutions have been achieved.

Another example of rethinking with a fresh result. One of the shibboleths of the housing world is low coverage, lots of open space. So where high density is required, i.e., large number of families per acre, the unavoidable answer has been tall buildings. But we have learned that for families with children this is an unhealthy solution, because the children are separated from their natural play habitat, on the ground. This is the current general impasse. In the La Puntilla low-cost housing development in old San Juan, Puerto Rico (see illustrations), architect Jan Wampler has gone back to his sources and articulated them in a forward direction. He produces a close-knit 5-story network of high coverage, a high degree of social interaction, a tropical urban pattern of interior courts and dense shade, akin in feeling to old San Juan itself, surrounded and penetrated by park and recreational space.

The next stopping point. By some mental quirk, housing, which is of course the very center and base of good living and of civic virtue, has in our consciousness a kind of status to one side as a necessity, is not seen as an opportunity for exuberant civic expression. In our enormous volumes of city construction, the glitter and the glamour go with the great office buildings, the monuments of corporate competition and identification, the outsized centers of various kinds. Housing at practically any level of income is by contrast undistinguished, and its neighborhoods in general are indistinguishable.

This is particularly true, of course, of areas of middle and lower incomes. It is characteristic of both large new developments and rehabilitated areas, which are absorbing more and more of our effort. In both types of undertaking, there is the same underlying assumption: if better creature comforts are assured and run-down exterior shabbiness is exorcised by repairs and fresh paint and tree planting, then we are achieving our purpose. This assumption, of course, determines policy. A new spiritual-architectural *lift* in the environment is not being sought. Indeed, it is sought to make new construction, as unobtrusive as possible, a "vest-pocket development." But creature comfort and cleanliness are far from satisfying the full need of people, as thirty years of public housing and some years of active rehabilitation have made clear. Personal and social identification have rarely been achieved except sometimes in a negative sense. The neighborhood has probably not deteriorated further, but no one claims or proclaims a psychological naissance or renaissance. It is true that lately, but as yet infrequently, some of these realizations have begun to produce some fresh answers, as we saw in Chapter 2.

In the present context, consider examples on two planes. The first deals with a large new housing complex in terms of impact on its own inhabitants and on its surroundings. The second is a sketched-in vision of what a much wider and more pervasive architectural-civic embodiment of hitherto invisible neighborhoods might be.

The first example is a preliminary site plan for the development of the Dike Park area of some 75 acres in Cleveland. This development is to be largely low-cost public housing, with some middle-income housing and a shopping center slated for probable inclusion: a large urban undertaking for some 2,000 family and elderly residences. At this magnitude there is the opportunity and challenge, within an over-all idiom, to develop interacting functional and architectural-landscaping design vi-

"La Puntilla":
Proposed Housing Community in Puerto Ri[co]

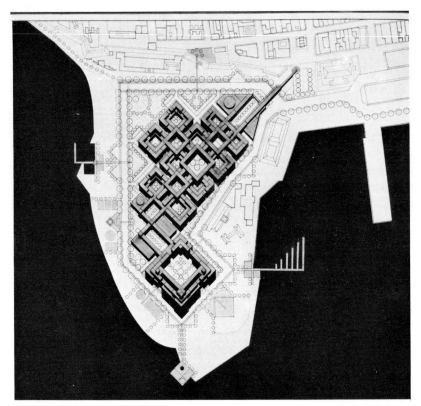

New thinking and design, projected forward from the old-familiar. In large cities, high residential density (families per acre) is often required, and has been generally attained by high-rise elevator buildings. For families they have proved socially undesirable. In San Juan, a new-old conception: higher land coverage as per custom in this city and climate, courts or quadrangles for social interaction, larger parks and recreation on the periphery.

1. *Photograph of the model*

2. *Typical views of physical-social life (courtyard, street, shopping)*

158

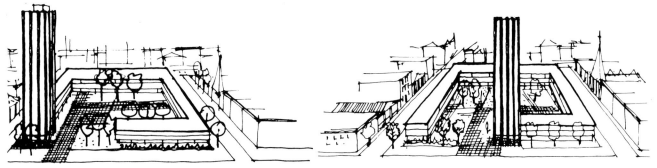

"Campanile Townscape" complexes can be integrally designed between blocks of existing housing.

tality in various groupings which allow social and personal choices, and varying architectural confrontations. The configuration is comprised of such elements as internal vista-ended streets, and residential courts ranging from the intimacy of eight families to larger courts of twenty-four families or more. There is also the choice of more impersonal street-fronted living. There are architectural subfoci, and a magnetic pedestrian Main Street, or promenade, threading through the development past the school, the community center, the subcenters. The streets surrounding the area are not ignored; some continue as internal pedestrian streets and some as roads into, but not through, the new residential neighborhood. Thus neither minuscule vest-pocket trivialities nor outsized mechanistic intrusion; instead, a brave new urbane world within the city is to be created, a world with a new spirit and spark, human and architectural-environmental.

We have still to seek and find a *total* new social-democratic-civic embodiment in architecture, and to think of housing itself as needing to be civic beacon, architectural-spiritual cynosure. We still have to create a decentralized and pervasive character of excellence and brilliance, with local peaks and beacons throughout the urban regional landscape, and in the hitherto invisible parts of that landscape. I have sketched out and present as one stimulating answer, in one kind of situation, the campanile townscape. The street scene and its accustomed relationships are accepted and retained, rehabilitated or new. The familiar is not abandoned, but endowed with new dimension, a new life-breathing vitality, a constant presence of nobleness not distant but here.

Architecture and Environment Shaping at the Urban Regional Scale

Now consider architecture in the great new dimension: the regional scale. This does not mean "local regional" architecture in the accepted sense,

fine and important as it is, characteristic of a region as it is, stemming from climate, materials, and ingrained human expression of regional living. Examples are the eighteenth-century houses of New England towns, possibly the antebellum architecture of the South, the work of Maybeck and his followers and architectural descendants in the Bay Area in California, Frank Lloyd Wright's prairie architecture. I shall not discuss at any length this inspiring work, because it is widely known, has been often and intimately discussed, and permeates our consciousness. I shall rather concentrate on the new regional scale of architecture and *opportunity* for architectural synthesis which are only emerging from multifaceted new requirements.

Now for two examples. One is from the Tennessee Valley Authority. Its architectural expressions nobly exist, and are shown here. The other is from the northeast Illinois metropolitan region. The example it presents exists only as a stirring presentation of an idea, an idea waiting to be transmuted into technical, physical, social, and architectural form. So it must be presented as a word challenge, as example of the still to be accomplished but as imminent potential, I hope.

Regional Challenge, Fulfilled and Potential

The TVA is cited here again as a noble substantive achievement of planning and development. In accomplishing this great concept, massive physical instruments were involved and evolved: river diversion, dams, powerhouses, impounded lakes. Architecture was the creative means for sublimating the mental efforts and the raw physical materials into unforgettable visual and emotional experience. Of course *any* big dam is an important experience. But the indigenous and integral expression of bold architectural content permeating the TVA structures is unique. Why and how?

Roland Wank was the constantly participating

regional architect and for fifteen years he was intimately connected with the thinkers, the planners, the engineers, the hydrographers—worked and argued and lived with them. He absorbed their thinking, their language, and their aspirations, and he posed his own analysis, infused into them his own feelings and interpretations. And because of this interaction, what would have been an impressive manifestation in any case has taken its place among the great architectural syntheses of our time.

The TVA represents fulfillment. But almost everywhere, regional opportunities for environment-shaping architecture, are not yet even in real existence. They still lie in formulations of challenges and problems, in hypothetical programs. Consider the following imaginative memorandum to the Planning Committee of the Chicago Chapter of the American Institute of Architects, from Matthew Rockwell, director of the Northeast Illinois Metropolitan Area Planning Commission. It deals with a universal, endemic problem arisen in the last two decades, which will be instantly and ruefully recognized.

> Specifically, we suggest that the Committee recognize the short-comings of a major highway interchange like the confluence of the Congress and Tri-State Expressways. Within the hundreds of acres of "dead" land [or efficient concrete] lies a design potential which, embodying lakes, hills, auditoria or other features, could augment use and attractive quality of a man-made environment of great variety, use, interest and large dimensions.
>
> The general area has periodic flooding problems. . . . For our economic advantage and for that of our downstream neighbors, we must detain all [the water] we can as long as we can. This in turn provides additional benefits, for as long as we detain the water it can be of service to us. As soon as the water has passed on downstream it is gone for good. . . . The management of surface run-off can be designed to preserve and sometimes augment the natural recharge to the sub-surface reservoirs. . . . The water that falls as precipitation is "free" water and an effort should be made to maximize the benefits that can be realized from it. In addition to recharge, we might arrange also for impoundment of storm run-off in excavated [man-made] lakes. . . .
>
> Six communities of differing size and characteristics meet at the interchange. Each taken separately has certain recreation needs—and similarly there are "collective" recreational aspects.
>
> The extensive land islands that result at such an interchange can be developed as a recreational area or areas. . . . The bordering lands would become most desirable for walking, hiking and picnicking. An outdoor amphitheater is also a possibility, as would be swimming facilities or other community requirements.
>
> The sanitary landfill method of refuse disposal can be used to add variations to the relatively uniform topography of Northeastern Illinois. . . . Such a program would tie in very closely with recreation, as the hills formed could be used to reduce or eliminate traffic noise in the amphitheater and could provide also hills on which toboggan slides and other recreation facilities could be provided. . . .
>
> From the above, it appears that many benefits may be obtained if the land trapped within a major expressway interchange is properly developed and managed. Preliminary estimates suggest that such development would provide economic returns which would more than justify their construction.

In the TVA situation there is a not often repeated opportunity for inspired architectural infusion and interpretation on a regional scale. The situation posed by the northeast Illinois planning body is a more commonly characteristic regional situation and in a sense a deeper challenge for the architect and his environment-shaping group. It involves for the architect, landscape architect, and their consultants the opportunity for inspired formulation of program in a field indeed ripe and waiting for it, and then the opportunity for inspiring interpretation.

Charles Blessing, director of city planning in Detroit, has recently written of another type of twentieth-century scale challenge: "Representatives of both HHFA [Housing and Home Finance Agency] and the Bureau of Public Roads have been unable to cite a single example in which a creative study of the form of the region, based on natural and man-made visual assets, has been made. We are trying to introduce a section in our Detroit Metropolitan Area Program Design covering this phase of the work." Perhaps this is excessively ambitious at the present stage of our social-physical-ecological-economic understanding. But it is an active or latent challenge. I am very sympathetic to this idea of trying *now*. The circumspectness of planners often needs tempering. I think of Napoleon's remark: "On s'engage. Puis on voit." Translated: "One moves into battle. Then one takes a look around."

Many Scales, All Regional: The Architect as Antaeus

In urban and regional development there is thus a myriad opportunity and need, at all the scales from the small to the full regional enterprise. All these cry out for the same penetration and dedication, the same searching for, and then winning of substantive social-physical-spiritual meaning, and then its expression. And full understanding of the substantive meaning of all development requires a full sense of the interconnection of all the scales, and of how they can be made to culminate in regional synthesis. To work toward this synthesis is of course what all the chapters of this study have been concerned with.

Ultimate expression and creation in architecture can be of the highest if and when the architect fully grasps this synthesis and also grasps all the social substance he is working with, is fully attuned to it, has a deep sympathy with it, and helps to arrive at it or helps to change it if he feels impelled to. The work of the TVA was evolved in the course of the architect's fifteen-year dedication to this region, and absorption in it. I believe that every gifted architect should be strengthened by such local absorption, attempt to fully understand an area, be steeped in it, belong to it. It may be a town or a city district or a subregion or whatever. No matter how many office buildings and cultural centers he designs in how many parts of the world, an architect ought to have a firm local base.

I think of the legend of Antaeus, who could not be vanquished while his feet were firmly on earth. Hercules finally conquered him after he had managed to get him to leave that source of strength. Not only does this deep local attachment strengthen the architect. It also gives to the grass roots or to the asphalt purlieus the benefit of the high talents and sympathies they deserve.

Architect and Program

Carrying this further, the architect group in our society, the environmental designing group must demand a much greater role and must prepare itself to fulfill it. The citizen and the body politic must permit and expect and demand much more of architecture and the architect than is the case now.

The architect is not yet the environment shaper that he must become, if we are to fulfill the social-physical discoveries and promise of our century. As of now, generally, he carries out the programs handed to him by his public or private client, and he does his best to produce something workable and pleasing and, most of all, striking. But the feeling of an architectural-human synthesis,

sense of inevitability, is generally absent. However gifted the architect, without this deep Antaean attachment, his works are arbitrary. Note the well-known castellated factory by Paul Rudolph. Note the moving depths of the Richards Medical Research Building in Philadelphia by Louis Kahn. But effective and romantic as they may be, and self-expressive, the forms they have assumed bear no particular relation to need and suitability and program.[4]

We are still far from achieving the crystallization in architecture and landscaping frame, of ecological facts and systems fully understood or at least fully struggled for by the environment shaper, in close continuing contact with the problem and the people, long before the particular commission came along. The environment-shaping team must have involved itself, together with the client and the client's client, the people, in producing and formulating a living program, so that the design and embodiment flow as a continuum from the very beginning; not as an injected element entering the picture long after the constituent elements have been put together and handed over for design as a package. In our complex pluralistic time it is only by this dedicated drawing together and synthesizing, involving the natural sciences, the social sciences, and the field warmth of contact with people where they are, that there can be found the equivalent of the emotionally satisfying state of man that was at hand in the Gothic epoch, or that was expressed in the vital religious art of primitive Africa. This state came as a gift, as it were, as a facet of circumambient life and vital tradition. We, on the other hand, have to *achieve* this state, by conscious pioneer work and by creation of program and program elements that we don't inherit.

Beautification Efforts: Importance and Limitations

There is a great deal of stirring, among architects and citizens at large and in the highest circles, about beauty in architecture and environment, and the lack of it. The Atlanta Chapter of the American Institute of Architects published a striking illustrated pamphlet, *The Mess We Live In*. It

---

[4] Bad working conditions are often found to be the price of striking composition. And it might perhaps be said of much of the most admired work of the last fifteen years that the effort has been to invent. The effort now needs to be more to discover, to be more humble in the face of the problem, to release it and let it do more of the speaking.

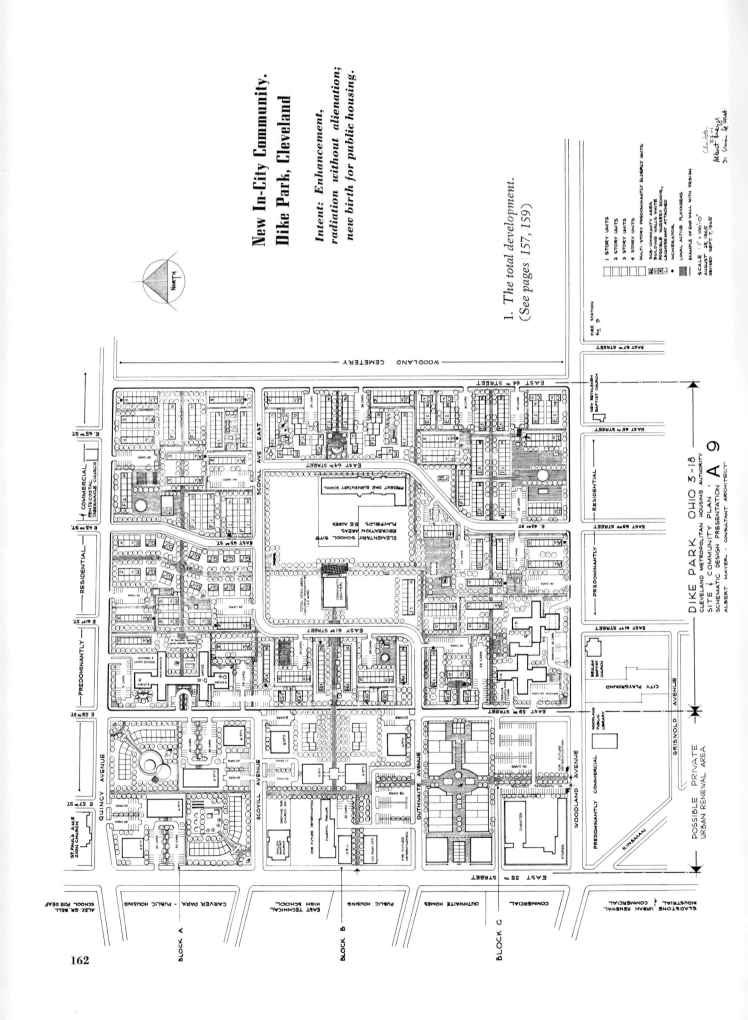

New In-City Community.
Dike Park, Cleveland

Intent: Enhancement, radiation without alienation; new birth for public housing.

1. The total development.
(See pages 157, 159)

DIKE PARK OHIO 3-18
CLEVELAND METROPOLITAN HOUSING AUTHORITY
SITE & COMMUNITY PLAN · A 9
SCHEMATIC DESIGN PRESENTATION
ALBERT MAYER · CONSULTANT ARCHITECT

162

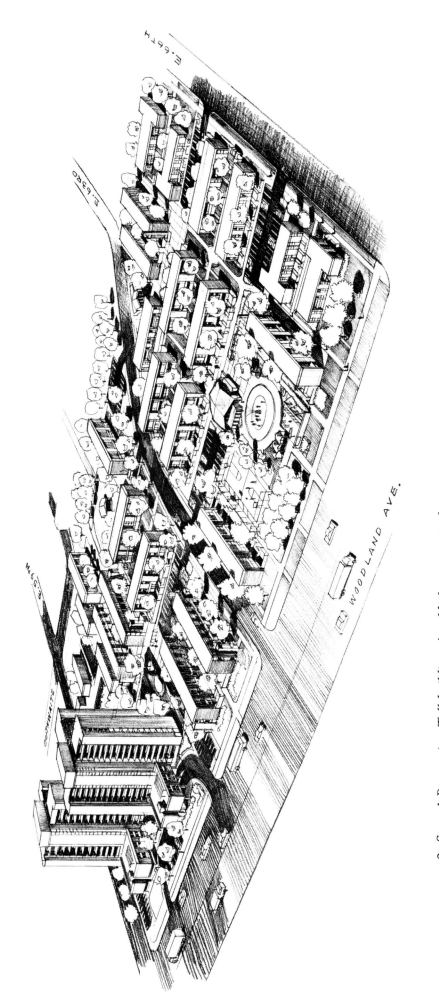

2. Stage 1 Perspective. Tall buildings for elderly to permit adequate range of services. Note low wings in foreground: visual tie to the low family community of which it is a part.

showed our normal gas stations, sign wildernesses, telephone-pole jungles, and some examples of better handling of environment. The New Mexico chapter's 1963 annual conference was devoted to "The Ugliness around Us." A major meeting of citizens and architects in New York a couple of years ago was devoted to this. And how many others. The high point of all these meetings was the White House Conference on Natural Beauty in 1965. All of this is symptomatic and hopeful. There are disgust and revolt and groping, widespread alarm at what we see around us, and steps being outlined or definitely proposed, or even taken, to deal with the ugliness.

There are Kevin Lynch's and Gordon Cullen's alertings and deeper observations, photographs, and analyses. Paul Spreiregen has done a skillful study, a stimulating illustrated manual for practitioners and laymen, on the principles and accomplishment of civic beauty.[5] In 1958, the New York Chapter of the American Architects, New York's regional Plan Association, and the American Institute of Planners put out a succinct book, *Planning and Community Appearance,* with this important proposal: "Recognize the need to provide over-all neighborhood context for the work of the ultimate designers of individual structures by creating and adopting generalized, three-dimensional district plans as integral parts of the municipal master plan."[6]

On quite another and essential plane, the White House Conference Educational Committee made a major recommendation that the public be educated by lectures and that the new generation be educated to a completely new and demanding outlook by creative curriculum in this field.

All these recommendations and developments are essential. They create and intensify a necessary atmosphere. And certainly let us have handsomer street lights; certainly let us have nonhideous gas stations, with flowers even. Certainly let us shout for joy at the Supreme Court's great dictum: "The concept of the public welfare is broad and inclusive. The values it represents are spiritual as well as physical, esthetic as well as monetary. It is within the power of the legislature to determine that the community should be beautiful as well as healthy, spacious as well as clean, well-balanced as well as carefully patrolled."[7]

[7] Justice Douglas's opinion in *Berman v. Parker,* 348 U.S. 26 (1954).
[5] Paul D. Spreiregen, *Urban Design,* McGraw-Hill Book Company, New York, 1965.
[6] P. 7.

But note the inherent limitation. These efforts are not fully involved in the organic process of creating new rational underlying conditions out of which a satisfying and challenging organic architectural environment will flow. In nature, appearance is the inevitable product and manifestation of organic process and structure. In architecture, true expression requires grasp of, and cradling in, the conditions of nature and social process. So proposals to set up better guides and rules and activity to enforce them can be deeply effective only when organic understanding and involvement are vitally present. In a sense, they are only "end-measures," the medicine for the situation. Underlying them there must be the ferment and the growth and the hard-won understanding which I have been trying to present and make vivid.

Beautification Efforts: A Warning

There are indeed two dangers in this "end-measure" approach. First: In such measures as eliminating electric poles and billboards and hiding auto graveyards—the traditional *bêtes noires* of garden clubs and other highly motivated organizations—we are eliminating only major or minor *irritations,* unpleasant but fairly superficial manifestations of deeper ills. If such irritations are considered the *real thing,* and such measures satisfy people's accumulated capacity for understanding and indignation, then harm will be done. We will concentrate on the negative actions which usually remedy such irritations—removal, burying, hiding. We will not ever reach the struggle for organic architectural fulfillment of valid accumulated or newly recognized human and social function. *This* is the real thing.

The second danger is this: Sometimes even the conventional and highly approved or even hallowed measures are irrelevant or wrong. Thus it has been counted an important forward step that organizations, public and private, increasingly allow ½ per cent or 1 per cent, or whatever, of the cost of a building enterprise for art. In a way it is. But where, as in many cases, art is not an organic imperative but a status requisite, it becomes a more or less irrelevant appendage of sculpture or mural which is not only not an organic expression but often an absurdity, as a dozen lobbies in New York office buildings pretentiously show. Let us consider another example. Doomed by our middle-class standards of fitness to be buried underground are the steel pylons striding boldly and proudly over the countryside, swiftly channeling incredible

1. *Immediate giant impact*

Architecture at Regional Scale

The great TVA dams are symbol and actuality of conversion from unharnessed potential to concentrated and disciplined action—in juxtaposition to nature, taking their place as powerful elements in perfecting nature's processes.

2. *Multi-Servant: power, communication, recreation*

3. *Merging into nature, modifying it and being absorbed by it*

amounts of electric energy, equally serving the greatest and the least. These are function and symbol together—the sinewy sculpture of function on regional scale supporting the incredibly delicate cables spanning the region and the continent. How sad if our beautifiers succeed in burying them at great expense and so make us unaware or less aware of this great assertion of Promethean power.

The Magic Ingredient: Organic Wholeness

We must grasp and act on the truth that vital visual impact can only flow out of a rationalized, humane, total environment extending from the small neighborhood nucleus to the total region. We must think and act in terms of decentralized and permeating excellence. We dare not settle for only the glittering central projects—which are in any reckoning of great significance of course—but which absorb too much of our effort and energy, and give great and delusive satisfaction to the prestige and pride of the powerful; nor for rationalizing and beautifying of all the signs and stores on Main Street. We have to place far more emphasis on the establishment and gifted design of many small parks and many, many, small social plazas and centers in obscure neighborhoods, where even "the least of these" is awakened and eager and significant.

Thus an indispensable element is emphasized: the equality of the small scale and the great scale in architecture. Beyond this, to achieve *any* architectural excellence, there has to be a struggled-for and participated-in basic agreed social matrix. And then we have to greatly struggle toward the birth of the total regional organism of which the great and small localities are to be living cellular parts.

In physics, it is of course understood that the great visible mountain range is a visual and analyzable entity, in terms of the all-important, all-pervasive atom and its subconstituents. I don't feel it is excessively forcing things to draw on this as an analogy to life and the region.

This brief last word is not a summation nor a summary. Rather it is a final underlining, and a fresh alarum to take up the vast unfinished business in housing, in community, in city-region building. This must immediately become current business of the very highest priority and scale. The legislation of 1964, 1965, and 1966 that took the first steps in effectuating the Great Society may be thought of as more or less *catching up with long-accumulated arrears,* bringing us approximately up to the starting line, as it were.

This has been an animating experience for our country, and now we dare not rest here and fall behind again so that we are again excessively pleased with just catching up or almost catching up in an emergency effort. (And on the urban region scene, specifically, we haven't by any means done even that.) The Demonstration Cities and Metropolitan Development Act of 1966 goes a short distance further, on a lamentably meager scale, absurdly inadequate to the objectives and the splendid language of its proponents. We have now to sustain and enhance the high mood which has been generated. We must now *catch up with the future,* immediately lay the basis for immediate great debate and action. And not only on the national plane, where the action has been serious, but on the state and local planes, where it has scarcely begun.

One awakening is particularly necessary on our urban scene. We have long equated modern technology with positive human gain, but in fact, as has been emphasized, technology is neutral, can accomplish good or ill. It may be just possible that technology can make megalopolis work after a fashion, at very great cost in resources and in human tensions. But equally, it now makes fluently possible the accomplishment of the great new adventures: the New Town, the new region, the re-created city. It can endow the smaller city with competitive equality, greater humanity, and ecological superiority. These things we must demand of technology. And we must see to it that we move off from the shadowboxing of demonstration projects to the muscular real thing: general and concentrated application. For tokenism is a characteristic deception not only in civil rights and integration but also in the urgent urban situation as a whole.

These are questions of *our* choice. Don't get the idea that these basic decisions are the domain of technicians, and lazily let it go at that. One great trouble currently is our unjustified modesty vis-à-vis the expert, the technician, our confusing his incomparably greater technical skill and resources with better basic judgment. Be clear about this.

CHAPTER TWELVE

EPILOGUE AND PROLOGUE: THE URGENT FUTURE

The expert commands many means. He has information and methods which we need to listen to and weigh. But we must distinguish between these and his personal opinions and conclusions, and we must distinguish between his opinions and conclusions and our goals and values. This is where we are or could be supreme. He will carry out almost anything, and on the urban scene often rejoices in piling up complications and then ingeniously making them work somehow. He works too, in general, in an orbit of opinion, and in underlying identification with a power structure whose objectives are well satisfied with public tokenism.

For example, in 1965, at a White House Conference on the Negro, A. Philip Randolph proposed a $100 billion "Freedom Budget" to eliminate slums. This was ridiculed or viewed with alarm, certainly not taken seriously. Why not? A value judgment, or a resultant of pressures of underlying dynamics. Expenditures of this order of magnitude are gladly authorized by Congress for roads, agricultural programs, space, etc. In terms of consumer health and comfort, in terms of employment created, in terms of *total equations,* the proposal makes important sense, demands our attention and follow-up, demands rigorous comparison with other such programs, if all cannot be afforded. In this book I have at various points tried to place feasibility in a money and resources focus in this customary way, by comparing and contrasting with other government expenditures, and indicating the high priority, among these, of the elements passionately emphasized here.

But actually, we now have to go much further, much further indeed. We must now go beyond this measure, into a more radical realm of measure and priority. The urgency of the requirements of the new world we must establish and of the old world we must re-create means that we have to push the whole question of raising total public expenditure at the expense of the unlimited private expenditure, particularly at the summit of private luxury, self-indulgence, and competitive acquisition.

Let me set forth very briefly what I have in mind. One reads almost daily of a $50,000 or $100,000 jewel robbery from some private house or hotel room or villa or lodge, in California or Palm Beach, on the Riviera or at Gstaad; and usually it turns out that the thief has missed a much larger haul. Again, anyone who has attended such fantastic parties as the April in Paris ball in New York, or various private balls, knows that they involve competitive display of, conservatively, millions of dollars worth of personal jewelry. I use jewelry, of course, merely as a convenient symbol— an indicator of a whole range and totality of absurdly huge expenditures for multiple homes, large staffs of servants, yachts, and so forth. Can it be maintained that this kind of façade and money allocation is really necessary as the incentive to make the private-enterprise system operate effectively? Are we not simply dealing with a system of power arrogation? Must we not siphon off very substantially more than we do from upper-level incomes? It is still a fact that the highest 5 per cent of the families in this country still get 20 per cent of total income; the lowest 20 per cent still is getting only 5 per cent. . . . We must write a new script. Guns versus butter is a perennial issue and always relevant. New and still more relevant is: diamonds versus slums.

Now, consider another level or quite different kind of value judgment: I have in this book described and advocated the concept of the New Town. A large part of the advocacy is based on the economy and convenience—the New Town will itself contain most of the cultural, educational, employment, and business resources it needs to make it a lively spirited entity—and a large part on the value judgment that the New Town can be a more deeply satisfying place to live than either the one-class residential-only suburb or the gargantuan city. Lately the Regional Plan Association of New York has developed and advocates a sort of rival concept, about as follows: Leave the normal substantially residential suburb as it is, but to avoid travel to the remote central city for work, entertainment, and culture, set up a number of subregional centers. These centers would in effect be a large expansion of the regional shopping center, but multifunctional in character. Now the question of whether to go for this concept or for New Towns is as of now really not a technical matter of comparative efficiency, or economy, for no alternative models have been set up, no capital and operating costs have been compared. Either is workable. Which to choose?

The subregional center could have the excitements and the sophistications of a large center, and it would have good accessibility by car or bus. But it would also have a good deal of the frenetic character of the metropolis, always in motion, and access would be *largely* from afar. In fact, it is argued that this center is justified because its character and scale justify more massive transit and converging road systems. But, by adopting this alternative, you are not altering but rather would be perpetuating and reinforcing the dormitory character and the sterility of the suburb. By contrast, a galaxy of New Towns would be a many-sided ensemble with its own characteristic range and vitality. The choice has to be, finally, based on a value judgment.

One must not belittle or ignore the expert. One must simply distinguish between his technical knowledge and his opinions, i.e., largely those of his backers. And so one major motivation for writing this book has been to address the layman, to rouse him to the desperate importance of the urban and regional drama and the urgent need for *his* high-priority active concern with its subject matter, and to equip him to grasp and measure the extent of his competence. Really, there is a new and expanding role for the layman, at local levels and upward. In fact, one may say that a major aspect of this book is in setting new roles for many of the participants, for the small-part participants, and for the hitherto nonparticipants in this urban regional drama.

We must call on the social scientist to alert himself and infuse his insights into sensitive permeating participation in planning decisions and physical design. We must call for the architect and the planner and the highway engineer to engraft into their intentions and design the social base, both as gained from the social scientist and as freshly understood and renewed by warm personal contact with the people. We must invite the landscape architect and the natural scientist to relate the old cities and the new cities and the new areas validly and vigorously to the natural forces, in whose web we are, and to infuse the natural spirit into the new creations.

We must all rethink our roles. And finally, we must emblazon on our banner that *trend is not destiny.* At the same time, we must be aware that trend has a tremendous momentum of its own. In striving to alter it or conquer it, we must be sure of our ground, and oppose to the momentum of trend the momentum of imagination, of intentions, of plans, of fervent conviction, of determination. A tough and exhilarating assignment.

To forestall any notion that I have put together a Utopia, I have in most cases cited examples of attained excellence, from our own country and from those other countries of the Western world that basically share our values, experiences, aspirations. Such examples are not yet predominant, it is true, but they now exist widely enough and come into being often enough to prove their feasibility and propulsive force.

The answer to the question of attainability in great measure lies in state of mind and of determination. Ada Louise Huxtable, the architectural critic, came back from a tour abroad full of admiration for what she had seen. She wrote in the New York *Times:*

> Seen on the spot, it becomes quite clear that the new and sometimes startlingly successful European housing and planning have grown out of a political, economic, sociological and cultural base that has no parallel in the United States. It is the product of a place, system and state of mind that are alien to the American way of life. Its lessons are legion, but they can be weighed only against what American society can absorb and achieve.[1]

But in its time, it was stoutly maintained that the income tax was incompatible with the American way of life. This was then said of social security, and it has recently been said of Medicare. They have one after the other been adopted. Let us bear in mind these stirring precedents, bearing in mind also that in our urban regional human dilemma the worsening conditions and prospects insistently demand boldness, concentrated debate, and action.

Gunnar Myrdal has a higher outlook and emphasis, in *Beyond the Welfare State:*

> There is in all planning, even if it were ever so earthily rooted in comprehensive studies of fact, an element of belief in reason as an independent force in history and in the freedom of choice by which man can change reality according to his design and so turn the course of future development. In essence, planning is an exercise in a nondeterministic conception of history, though it recognizes the limitations put up by existing conditions and forces and their causal interrelations.

Let us move forward boldly and resolutely, in this awakened spirit.

What may make us seem utopian is this. The technological pace of this century has accelerated and is accelerating at an unbridled rate; and technology is moving in many bewildering directions. We must gear ourselves to equal it, outstrip it, harness it. We must sharply accelerate *our* pace, the pace of human, social, political decision and devotion, not just in emergency but every day. We must, and we can, convert the aimless dynamics of Pandora's box into a magnificent surge of human dynamism. This is attainable Utopia.

[1] New York *Times,* Nov. 22, 1965.

APPENDIX

HOW HOUSING AND URBAN PROGRAMS ARE REGROUPED UNDER THE DEPARTMENT OF HOUSING AND URBAN DEVELOPMENT [1]

UNDER DEPARTMENT STRUCTURE	ADMINISTRATIVE UNIT UNDER PREDECESSOR HOUSING AND HOME FINANCE AGENCY
Assistant Secretary for Mortgage Credit and Federal Housing Commissioner	
FHA mortgage insurance programs	Federal Housing Administration
Rent-supplement program	Federal Housing Administration
Community disposition staff	Office of the Administrator
Assistant Secretary for Renewal and Housing Assistance	
Urban renewal projects (Title I)	Urban Renewal Administration (URA)
Rehabilitation loans	URA
Low-rent public housing	Public Housing Administration (PHA)
College housing loans	Community Facilities Administration
Loans for housing the elderly and handicapped	Community Facilities Administration
Workable program for community improvement	Office of the Administrator and URA
Relocation	URA and PHA
Neighborhood facilities	URA
Urban beautification	URA
Urban parks	URA
Open-space, central city	URA
Project social service activities	URA and PHA
Coordination of problems of elderly and handicapped	Office of the Administrator
Assistant Secretary for Metropolitan Development	
Urban planning assistance program	URA
Planned metropolitan development (proposed)	(not previously assigned)
Comprehensive planning requirements	Office of the Administrator and URA
Metropolitan area planning coordination	Office of the Administrator
Mass transportation grants and loans	Office of the Administrator
Basic water and sewer facilities	Community Facilities Administration
Open-space land (outside central city)	URA
Urban beautification (outside central city)	URA
Advance land acquisition for urban growth	Community Facilities Administration
Public facilities loans	Community Facilities Administration
School construction	Community Facilities Administration
Academic facilities	Community Facilities Administration

[1] Department of Housing and Urban Development, Washington, D.C., Feb. 25, 1966.

Assistant Secretary for Demonstrations and
Intergovernmental Relations

Demonstration cities program (proposed)	(not previously assigned)
Low-income housing demonstrations	Office of the Administrator
Urban renewal demonstrations	URA
Metropolitan desks (proposed)	(not previously assigned)
Intergovernmental relations studies	(not previously assigned)
City, county, state coordination and liaison for department	(not previously assigned)
Federal-state training program	(not previously assigned)
City planning fellowships	(not previously assigned)
Development of proposed institute for urban development	(not previously assigned)
Clearinghouse service	(not previously assigned)
Urban studies and housing research	Office of the Administrator
Open-space land and urban beautification studies	URA
Urban planning research and demonstrations	URA
Public facilities technical advisory services	Community Facilities Administration
Surveys of public works planning	Community Facilities Administration
Study of codes, zoning, etc.	(not previously assigned)
Natural disaster study	(not previously assigned)
Comprehensive market analysis	Office of the Administrator
Defense planning	Office of the Administrator

Federal National Mortgage Association

The FNMA, a government corporation, will continue unchanged under the direction of its board, of which the secretary is chairman. The Assistant Secretary for Mortgage Credit, a member of the board, will assist in coordinating FHA activities with those of the FNMA.

Assistant Secretary for Administration

This office will direct the administrative management functions of the department, including budget, personnel, accounting, and audits.

It is customary and important that a serious book dealing with our field should have a bibliography for those who want to penetrate further and into constituent or associated fields. The standard bibliography lists the solid sources which add up to a well-rounded totality. I believe this is neither necessary nor useful here, because this kind of systematic bibliography can be found in almost any book including a number cited here.

The bibliography which follows is quite unorthodox; it makes no effort at being complete or well rounded. It is diverse in character and very uneven in coverage. One of its purposes is to pick up sources, not standard or generally known, that would not otherwise usually be encountered by the reader. These bear on sections of this book or on specific examples cited in it which are special or embryonic. In this aspect, it is a pinpointed selection which might in a way be considered rather as a freewheeling extension of footnote references than as a bibliography. For instance, in Chapter 5, in connection with the proposition that racial integration must and can be a major and permeating ingredient in development, the large, integrated Rochdale Cooperative was noted. In this bibliography there is a first-hand report of actualities there called "When Black and White Live Together," which brings us up to 1966, three years after first occupancy.

In this sense, the footnote references are an integral part of this bibliography. Only a few of these have been repeated here, where a different purpose was to be served.

At the other end of the spectrum, the nonspecific end, there are noted periodicals and periodic reports and bulletins through which, if the reader peruses them, he will be alerted to a whole range or catchall of events, issues, and developments with which he ought to be in fruitful touch.

BIBLIOGRAPHY

Guidance to Citizens on Various Planes (*Some examples of what every citizen needs and every city owes itself*)

A Citizens' Handbook of Housing, Planning and Urban Renewal Procedures in New York City, Community Education Program, Pratt Institute, Brooklyn, N.Y., 1965, 186 pages, four Appendices, and Bibliography. Excellent objective, and a compendium is much needed. But whoever can make his way through this quite long guide probably doesn't need its help. A much condensed version, please.

A Citizen's Guide to Housing and Urban Renewal in Philadelphia, 2d ed., Philadelphia Housing Association, 1601 Walnut Street, Philadelphia, Pa., 1960, 72 pages, Bibliography, Directory, etc. Revision being prepared for publication in 1967, pending which a series of special memoranda have appeared (fourteen in all through October, 1966). This is intended not only to help the citizen to be more effective in a practical sense, but also to understand policies and to help him form opinions.

The Citizen's Guide to Town and Country Planning, 1966, 66 pages. From the Planning Bookshop, 28 King Street, Covent Garden, London, W. C. 2, England. "Intended primarily to help local councillors, leaders of voluntary societies, schools and colleges." Obviously, not directly of use here, but very much the kind of thing we need and worth consulting for a compact consideration of needs, policies, and politics. Broader, less bread-and-butter than the preceding two. Chapters include modern development of town and country planning, the administrative machinery, local and regional planning problems, and effect of planning on land values. As far as I know we have nothing here as succinct, on this plane.

Spiraling Prices in a Speculative Land System

Raw Land: How to Find, Finance and Develop It, P-H Editorial Staff, Copyright 1966, Prentice-Hall, Inc., Englewood Cliffs, N.J.

The character of this report is underlined by excerpts from a sales letter sent out by Prentice-Hall: *"The big profits still to be made in raw land today."* Quoting further: "By moving in fast for a share of this action, you can latch on to a gold mine." And, "You get 6 tested angles that help you line up the most desirable raw land and rake in top profits from it." This is underlying dynamics with a vengeance and sadly bears out the pessimistic observations in Chapters 4 and 6, concerning the private entrepreneurial land-disposal system.

"NEW TOWNS: Are they just oversized subdivisions with oversized problems?" *House and Home,* June, 1966, pp. 92–103. Useful review of certain troublesome aspects of New Town development by private enterprise. Regarding land: "More and more investors are realizing they can take the risk out of financing a new town if they can get control of the appreciating land. And the land does appreciate at unbelievable rates. El Dorado Hills land has climbed from $6.7 million to $29 million in six years.

"Investors have also learned that they don't have to own land to control it." From p. 94.

New Towns; Environment and Region

Creese, Walter L: *The Search for Environment. The Garden City Before and After,* Yale University Press, New Haven, Conn., 1966. Philosophic outlook and questioning as to the nature of new community and new city, the nature of social and private life, the alternatives available to the environment shaper and the consumer; the relations of sociology, technology, and art; the repeated interplay of the creative manifestations in community and community creation from country to country. Covers the past hundred years. A vital contrast with the dernier cri or born-yesterday limitations of American analysis and architectural criticism today. Too long, but rewarding. Profusion of excellent illustrations.

Lubove, Roy: *Community Planning in the 1920's: The Contribution of the Regional Planning Association of America,* The University of Pittsburgh Press, Pittsburgh, Pa., 1963. This covers much more ground than just New Towns; it includes them as part of a total social-economic-physical community-regional conspectus. It gives an excellent background of the development of forward thinking in this country, intimately introducing the theories, achievements, and influence of such men as Lewis Mumford, Clarence Stein, Henry Wright, Benton MacKaye, and others. A brilliant memoir. Disturbing question: Why has this thinking not had more impact?

Mayer, Albert: "Greenbelt Towns Revisited in Search of New Directions," series of articles in *Journal of Housing* beginning January, 1967, based on 1966 field study and report made for the National Association of Housing and Redevelopment Officials. What happened to the three New Towns started under the New Deal in 1935, and what can we learn?

Osborn, Sir Frederic J., and Arnold Whittick: *The New Towns: The Answer to Megalopolis,* McGraw-Hill Book Co., New York, 1964. The definitive book on the background and growth of the New Town movement in Great Britain and on the creation of each of the British New Towns, with plans and photographs. Sir Frederic Osborn has been a central participant in all phases of the movement and its effective work, including the first prototypes of Letchworth and Welwyn Garden City early in the century.

Stein, Clarence S: *Toward New Towns for America,* The M.I.T. Press, Cambridge, Mass., 1966, reissue in paperback and hard cover. Account by the man who, with Henry Wright decades ago, developed the penetrating insights and the disciplined imaginative concepts which constitute the physical, technical, and social premises for new towns. Copious illustrations from "partial forerunners" Radburn, Greenbelt, Baldwin Hills, Chatham Village, etc.

Some current new towns by private enterprise in U.S. Publicity, brochures, photographs, and much graphic material by the developer of each. Informative and stimulating.

Columbia: New Town between Baltimore and Washington. Materials available from Information Department, The Rouse Company, The Village of Cross Keys, Baltimore, Md. 21210.

Litchfield Park: outside of Phoenix. Materials available from Walter F. Wiener, Doherty Associates, 551 Fifth Avenue, New York, N.Y. 10019.

Reston: New Town in the Washington orbit. Materials available from Bernard E. Norwitch, Executive Office, Reston, Va. The furthest along in construction and occupancy of those cited here.

Maumelle: New Town in a "new" region. Materials from Jess Odom Development Corporation, Little Rock, Ark. In the planning stage. The planner, the author of this book, is particularly gratified at being creatively connected with the first new city in a new region not in the orbit of a great metropolis. This is "twentieth-century pioneering" as explained and ardently recommended in Chapter 10.

Restructuring the City and Sublimation into Architecture

Chermayeff, Serge, and Christopher Alexander: *Community and Privacy—Toward a New Architecture of Humanism*, Doubleday & Company, Inc., Garden City, N.Y., 1965. "It is our contention that . . . an entirely new anatomy of urbanism is needed, built of many hierarchies of clearly articulated domains." A brilliant book—fresh analysis and synthesis of macro- and micro-scales. Equally provocative and useful for the searching designer of environment and for the lay searcher seeking a rational basis for selecting his piece of environment—the home.

The Pedestrian in the City, David Lewis (ed.), D. Van Nostrand Company, Inc., Princeton, N.J., 1966. The subject matter of this book is very much more extensive than its title. It is a very freewheeling series of freewheeling articles of varying merit. But, perhaps for this very reason and because of its numerous effective photographs of urban situations and creations, it is immensely stimulating. It loosens up one's imagination and thinking.

How Much Can We Manage to Do and in What Period of Time?

Two very opposed views are presented in these two references.
A "Freedom Budget" for All Americans: Budgeting Our Resources 1966–1975 to Achieve "Freedom From Want," Pamphlet of A. Philip Randolph Institute, 217 West 125th Street, New York, N.Y. 10027, 1966.

Goals, Priorities and Dollars—The Next Decade, Lecht, Leonard A., et al., for the National Planning Association, The Free Press of Glencoe, N.Y., 1966. Hardbound $6.95; paperback $2.95.
The latter takes as a point of departure the goals formulated in 1960 by President Eisenhower's Commission on National Goals ("Goals for Americans") and brings it up to date. It concludes that the GNP, even though growing by some $425 billion by 1975, will nevertheless be 15 per cent or $146 billion short of being able to meet them all. A reviewer notes *:

"It is all very well to affirm that even the richest country in the world cannot, within the space of ten years, satisfy all the aspirations of the society, and that priorities are therefore necessary. But to incorporate within the tally of aspiration standards a large component of luxury, ostentatious, meretricious and wasteful consumption is to imply—unintentionally, I am sure—that this is entitled to equal consideration in the priority determination process, especially so because this inclusion has not been made explicit."

On the other hand, A *"Freedom Budget"* in whose formulation such eminent economists as John K. Galbraith and Leon Keyserling participated, concludes that we can accomplish much more than the "Eisenhower goals" including, for example, a decent home for every American family within a decade. Some statements from the introduction to this remarkable pamphlet:

"The *'Freedom Budget'* differs from previous worthy

* Walinsky, Louis J: *International Development Review*, September, 1966, p. 31.

efforts to set forth similar goals because it fuses general aspirations with quantitative content, and imposes time schedules. It deals not only with where we must go, but also with how fast and in what proportions. It measures costs against resources, and thus determines feasible priorities. It is not only a *call* to action, but also a *schedule* for action.

. . . The *'Freedom Budget'* contends that this nation has the resources to abolish poverty, for the first time in human history, and to do so within a decade. Indeed, the very process of abolishing poverty will add enormously to our resources, raising the living standard of Americans at all income levels. By serving our unmet social needs—in slum clearance and housing, education and training, health, agriculture, natural resources and regional development, social insurance and welfare programs—we can achieve and sustain a full employment economy (itself the greatest single force against poverty) and a higher rate of economic growth, while simultaneously tearing down the environment of poverty. All of these problems interact, whether viewed as causes or results, and they are in truth both.

. . . The fundamental proposition is that the broad approaches of the *'Freedom Budget'* can and should be implemented, whether or not an early termination of the Vietnam conflict is achieved, or even were there to be substantial increase in its economic and financial burdens."

Thus, from this sharp conflict between experts, resulting in large measure from their quite different premises, we see exemplified a major thesis of our book: These life and death matters are not neutral, and as deeply involved persons and citizens, we must step in with strong conviction and determine our destiny.

Issues of Conscience

The Urgent Future has maintained the importance of emotional-moral commitment in creating a more worthy environment for all. In the immediately previous paragraphs we have seen how indispensable this is to attain the kind and scale and rate of transformation we seek.

The Interfaith Housing Corporation in the Boston area, whose work has been noted in the text, is an example of this kind of commitment in specific action.

There is a remarkable pamphlet which brings to life the religious-moral imperatives involved, galvanizes the current and the ancient-latent ethical springs of action. This is entitled *Judaism and Cities in Crisis*, one of a series on Issues of Conscience, by Rabbi Richard G. Hirsch. First appearing in 1961 (second printing 1964), it is the work of the Commission on Social Action of Reformed Judaism, 838 Fifth Avenue, New York, N.Y. A stirring document, completely up to date in information and awareness, it also evokes the thundering voices of the prophets to whom the same kinds of issues were contemporary and a cause of white-hot indignation.

Three Miscellaneous Items

Peabody, Malcolm E., Jr.: "Massachusetts Expands State-aided Program," *Journal of Housing*, no. 9, 1966, pp. 498–

501. In Chapter 2, it was urged that state and city must genuinely bestir themselves to imaginatively formulate, finance, and activate low-rent subsidized housing, rather than confine themselves to quite inadequate Federal help. In 1966, Massachusetts enacted legislation undertaking a major share of responsibility for public and other forms of low-rental housing. Provisions take account of the accumulation of experience and of the latest thinking. This is the most refreshing forward-looking action in years by any state. It deserves study and emulation. Peabody's statement is a succinct and stimulating summary and analysis.

Swados, Harvey: "When Black and White Live Together," *New York Times Magazine,* Nov. 13, 1966. Close-up account and analysis of the first three years of the Rochdale Cooperative, the 6,000-family, integrated community in a heretofore all-Negro slum in New York City. An over-all success, one gets from this account the daily flavor, the problems solved and not yet solved, the richness of relationships. The chief unsolved impinging questions are in and from the surrounding areas. And this, with 6,000 families. Just imagine what happens with the now so fashionable vest-pocket jobs!

"Where Metro Government Works," an article in *Baltimore Magazine,* December, 1966. This brings up to the minute, the account of the two-tiered metropolitan government of Toronto, now thirteen years old. In important contemporary or recent developments, it is an inestimable advantage when one can closely follow a few years later what *really* happened, how the later actualities live up to the original expectations, what are the pluses and minuses. An index of Metro's success on balance is the increasing number of subjects of jurisdiction that have voluntarily been made and are being made over to it (one of which is public housing). Its planning jurisdiction now goes far beyond the administrative limits of 240 square miles, to cover a surrounding area of a total of 720 square miles.

Periodicals and House-Organs *
A wide-ranging miscellany

American Behavioral Scientist. Published ten times a year. Special number Urban Studies, February, 1963, contains well-selected bibliography of the last ten years' books.

Cooperative Housing. Quarterly, published by the National Association of Housing Cooperatives, 59 East Van Buren St., Chicago, Ill. 60605, $4 per year. Informative journal dealing with this creative burgeoning field and with linked urban-social-consumer subjects. To date, a largely middle-class movement of important liberal content, it may be on the threshold of much deeper economic penetration by virtue of the new rent supplementation. Keep well in touch with this major and very potential element of THE URGENT FUTURE.

Cry California. Quarterly journal of the organization, California Tomorrow, Forum Building, Sacramento, Calif. Dues are $9 per year including subscription. Though specifically for California, it is provocative and enlightening for anyone in the U.S. Gamut of articles from "Reshaping Super-City: the Problem of Los Angeles" to "Confessions of a Highway Commissioner."

* The really well-known periodicals in our field are omitted because everyone knows about them.

"California Tomorrow is a non-profit educational organization dedicated to bringing to the public a greater awareness of the problems we must face to maintain a beautiful and productive California. Contributors to *Cry California* and other California Tomorrow publications are chosen for their ability to illuminate those problems, and to discover possible solutions to them."
Also publishes special pamphlets such as the excellent and hair-raising "Phantom Cities of California" (1963).

Event. A journal of public affairs. Published quarterly by University College, Adult Education Division, Syracuse University. An excellent journal of opinion and events on the local scene, often controversial. Example: article in the issue of Summer, 1965, "The Unfinished Business of Human Rights in Syracuse." This publication is cited as an example of sophisticated and provocative local magazines that have sprung up around the country, a number of them in middle-sized cities.

Flatland. A biweekly newspaper written and published by and for the Oakland (California) poor. Typical of a growing number of these.

Journal of Housing. Published ten times a year by the National Association of Housing and Redevelopment Officials, 1413 K Street N.W., Washington, D.C. Spotty, but indispensable both to keep up with its fields and because of sometimes excellent articles.

Landscape. Published three times yearly, Box 2323, Santa Fe, N. Mex. Subscription $3. Stimulating, varied. Articles with topics both within the confines of its title as well as almost anything else.

Looking Ahead. "A monthly report by the National Planning Association on forward-looking policy planning and research—announced, under way, and completed—of importance to the nation's future." 1606 New Hampshire Avenue N.W., Washington 9, D.C. Frequent articles on urban development and housing and cost and financing. Interesting as a running insight into the views of an unusually progressive (but still fundamentally conservative) group of businessmen and some labor leaders and academicians.

Pratt Planning Papers. Published quarterly by Pratt Center for Community Improvement, Pratt Institute, Brooklyn, N.Y., $3 per year. Articles discuss incisively, not in great depth, a range of urgent current planning-development proposals and programs, with special attention to New York.

Town and Country Planning. Monthly publication of the Town and Country Planning Association, 28 King Street, London, W. C. 2, England. A stimulating and very influential journal devoting much of its space to regional development and to the British New Towns. Each January issue contains tables showing progress in the growth of population, housing, industry, shops, schools, etc. Important source of current information and opinion. Also, right along, current significant material from other countries.

Trans-Action. A bimonthly journal to further the understanding and use of the social sciences, published by the Community Leadership Project, Washington University, St. Louis, Mo.

Trends in Housing. Bimonthly news bulletin published by the National Committee against Discrimination in Housing, 323 Lexington Avenue, New York, N.Y. 10016. Subscription $2 per year. Keeps one closely abreast of the struggle for integrated housing and cities, its progress and setbacks. This organization also publishes excellent pamphlets, treating specific subjects more deeply. One is "Operation Open City," October, 1965, a comment by Eunice Greer on a determined program to open all neighborhoods to minority occupancy. The locale is New York City. Lessons and successes of the program now being extended to eight additional cities by the National Urban League's "Operation Equality," of which Cleveland and Seattle are underway (1966).

Department of Housing and Urban Development. Numerous pertinent publications. Up-to-date listing not yet available. There is a bimonthly leaflet entitled *H.U.D. Notes,* the new title of *Urban Renewal Notes,* which the department has been issuing for some years. While this is very brief, and naturally slanted toward a favorable view, it is of considerable value in keeping one au courant as to varied developments over the country. Until recently, there was a similar publication *Public Housing Highlights,* which significantly has been discontinued.

Ford Foundation Publications. Ford Foundation, 477 Madison Avenue, New York, N.Y. 10022. Their reports, capsulizing the nature of wide-ranging programs and sometimes the indicated results of grants for research and experimentation in diverse but interrelated urban programs and directions, are stimulating to read. Some titles:

"American Community Development," 1963. Preliminary reports on comprehensive community projects assisted by the foundation in Boston, New Haven, Oakland, Philadelphia, and North Carolina.

"Cross Sections," 1965. Multiple foundation programs illustrated by activities in a single city (Pittsburgh).

"Metropolis," third printing 1963. Grants covering urban and regional problems. Includes work in the metropolitan areas of Boston, Kansas City, Peoria, Dayton; Pennsylvania–New Jersey–Delaware Metropolitan Project; Southeast Michigan metropolitan area; Piedmont Industrial Crescent in North Carolina; Appalachian Mountain Region.

"Urban Extension," 1966. Efforts to attain in urban conditions some of the fruitful results that agricultural extension and home economics have achieved over the last half-century. Various combinations of research, teaching, and extension explored in the University of Wisconsin, Rutgers, the Universities of Delaware, California (Berkeley), Missouri, Oklahoma, Purdue, Illinois; and ACTION-Housing (Pittsburgh).

"Society of the Streets," June, 1962. Activities in youth development.

Special Category

Library of Urban Affairs, Riverside, N.J. This recently formed organization is an urban Book-of-the-Month Club, which provides a way of keeping abreast of current books. Selections are made by an eminent committee.

DESIGN
AND
ILLUSTRATION
CREDITS

3. New Haven Redevelopment Agency. *Photograph by Earl Colter Studio, Branford, Conn.*

4. New Haven Redevelopment Agency. *Photograph by Charles R. Schulze, New Haven.*

Page 68
1. *Photograph by Washington Center for Metropolitan Studies.*
2. *Photograph by Washington Center for Metropolitan Studies.*
3. *Photograph by Eric Maristany.*

Page 78
1. ARCHITECTS: Clarence Stein and Henry Wright.
2. ARCHITECTS: Clarence Stein and Henry Wright. *Photograph by Gretchen van Tassel Shaw, Kensington, Maryland.*

Page 79
1. Stevenage Development Corporation.
2. Cumbernauld Development Corporation. ARCHITECT: L. Hugh Wilson.
3. Basildon Development Corporation. *Photograph by Stanland, Chelmsford.*

Page 80
1. Crawley Development Corporation. *Photograph by D. L. Buckland.*
2. Hemel Hempstead Development Corporation.
3. Harlow Development Corporation Design Group. *Photograph by Wainwright.*

Page 83
1. Cwmbran Development Corporation.
2. Basildon Development Corporation. *Photograph by W. Suschitzky, London.*
3. ARCHITECT: Frederick Gibberd. Harlow Development Corporation Design Group. *Photograph by Wainwright.*
4. Crawley Development Corporation. *Photograph by Sidney Newbery.*
5. Harlow Development Corporation.

Page 85
1. East Kilbride Development Corporation.
2. Stevenage Development Corporation.
3. Crawley Development Corporation. *Photograph by Sydney Newbery.*

Page 87
1, 2. Consulate General of Finland, New York.

Page 89
DESIGNERS: Gordon Cullen and Richard Mathews, for Alcan Industries Ltd.

Page 90
1, 2. Simon Enterprises.

Page 92
1, 2. Community Research & Development Corporation.

Page 97
1. Planning Commission of City of Stockholm. *Photograph by Hugo Priivits.*
2. Planning Commission of City of Stockholm. *Photograph by REFOT.*
3. *Photograph by Reportagebild Klara KYRKOGATA.*
4. *Photograph by per-olle Stackman.*
5. *Photograph by Harvey Barton, Bristol.*
6. *Photography by Pace, Sidcup, Kent.*

Page 100
1. ARCHITECTS: Robert Alexander, Reginald Johnson, and Lewis Wilson; CONSULTING ARCHITECT: Clarence Stein.
2. East River Houses, New York City.
3. ARCHITECTS: Holden, Egan, Wilson, and Corser; ARCHITECT FOR THE OUTDOORS: Albert Mayer.

Page 101
4. ARCHITECTS: Holden, Egan, Wilson, and Corser; ARCHITECT FOR THE OUTDOORS: Albert Mayer. *Photograph by Ed Bagwell.*
5. ARCHITECTS: Holden, Egan, Wilson, Corser; ARCHITECT FOR THE OUTDOORS: Albert Mayer. *Photograph by Ed Bagwell.*

Page 102
1. ARCHITECT: Brown & Guenther; ARCHITECT FOR THE OUTDOORS: Albert Mayer. *Photograph by New York City Housing Authority.*
2. *Photograph by New York City Housing Authority.*
3, 4, 5. *Photograph by Ed Bagwell.*

Pages 104, 105
Conception and drawing by Albert Mayer.

Page 111
New York Civic Center. From pamphlet.

Page 113
1. Detroit City Planning Commission.
2. Detroit Medical Center. ARCHITECTS: Crane & Gorwic.

Page 121
1. National Capital Planning Commission, National Capital Regional Planning Council.
2. *Washington Post.*

Pages 124–126
1–6. Northeastern Illinois Metropolitan Area Planning Commission.

Page 132
1. New York Times Company, 1965. Reprinted by permission.
2. *New York Times. Photograph by Allan Baum.*
3. *Christian Science Monitor* adaptation of U.S. Bureau of the Census map.

Page 135
1–3. Report on Physical Planning in the Netherlands. Netherlands Printing Office, 1961, The Hague.

Page 136
1, 2. France Town and Country Environment Planning 1965.

Pages 138, 139
1–6. Zurich. Swiss National Tourist Office.

Pages 142, 143
1, 2. ARCHITECT: Nervi; City of Norfolk.

Page 144
1, 2. Institute for Research in Social Science, University of North Carolina.

Page 146
1. Roberson Memorial Center, Binghamton, N. Y.
2. Marine Midland Trust Company of Southern New York.

Page 147
3. Roberson Memorial Center, Binghamton, N. Y.

Page 151
1. *Photograph by Bruce Davidson, Magnum Photos.*
2. *Photograph by Ewing Galloway, New York.*

Page 152
ARCHITECT: Matthew Nowicki.

Page 155
ARCHITECT: Meathe Kessler & Associates.

Page 156
ARCHITECT: Albert Mayer.

Page 158
1, 2. Puerto Rico Urban Renewal & Housing Corporation. ARCHITECT: Jan Wampler.

Pages 162, 163
1, 2. Cleveland Metropolitan Housing Authority (Ernest Bohn, Chairman). ARCHITECTS: Damon Worley Cady Kirk; CONSULTING ARCHITECT: Albert Mayer.

Page 159
Conception and drawing by Albert Mayer.

Page 165
1–3. ARCHITECT: Roland Wank. *Photograph by TVA.*

Back endpapers
American Electric Power Company.

INDEX